Cuban
Palimpsests

Cuban Palimpsests

JOSÉ QUIROGA

UNIVERSITY OF MINNESOTA PRESS

MINNEAPOLIS • LONDON

Volume 19 in Cultural Studies of the Americas Series
George Yúdice, Jean Franco, and Juan Flores, series editors

Published by the University of Minnesota Press
111 Third Avenue South, Suite 290
Minneapolis, MN 55401-2520
http://www.upress.umn.edu

Printed in the United States of America on acid-free paper

Library of Congress Cataloging-in-Publication Data

Quiroga, José, 1959–
    Cuban palimpsests / José Quiroga.
        p. cm. — (Cultural studies of the Americas ; v. 19)
    Includes bibliographical references and index.
    ISBN 0-8166-4213-3 (hc : alk. paper) — ISBN 0-8166-4214-1 (pb : alk. paper)
    1. Cuba—Civilization—1959– I. Title. II. Series.
    F1788.Q57 2005
    972.9106'4—dc22

                                                    2005019767

The University of Minnesota is an equal-opportunity educator and employer.

12 11 10 09 08 07 06 05   10 9 8 7 6 5 4 3 2 1

Contents

Preface: Stuck in Time

IN LIMBO

Most of the pictures I took the first time I returned to Cuba in 1980 were lost because I never had them developed. By the time I got around to developing the film, it had suffered too much in tropical weather: too much heat, too much rain, too much corrosion. Back then, I was more interested in "living" the experience than in forming a memory of it. Years later, when I realized I somehow hadn't lived it enough in my mind, I started searching out anything that could give me access to that month on the island, and that's when I found the film was now useless. I then reexamined the objects that I had brought back: notebooks scribbled in a handwriting that I could barely read, a Marxist novel given to me by one of our Cuban "hosts," a postcard signed by my traveling companions at Soroa Park. And handling them again and again, it slowly became clear to me that everything regarding Cuba had become too layered over time, and that a chronological narrative would not do justice to it. Deciphering a travel account that got written and rewritten so many times over the course of so many years that its prose was already flattened by overrevision was not going to do the trick. The notebook itself was all internal perception: it gave a good account of my states of mind, but no concrete information as to what I was doing. I have no recollection as to the names of our hosts, and only here and there, in one academic setting or another, do I encounter a name that I can reconnect as one of those Cubans who also, back then (we were all much younger then) made the trip from the United

States to the island. Not having anything in my possession that could trigger a sense of recall, the only thing possible was to go "back" to the island.

Out of time, on a time of its own, stuck in time. For those of us with a strong personal investment in Cuba, these phrases kept reappearing after the Soviet bloc collapsed and the United States engaged in diplomatic and commercial relationships with all of its former enemies except Cuba. The personal investment I am thinking about can come in many ways—memories of having been born or having lived on the island, relatives still living or dead. Others are invested as Cuba scholars, or Latino scholars, or are part of the more generalized cohort of those raised during the Cold War who recalled Cuba's revolution and its promise. I cannot call it a tight and cohesive group, but then again some bonds are predicated on common concerns. Twenty-five years after my first return, the island had somehow sedimented into its own temporality for the image banks of the West. Time itself, and history, have been codified by the memory of exile, frozen by the memory of empire, and placed on a permanent soft focus with nostalgias of meaning lost.

For the United States, Cuba is so out of time that the government placed "enemy combatants" in the no-man's-land of Guantánamo during George W. Bush's administration without any kind of legal recourse. Guantánamo itself is a piece of real estate fraught with problems: a piece of land claimed by Cuba, given as the result of an unfairly negotiated treaty, not officially subject to U.S. laws and not subject to Cuba's either. The base was initially established in 1898, at the end of the Spanish-Cuban-American War, with the lease for it signed on February 23, 1903, and then renegotiated again in 1934. The United States treats it as real estate: it pays about forty thousand dollars a year in rent, but since coming to power Fidel Castro has symbolically refused to cash the checks. Guantánamo is a cut-up place, a border of sorts, a piece of the United States in the territorial insularity of the island—an island within an island. Gitmo (as Guantánamo is sometimes called in English) has shed its skin as a surveillance center and also as a primary destination of sorts. During the 1960s, as Reinaldo Arenas recalled, it was the place for daring escapes, though at the risk of being electrocuted or caught by sharks or alligators. Arenas was the most brilliant writer of his generation, and in the early 1960s it seemed as if he was going to be the revolution's model writer—country boy who embodied the revolution's promise and its mission.

Things turned sour very fast, and by the early 1970s he was ostracized, incarcerated, unpublished in the island, and eked out a living as a damned homosexual writer. Arenas tried to make it there, as he recounts in *Before Night Falls,* but he was trumped by the heavy security: infrared lights, cars full of dogs, minefields. It was all part of a terrible, beautiful, surreal landscape of fear: "This time I entered the water and by the light of the moon I was able to see where the crackling sounds had come from: the river was infested with alligators. I have never seen so many sinister-looking animals in such a small expanse of water. They were just waiting there for me to get in so they could devour me. It was impossible to cross that river."[1] Some made it and some did not; the point is they all wanted to leave. In one of his last novels, *La loma del ángel* (*Graveyard of the Angels*), there is a contraption that purportedly sends slaves back to an Africa they all want to go back to. For Arenas, reimagining Cuba from his exile was related to the act of understanding how it was all becoming undone. Writing one manuscript on top of the other—not so much reproducing the nineteenth-century Cuban masterpiece *Cecilia Valdés,* but actually writing over its text. One could never hope to displace the original, but one could write in such a way that both texts could be read at the same time. Arenas's work abounds in these gestures: from his early *El mundo alucinante* (*Hallucinations: Or, the Ill-Fated Peregrinations of Fray Servando*), where he created the palimpsest out of which readers could make out the memoirs of Fray Servando Teresa de Mier, all the way up to *Viaje a La Habana* (Voyage to Havana), where the text cannot disguise Martí's life story as a running thread. The palimpsest does not reproduce the original, but it dismantles it, writes on top of it, allows it to be seen. It is a queer form of reproduction, one where two texts, two sites, two lives, blend into one continuous present.

Cuban Palimpsests writes the text of the present in a way that allows the older text to come to the fore. Its method is not displacement but rather dismantling—both the privilege of the past and the timelessness of the present. The dismantling it produces came to me one afternoon, coming out of a Cuban restaurant in Madrid that was full of artifacts brought in from a nineteenth-century Cuban mansion—washbasins, wicker baskets, rocking chairs, original paintings of native landscapes, modernist portraits, and silver bells. It was strange to see so much in one place, and to decide whether I was in a nineteenth-century museum or in a place where I was about to be served rice, beans, shredded meat, and fried plantains. When I asked how it had all gotten there, the waiter shrugged and did not say much. But when I came upon him a couple of hours later on a street corner and he offered to show me some nineteenth-century stamps and books, there at the market of the Plaza Mayor, in Madrid, it dawned on me that all around there was a slow dismantling taking place, like the one that Antonio José Ponte talked about in *Las comidas profundas* (*Wanting to Eat*), where a Spanish countess lives among fragments of the island meticulously transported to the arid Castilian plain: "The Cuban woods, that near Madrid, at the Escorial, had their own temple as doors, and closed in that very same city the basilica of Saint Francis the Great, penetrated their mouths to fulfill their appetite."[2] The yin-and-yang quality of these parallel dynamics fascinated me. There was the reproduction of Cuba and at the same time its ongoing dismantling. The two situations are complementary. The restaurant in Madrid was living off furniture and objects taken out of Cuba during the 1990s by Cubans who needed to get access to hard currency. But, at the same time, the revolution was heavily investing in selling itself as a franchise. There are many places in the world called La Bodeguita del Medio, for example, using a trademark adopted by a semigovernmental agency that exports ambiance, recipes, and rum, but also cooks, bartenders, managers, and sometimes waiters. It is sort of a Hard Rock Café, though here the symbolic capital treads a fine line between revolutionary panache and the merchandising of fun and sun. For every restaurant that reproduced Cuba from Havana there was someplace else where pieces of Cuba were being sold off by anybody who needed to make some hard currency—which was everybody in Cuba during the 1990s.

Disappearance, dismantling, and reproduction are the elements I want to focus on. Nobody can quite say how much has disappeared, how much of it just got sent out somewhere, and what quintessentially tropical wood is adorning what commercial venue somewhere else in the world. During the 1990s, booksellers in many countries were offering rare Cuban books taken out of private collections, and stacks of film taken from the film institute's vaults reappeared in a Miami nightclub for nostalgic exiles. One could say that these objects reflect how the memory of the colonial past and of the republic is slowly disappearing. But, at the same time, there is a way of seeing this whole situation as one where the dismantling

that takes place on the one hand is matched by self-invention and reproduction on the other—that the operation is not merely subtraction, that
the island is always being reinvented somewhere else.

Processes that are hard to explain are evident in the selective news we
hear from the island, in what we know about, as compared to what we
almost never pay attention to. In the United States, the gripping tale of
Elián González shared media space with other events, big or small. In
Havana, Elián brought the country to a virtual standstill. All formal developments of the case, within a context of extreme pedagogy by the government, demanded mass rallies and marches in every city and every town,
where every cultural worker, electrician, cabaret show dancer, bellhop—
every man, woman, and child (especially every child)—exercised their at
times free, at times coerced, at times implied, and at times suggested right
to become one as a people, and demand the return of the child. It was
a very visual spectacle that impacted upon material culture: television
demanded roundtables, marches needed T-shirts, education offered little
books of stamps that explained the situation to children, complete with
reenactments followed by assignments or compositions, book reports, and
so on. Billboards were expressly created for the case: visual reminders in
cities and highways of the child, of the father, and of the father with the
child. These were followed by still more educational projects meant to
remotivate the past (the early years of the revolution, its collective works).

The Elián González saga deserves to be included as an important marker
for the Cuban 1990s. It illuminated history and collective memory; it was
specific and, at the same time, broad. It allowed exiles to revisit the child
exodus of the 1960s called Operation Pedro Pan, and this brought back
the life and works of Ana Mendieta, and it also accounted for Carlos Eire's
National Book Award for *Waiting for Snow in Havana*.[3] The spy case in
Miami that from 1998 to 2001 was called "Web of the Wasp" was in many
ways the follow-up to the Elián González drama. This was a situation not
necessarily or overtly complicated by family ties, or by the sentimental
mass appeals of fatherhood. It impacted on political identities and citizen-
ships on both sides of a political division, and it went to the heart of the
visual because of surveillance. If at any point during the Elián González
saga, citizens on both sides of the U.S.-Cuba divide were interpellated
as lost children, the spy chase went to the heart of self-identification as a
chase between performance and essence. Those who professed their own

Cubanness in order to fit within the Miami exile community articulated a version of what Cuba was. They could blend in because being Cuban was understood as forming part of a community of belief that only needed a political position in order to be enacted. The fact that the spies could blend in pointed to a common Cuban culture; the fact that they were spies signaled a political divide. What culture brings together, politics divides, as the axis of resemblance intersected with the axis of difference. Within these two bisecting lines, insisting on one's Cubanness demands also staking a position as to where and under what circumstances one performs the act of being Cuban. Who is Cuban and who is not? The question apparently needs to be answered by taking both categories into account. From the political point of view of the Cuban state, allegiance to the social project of the revolution is the mark of *cubanía,* just as, from the political point of view of exile, opposition to the project is the essence of what being Cuban is all about. What culture brings together, politics divides.

Over and beyond these two terms, the mechanism of political categories dismantling cultural ones points to the fact that dismantling Cuba is always predicated on the fact that Cuba is always already dismantled.

REPETITION

Cubans have seen each other with fully developed scripts for these encounters for more than four decades. In Havana in 1980 I came across a man and a woman—thirty-something-year-old Cubans living in Miami—while they were in the process of negotiating their nostalgia with the realities of a revolutionary city. It was a painful experience for them, though pain itself does not do justice to the complicated networks of affection that Havana brought back to life at that time, when Cubans who had left for the United States were first allowed to go back after twenty years. It was not clear whether Havana was the illness or the medication; whether this trip was the conclusion of exile or the symptom of their exile. It was not even clear what was it that Havana brought back to life or what—if anything—the physical return to Havana was allowing them to bury, once and for all. They had left the city for a different life and a different "way of life" and they felt and looked like beings from another planet, coming from a Miami they had welcomed in the early 1960s as a future, back to a revolutionary city that had proclaimed itself as the vanguard of change but now looked hopelessly outdated, flat, lifeless compared to smaller tropical cities like Cartagena, Mérida, Santo Domingo, or San Juan. It was clear that the temporality that organized their lives ran counter to the ideologies and political histories of the revolution. They were coming back to *the* past, to *their* past. But all they could perceive was the failures of a future perfect—its dour lives fully controlled by the state and with no signs of private enterprise amid the city's eternal beauty. For them, Havana was a city lost; it mirrored a past where already, in 1980, that first cohort of Cuban exiles could not really gaze at their own reflection.

In general terms, and aside from the many poignant reconciliations that took place then, there were many jokes, and there was much laughter about these visitors, from the Cuban press but mostly by word of mouth. The Cuban press and government spokespersons discredited the community as participants in and fabricators of an empty nostalgia—and nostalgia itself was anathema to the revolutionary way of seeing things. What was more revealing was the fact that there was no vocabulary, no language, for the interactions produced at that point. For its first attempt at national reconciliation, the government experimented with dollar stores so that Cuban exiles (euphemistically and somewhat formally called the "Cuban Overseas Community"—Comunidad Cubana en el Exterior) could buy products their relatives needed on the island: a refrigerator or a fan, a pair of jeans or a bar of soap. And because there was no vocabulary with which to name these interactions, they were rapidly pitted as the struggle for material possessions versus the overall possession of "dignity." The two people I saw in Havana were part of that dynamic—as I was—in spite of my different political viewpoints and the different perceptions we had.

Since the early 1980s, these encounters between Cubans who live on two different sides of a geographic and economic divide have had their own push-and-pull dialectics, their own forms of conciliation and reconciliation, their exchange of symbolic or real goods. In 1980, the myth of an alternative to consumer capitalism was still present for many in Cuba, as well as abroad; by the 1990s, the narrative was, tragically perhaps, harder to sustain. In the 1980s, going to Cuba was a contentious experience, part of an immense and at times violent and tragic debate as to whether exiles were propping up a regime many considered distasteful and illegitimate. In the 1990s, though the debate about supporting the regime would still come up often, visiting the island was somehow part of life, it was talked about in radio call-in shows, it could be commented on television and written about in newspapers. In the 1980s, the couple I met in Havana insisted on a past that had authority, validity, and ownership; they created picture albums labeled according to what a certain construction used to be, before 1959, instead of what it actually was. In the 1990s, Cubans from Miami (and Miami is here just a shorthand for a much broader "exile") came back with a fully developed script of the city preserved and disfigured amid the ruins.

If the experience was always more painful for Cuban exiles, I am sure that for Cubans in Havana then, as well as now, the other's gaze upon the city at some point reflected what they themselves could never bring themselves to see—just as many in Havana pointed out that the film *Suite Habana,* which is a visual homage to the city, revealed to them the poverty in which they live daily. These self-perceptions as they are seen from different viewpoints colored all these interactions. Thus, from the outset and in the daily interactions, two populations were locked in time, looking at themselves as they are looking at the other, and searching for something in the other that could or would have been there in the self.

The political situation in the spring of 1980 was unique. It was a sunny afternoon, but the city had a darkened feel to it. Cubans were leaving the island, an exodus that started with ten thousand Cubans crammed into the Peruvian embassy and that ended up with a hundred thousand Cubans leaving from the port city of Mariel. There had been demonstrations and, while some Cubans demanded to leave, their neighbors were called upon to stage mass actions in front of their houses, with those houses themselves all boarded up, their inhabitants called "traitors" and worse. To this day, when I look at the pictures of the time, the ones distributed as part of the propaganda machine that twenty years later orchestrated the Elián González rallies, and I see a child in the mass demonstrations, I realize that, in Cuba, shouting for someone to leave is a powerful act.

As Román de la Campa says, "[l]eaving Cuba is a story one tells over and over, often looking for details that reveal themselves only through repetition."[4] My own departure was uneventful because it really does not feel like an experience lived, but rather like an experience lived by another who was back then a child. The memory, in fact, is totally collapsed as one more part of the collective memory project that exiles created for us children—always with us in mind. And because the memory, and not

necessarily the reality, of Cuba needed to be preserved, the first generation set itself about producing memories: albums, picture books, postcard
collections, records and record covers, restaurants named after streets, corners, city blocks, natural landscapes. Toponyms were decorated with all
sorts of authentic motifs, naming illusory or real sites and giving reality
to furniture stores, auto franchises, upholstery shops, dry cleaners, video
stores, and beauty parlors that in turn had matte reproductions of the
Capitol building, of the Morro Castle, of the bay of Manzanillo, of the
Valley of Viñales, of orchids near the waterfalls in Soroa. It was an un-
reachable, other landscape because of the political situation, but it became
as real as *fact.* It created a place to live by, alongside whatever flattened
scenery was actually lived in Miami, and they were real fragments of something that intervened within the tenement in upper Manhattan, that surrounded you during the snowstorms of Iowa, or that created an uncanny
sense of reproduction in Puerto Rico.

Child in demonstration: the Cuban government staged mass rallies during the
exodus from the port of Mariel in 1980.

Back in the 1980s, I am sure that, as popular tales have it, many of those who came from Miami flaunted their wealth to family members, old neighbors, and former coworkers. (This is Cuba, after all, part of what Antonio Benítez Rojo has labeled the Caribbean performative space, where jewelry is meant to be flashed and wealth meant to be seen.) But the man and the woman I saw that afternoon in Línea Street in Havana were not really flashing their wealth, but rather crying behind dark sunglasses. They were walking around dazed. They looked at me and recognized me for what I was: one of their own kind, one of the ones from the other side. The woman turned to me and asked, "Do you like this?" and I said, "Yes, I like this," and they said, "What is there to like? There is nothing here." They couldn't see a thing, not even the invented memory of a life they could have lived. The only thing they saw was a past that was no more and that could not be brought back to life in lifeless buildings. It was relatively easy to dismiss them back then, though I guess time has softened me too, even if I always saw possibilities in a future perfect that still seems elusive, even after all these years.

MUSEO DE LA REVOLUCIÓN

I used to go to a bar in Washington, DC, called Havana Village. It had a sign in Spanish that can roughly be translated as "If you drink to forget, pay before you start," although the translation loses the original's sense of rhythm and rhyme ("Si bebes para olvidar, paga antes de empezar"). I've seen signs like these before in bars, so it is not entirely an original work of art in any way (in fact, it could be a cliché sign for a bar to have, signaling a lot of drunkards telling sad stories, the owner having to drag them away, and so on). It was a strange sign in a strange place because, if you are going to have a bar called Havana Village in Washington, DC, every drink you have is a bet you place on memory and forgetting, with a dose of self-invention involved.

How much pleasure does the clandestine (and illegal) trip to Havana taken by U.S. tourists every year paradoxically owe to the intransigence of the Cuban community in Miami, and its stubborn creation of a nostalgia? Or is the creation of nostalgia part of a revolutionary appeal to those same tourists? It's as if those U.S. citizens were strangely participating in part of the nostalgic exile project: looking for, and finding, the bars of the past in the same street where the present bars are located. Speak to those same U.S. citizens these days and mention Cuba, and invariably you come across the consumer product, the trademark—and, at some level, mixed with respect and validation, the sense of imperial possession—but also (yet another paradoxical gesture) a Cuba where the capitalist and the consumer are offered a kind of unspoiled site where there is no capitalism. It brings up a kind of self-hatred of capitalism—hence its allure—as if the hunger for that which is not "ours" were also manifested in the displeasure with what actually belongs to "us." No fast-food joints, no trinkets: if there is a space close by where we can flee to from the culture of capitalism, then Cuba is the place. The travel happens in the midst of another event: the unconventional war that both sides of the Cuban political class in Miami and Havana have waged among themselves. In that territory, the U.S. tourist is not going to be angry at his or her own imperial state with its arrogant decrees about what business or political interests might be expedient at a given point in time, but at the population of Cuban exiles that that same state created as a symbolic mirage stuck in a broader geopolitical landscape. That return, so much desired, never quite happened in the heroic way in which it was supposed to have happened. There may still be some Miami corners where disenchantment is the preferred mode of communicating the fact that no victory parade will ever welcome that generation of Cuban exiles, and that for many, "returning" at this point needs to be placed on hold.

And it is all at this point suspended, as if on a tightrope. When people ask me to look into the future, I respond with a bit of black humor, recalling the famous rumba where Papa Montero is celebrated and insulted upon his death, the music itself at once celebrating and mourning. So, this is how I recount my vision of the future: by recalling one summer afternoon in Miami, around 1998, when one of the male callers to the Rico Pérez radio show that my uncle used to listen to—Rico Pérez sold all kinds of medicines for a broad array of real or perceived illnesses—described the situation. The caller said that his wife was Dominican, and that her mother (his mother-in-law) had died a couple of months earlier. She was buried faceup but, at some point, for some reason I can't remember, they had to open the casket and that's when they discovered that the cadaver was lying facedown. It turns out the woman was not dead after all, the caller says, and he looks for the word, because it is a condition that has a name, and that describes people who seem dead but are not dead at all. Rico Pérez explains that the name is "catalepsy" and at that point the caller asks the question that has been haunting him: he wants to know if this is a hereditary condition, because he really doesn't want this to happen to his wife. Rico Pérez says that, no, there is no proof that this is a hereditary condition, but he also adds that it happens and that it is a horrible thing, and that he does not wish it upon anyone. But then he pauses and says that the only person he wishes this might happen to is You-Know-Who. This thought gave the caller and the doctor a moment's pause. It was a very brief radio silence, and Rico Pérez went on to the next call.

Introduction: Untimely Cuba

MANAGING THE PRESENT

Cuba is one of the last socialist countries in the world still at odds with the United States, it has sustained one of the longest one-man regimes in the world, and it still defines nationality in terms of geography, although it has a diaspora of at least three generations of exiles. In the early 1990s, it seemed totally lost in a world that had abruptly changed since that distant January 1, 1959, when young, bearded fighters—*barbudos,* as they were then called—forced the dictator Fulgencio Batista into exile. A legacy of a Cold War that neither the island nor the United States can conceive as having really finished, the Cuban ruling class still explains the world in terms of *us* versus *them* with an official discourse of resistance against all odds that has allowed the state to survive in a region dominated by American capital.

The Cuban Revolution was an event captured in images and heroic gestures.[1] From these, the state and its intellectuals developed a clearly delineated national and collective memory that led from a colonial past to a promising future. Articulated first during the 1960s, the memory of historical grievances collectively suffered motivated the population to work toward liberation, equality, and progress. But this narrative came to a halt in the early 1990s, when the only image left of that heroic struggle was the sense of an expanded present. The collapse of the Soviet Union and the socialist bloc did not produce a time understood exactly as a "transition," but a period of uncertainty that still meant to connect past to future while suspending the time between the two. It was called in Cuba the

"Período especial en tiempos de paz," roughly translated as the "Special Period in Times of Peace." It is a euphemistic term that sought to give a name to a situation that was never anticipated in the long march toward egalitarianism and social progress that the revolution promised Cubans. Even though at first many thought this was the government's death knell, over time it is best seen as a transformation, and not a transition: a moment during which different outcomes can take place and differing reactions are meant to be expected—an uneven process with progressive dynamics but also regressive gestures.[2] If the period were to be seen as a grammatical construction, it would best be apprehended as a verb tense that selectively incorporates the past while prescribing, yet closing off, alternative visions of the future. But in fact, it has been clear throughout the "Special Period" that there is no stable grammar to describe the Cuban condition after more than four decades of revolutionary life. As in the world-famous Cuban cinematic hit *Strawberry and Chocolate* (1994), verbs, like concepts, and even hardened political positions, tend to melt like ice cream under the Cuban heat.

How can the future of Cuba be debated without taking into account the enormous affective links the revolution produced during the 1960s? Utopia in the past may never have been a utopia at all, yet it was photographed for the future (for us, in the present) to look at precisely from that angle. In a paradoxical manner, memory and not history will allow us a more perceptive vision of the Cuban present and of its future. Where history focuses on an economic and political project that still in the 1990s commanded a broad degree of support, memory will allow us to understand the direct and discrete ways in which the state sustained itself by interpellating its population *both* in the past and in the present. The state was not simply using coercive mechanisms, but commanding a symbolic language that registered with the people, always addressed in the plural. This tactic demands an approach that focuses on the representation of memory and culture, and on the broad effects ideologies and policies have had on all forms of expression within the collective lives of Cubans who live not only on the island, but also outside of its territorial boundaries.

One of the tasks that makes focusing on Cuban memory difficult—as opposed to, but in relation to, Cuban history—is the internationalist dimension to the island since the early 1960s. Cuba belongs to what Andreas Huyssen has called an "expanded field," which involves a "cross-national memory discourse" situated between the global and the local and not simply within a geographic boundary.[3] Hence, Cuban history and memory are not simply written from and within the island, but they force us to cross geographic and artistic borders. I have wanted to take note of this effect throughout: during Fidel Castro's 1960 visit to Harlem, and then during his 1995 visit to the same site; in the political and ideological conflicts around image and memory; in the complicated tales of espionage; in the search for the pieces that Ana Mendieta carved in Cuba; in the difficult context for books and literature; in the discussion of the role of music in contemporary Cuban society; even in the acts that surrounded the reburial of Che Guevara in 1997 and the death of Celia Cruz in 2003. The media archive devoted to Cuba at some point has been collapsed into the dreams and projections, hopes and resolutions of broad segments of Western and Third World imaginaries, and this is certainly one of the strongest implications scholars must face when treating Cuba. At the moment it became involved in an East–West confrontation that Cubans themselves were not prepared for, the island became a symbolic site and Havana a symbolic capital. What Cuba is, or was, is intimately linked to what it *represented* and what it still does represent.

In pictures and words—in photography, literature, recorded music, and film—this book explores collective memory and memorialization, and their effects on the perception of time in Cuba. I have selected seven sites— I am not necessarily defining "site" as a concrete, physical *place*—where memory bears upon collective history in ways that may shed light on the present situation. I am not necessarily following different moments of the revolution in a chronological fashion, but trying to reproduce the temporal shifts that I see acting in the present Cuban cultural situation. Readers can follow, of course, a historical line. After all, it is not my intention to do away with history altogether: the revolution *is* historical time, and it has concretely acted upon people, places, and things. But I would like to leave open the relationship to history that these essays *do* have, so that readers may pursue other, hidden connections.

MEMORY AND MEMORIALIZATION

Events in Cuba during the 1990s forced the state to turn the discontinuities created as a result of the socialist collapse into a narrative line that leads to an "expanded" present. Past and present, memory and memorialization are related to the project for a collective, cohesive, and *national* memory that the state produced back in the 1960s. At that point, state ideology fashioned a Cuban history that was different from that of the republic, though at the same time bearing an organic relationship to it.[4] This historiographical shift was fundamental in an island that was so close to the United States and to its markets, and with middle and upper classes (to which the early *revolucionarios* belonged) so embedded within the promise of the American Way of Life. The memory constructed by the revolution was that of a nation eternally at war, fighting for justice and liberation, and thus projecting itself toward a future that would always be marked by struggle.[5]

In the 1990s, the state continued to write the text of Cuban nationality as it always had, by appealing to a cohesive set of symbols geared toward a future teleology. But at this point something changed. It was the revolutionary past itself—the recent past, not the distant past of the nineteenth century—that gave the nation its sense of identity, and created a sense of cohesive nationalism. At some level, one could say that as a result of the "Special Period in Times of Peace" the present folded upon itself. It was not engaged in memory, but in memorialization, while at the same time it produced the sense that things that had not been said before were now being said.

Memory in the 1960s was deployed as part of a long narrative leading toward a future, whereas the memorialization of the 1990s celebrated and critiqued the past in order to gain some time in the present. The cohesive memory enacted in the 1960s entailed a clear sense of the future; the act of memorialization speaks to a loss of that image. Memorialization thus was a way of buying time for the revolutionary regime. It allowed the state to relax censorship controls for the sake of a mediated openness. The state was, in fact, managing the past, while also managing the civil society that was entrusted to create its narrative. The picture was carefully crafted—again, one has to see this in terms of managed processes—in order to criticize the state for errors committed in the past (for example, in the 1970s) that were at no point seen as policies of the present. Or, if they were policies of the present, they were undertaken by actors so different that one could reasonably wonder whether the *same* state was amending its ways, or whether this was a different state altogether. The mechanism was complex, for ideologically the past and the present could not serve as commentaries on what the future had failed to deliver—but rather as a way of opening up once again the possibility that the future *may* still deliver. If debates on the past illuminated errors, they did so by implicitly positing the past as antediluvian, a past for which none of the people in charge of present-day policies bear responsibility. If these "negative pasts" were seen as the source of the present malaise, an implicit code demanded not to dwell too much on the relationship between then and now, but rather to ask for more state intervention in order to rectify present-day problems. With the conversation so firmly structured in this way, one had the vague, discomforting feeling that the "Período especial" was simply a proxy for a future that never quite seemed to have arrived.

One is certainly entitled to think cynically of this process as just empty memorializing, expressing itself in a kind of cultural hard currency that allowed Cuban authors, singers, or painters to earn much-needed cash abroad. And one is also entitled to remark that these complicated ideological shifts were responsible for renaming governmental organizations as nongovernmental organizations (NGOs), without having to dislodge these from the state altogether. Even if one justifies these as measures arising out of necessity, the point here is not to condemn them but to uncover their strategic value and their effects in the cultural atmosphere of the island. For the Cuban Revolution, the 1990s demanded some kind of course correction. That this present had a name—the Special Period in Times of Peace—allowed it to be read as a kind of interregnum, in which other temporalities could always intervene. It was a present accompanied by some of the most difficult economic conditions in the country's history, and as Cubans lacked basic foods, transportation, and medicine, they were also given the sensation that multiple temporalities were coexisting in the same space—a space that could not fashion the future except as the return of the most odious forms of the past that the state had always tried to eliminate.

ECONOMIC COLLAPSE

The Cuban state still mistrusted perestroika and glasnost when the Berlin Wall collapsed on November 9, 1989. And, as the Cuban writer Eliseo Alberto has recalled, that very same day, the official Cuban newspaper

Granma gave front-page coverage to the production of plantains in an area called Güira de Melena.[6] But the impression that nothing was happening did not last long. Because the world changed, the Cuban government was forced to make what it termed "concessions," though some of these changes had been contemplated, or even experimented with, earlier. In the late 1970s, for example, the government created "dollar stores" in order to serve the needs of Cuban exiles who returned on visits and wanted to buy consumer goods for their relatives. In the early 1980s, responding to popular discontent, the revolution authorized open farmers' markets and allowed state enterprises to hire their employees freely.[7] But the government at that point retreated from its experimental policies for fear of unleashing capitalism. This fear was so strong that even as late as 1986, in order to counter Mikhail Gorbachev's perestroika, the state launched the "Rectification Campaign" and moved the economy away from the market by reducing material incentives for the sake of moral imperatives, and once again recentralized economic decision making. It was totally against the grain of what was happening elsewhere, particularly in Eastern Europe. As Carmelo Mesa-Lago recalled, "After decades of central planning, intercepted with periods of anti-market radicalism and experimentation with moral stimulation, in 1989 Cuba had the most collectivized, egalitarian, externally dependent and Soviet-subsidized economy within the socialist world."[8]

The internal political context that surrounded the economic debacle in the late 1980s was no less difficult than the events in the former USSR. In 1988, the Angolan peace accords ended the involvement of the Fuerzas Armadas Revolucionarias (FAR) in internationalist missions. Many Cubans who had been trained and deployed overseas were now returning to an economic situation best described as critical.[9] On July 26, 1992, while commemorating the attack on the Moncada barracks that is the official start of the Cuban revolutionary struggle, Castro announced that new reforms would be put in place—and in the following years it was, indeed, hard to keep pace with the wide-ranging nature of these changes. In 1992, the government established a constitutional reform legalizing associations with foreign investors, with the first joint venture being a hotel in Varadero beach with Spain. These joint ventures doubled between 1994 and 1995. In 1993, reacting to popular discontent, the government legalized the U.S. dollar and authorized certain forms of self-employment. In 1994, farmers' markets were reopened (they had functioned in the early

1980s but had been shut down in 1986); and in 1995 the government introduced a "peso" that could be converted to foreign currency (alongside the regular "peso" that Cuban citizens used). Cuba expanded self-employment, legalizing small restaurants called *paladares*, even if these were subject to enormous and belabored government controls. In 1996, the government created free zones and industrial parks.[10]

The state tried to address potential armed forces restlessness by involving them in joint ventures with foreign capital. In order to facilitate that, in 1988 it formed the Gaviota Tourism Group S.A., an umbrella association that managed all sorts of foreign contacts. The state was assured of the army's loyalty and felt free to create a new class of military entrepreneurs after condemning to death in 1989 Arnaldo Ochoa—the highest-ranking and most decorated hero of the Angolan campaigns—as well as Antonio de la Guardia, Amado Padrón, and Jorge Martínez.[11] The military ended up managing the most critical sectors of the economy—going as far as to control the TRD subsidiary—(the Tienda de Recaudación de Divisas), stores that collect hard currency.

With the military firmly involved in the economic restructuring of society, the government could devote its energies to the tense relationship with the United States. It worked closely with members of the U.S. Congress, as well as with interest and policy groups in the United States, to slowly chip away at the more damaging provisions of the embargo. It succeeded over the course of the decade to the extent that agricultural interests in the United States can now sell food to Cuba—even though these commercial transactions cannot be done on credit. After 1994, the Cuban government entered into a new migration pact with the United States and streamlined its emigration agreements, though it still complains that the Cuban Adjustment Act—which grants Cuban residents who arrive in the United States legal status after a year and one day—fosters illegal emigration that results in deaths as Cubans try to cross the Florida Straits in flimsy rafts.

By 2001, the situation had dramatically changed. There is ideological and political repression on the island, as indicated by the incarceration of journalists and human rights activists in 2003. At the same time, there are now direct flights between Havana and such U.S. cities as Miami, New York, and Los Angeles, and this has created a population that surmounts all kinds of bureaucratic obstacles in order to give some sense of normalcy to yearly visits to Cuba or Miami.[12] There are now *balseros* who come and go in rafts or even boats, and make the treacherous crossing between Cuba and the Florida Keys—most of them paying considerable sums in order to do so. Top-level diplomatic overtures also took place. In May 2002, Jimmy Carter became the first former president to go to Cuba since 1928—a fact that eloquently expresses the lack of importance accorded to the island by the U.S. government throughout the Cuban republic. Carter met both government functionaries and dissidents, and he was allowed to speak on national television. The Guantánamo base in Cuba, meanwhile, was receiving Al Qaeda fighters shipped from Afghanistan without much complaint from the Cuban government. The departure of U.S. Treasury Secretary Paul O'Neill in late 2002 undoubtedly had its roots in President George W. Bush's internal economic policies, but O'Neill had openly declared in March 2002 that he favored loosening travel restrictions to Cuba—a comment for which he was attacked by Florida congressional representatives Ileana Ros-Lehtinen and Lincoln Díaz-Balart.[13]

Even if at some level Cuba did not seem to have changed much, nothing would ever be the same in Cuban life in the 1990s.

CULTURAL PALIMPSESTS

The new economic policies implemented in the 1990s created strange aftereffects. The historical promise that the revolution had made since the 1960s rendered Cuban socialism in the 1990s "out of joint": the promised future never quite arrived, and it was clear that the road ahead was fraught with difficulties if the revolution was to survive a possible onslaught of capitalism.[14] As the state prepared the population for the possible "return" of the past, it turned Cuban life into a morality tale about what could befall under capitalism. Prostitution—hidden in the past and occluded from the view of the average Cuban—was allowed to flourish, while the general framework of economic equality was ruptured by new economic agents.[15] The situation became more critical as the country opened up to tourism and, in 1994, the government had to stop penalizing access to dollars by ordinary Cubans.[16] This latter measure was reluctantly implemented as a result of open rebellion in the streets of Havana in 1994, which led to the departure of thousands of Cubans in makeshift rafts—an event that was photographed, filmed, and transmitted throughout the world.[17]

While the Cuban countryside was mired in poverty, Havana became
a verb tense all unto its own, a mixture of the Spanish past and future perfect.[18] Nightclubs that traded on the old glory that was Havana before
1959 appeared in the central areas of the city, while the city around them
was in ruins. Cuba published glossy magazines celebrating the past, such
as *Opus Habana*, and these could be read and admired next to now useless
Marxist-Leninist manuals of the 1960s sold in the streets. Many houses
in central Havana had little running water and no electricity for days at a
time, but European fashion photo shoots increasingly used those ruins
as backdrops, and joint enterprises with foreign and Cuban capital built
hotels and restaurants next to rundown buildings. Even the texture of the
city changed: Old Havana became the place where tourists roamed and
performers sang; the new city gravitated to the plush suburbs of Miramar
or Siboney while central Havana remained a no-man's-land where people
are packed in tenements.

To the north, Miami also changed during this period, in subtle and not
so subtle ways. To be sure, one still encounters the same loud intransigence

Cuba faced yet another refugee crisis in 1993. Photograph by Farah Rivera.
Copyright Star Photo.

that has pursued the Cuban dynamic since the revolution, but Little Havana has also turned into a relic of its own, as the historical exile has moved to the middle-class prosperity of Kendall, or the tight urban enclave of Hialeah. Unable to let go of a trauma too immense to fully understand at this point, Cubans on both sides of the clichéd ninety miles of bitterness cling to the roles they know best, understandably afraid of the new world to come.

The scene in Havana and, to a lesser extent, in Miami has been radically altered in so many ways that there is no dearth of books, documentaries, and travel accounts that seek to understand these shifts.[19] In spite of the very clear temporal narrative deployed by the revolution, with its insistence on a vanquished political and economic system, and then on a forward march toward economic equality and prosperity for all, the new moment in time left Cubans with a sense of a life that could not be easily understood within the revolution's own temporal frameworks.

The city was collapsing, but it was essentially, in architectural terms, the same city the revolution had inherited from the republic in 1959. The population had changed, but that population was still living within a collective project that always seemed to be moving forward. There was a way of viewing these events, a manner in which they could be apprehended. But then again, Cubans could not quite make sense of a logic where revolution and collapse could be put onto the same grid. Literature and literary criticism clearly stated that events were not to be seen in linear terms, and that the best way of apprehending time and circumstance was by combining different texts into one. This entailed not only the use of pastiche, but also the art of combining different genres, modes, and even historical texts into one. Margarita Mateo Palmer's most important work as a critic is still her 1995 *Ella escribía poscrítica* (She used to write post-criticism), in which she combines a sharp reading of postcolonial fictions and testimonial narratives with a personal account of the intellectual difficulties of the "Período especial." The past was not quite dead, though it seemed that the dead occupied the space of the living and that different temporalities colluded within the same geographic space. As Antonio José Ponte keenly perceived in his 2002 novel *Contrabando de sombras* (Contraband of shadows), past and present bled onto each other: lives threaded in different configurations in an ahistorical moment of coexistence. The linear discourse, the elliptical morality tale that the revolution was constructing in terms

of this scenario, was transformed in literature and the arts into simultane-
ous movements toward progression and regression. The weird temporality
they created turned Cuba into a massive jigsaw puzzle where the pieces
never quite fit.

Juxtapositions are the main element in Cuban works from the 1990s.
Pedro Juan Gutiérrez places a poor, young drifter called Rey—who lives
from day to day in the most sordid circumstances imaginable—in the
midst of the tourist "dollar zone" of the Cuban economy. In *El Rey de
La Habana* (The king of Havana) published in Spain in 1999, Rey walks
around the carefully manicured lawn of a hotel and stumbles upon a gardener. He needs employment and he begs the gardener for a job water-
ing plants. But the man then explains what he needs to have: certificates
of ideological purity, impeccable party credentials from all imaginable
sources, a high degree of education with at least a second language, an
amiable disposition, and delectable physique. The gardener is baffled by
Rey's ignorance of these requirements, and kicks him out of the grounds
as an undesirable.[20]

Gutiérrez's dirty realism is in many ways more of an aesthetics than
"realism" per se. But it is true that the most menial job in the Cuban "dollar zone" is a coveted luxury, and a source of fierce competition, within a
country that can actually boast of having workers who fulfill those credentials. What Gutiérrez created was a comic scene providing no sense of
liberation. The clash between what Rey actually is and the realities of the
Cuban labor marketplace is not resolved. The historical layers of memory
and amnesia that pertain to that scene (education and sociability versus
marginality) are presented in a deadpan fashion whereby readers laugh
while resigning themselves to a social circumstance that seems unreal. As
the Cuban writer Arturo Arango has explained, "The Cuba where we used
to live, which we have struggled to construct and to comprehend for the
better part of our lives, no longer exists."[21] The Cuba where Arango used
to live was a player on the world stage during the 1960s, a beacon of solidarity for liberation struggles throughout the Third World, a model for a
new Latin American culture. There is nothing of that, and no memory of
it, in the world of Rey that Gutiérrez depicts.

In the 1960s, Cubans basked in a glory that can only be recalled with a
bitter sense of defeat in contemporary accounts. The literacy campaign, or
the struggle against colonialism and imperialism, was memorialized in art

that was challenging and new. Havana was the epicenter of a new society: travelers came to Havana to escape capitalism and get a dose of what the world could look like. Writers, painters, and filmmakers were "intellectual workers" with affective links to a revolutionary process, which in turn validated their work as the vanguard of Latin American cultural expression. This is the world registered most of all in photographs and film, which documented the changes of a revolutionary society.

In literature, that narrative is juxtaposed to a darker process, as the revolution very soon started demanding unquestioning allegiance from its youth. The younger generations in 1959 were combative and iconoclastic, and they were slowly marginalized, ostracized, or forced to acquiesce. The generational dispute was first felt in the elder members of the historic revolutionary generation, and they produced over time two names that stand out at opposite ends of the political spectrum: Guillermo Cabrera Infante, author of *Three Trapped Tigers* (1967), who since the 1970s and before his death in 2005 became one of the most vocal critics of the revolution from his exile in London, and Roberto Fernández Retamar, editor of the magazine *Casa de las Américas* and author of *Calibán*, the canonical text of the Latin American left.[22] He is, to this day, perhaps the clearest example of an "official" Cuban writer.

As many have observed, the 1970s represented the darkest period for Cuban culture. For Fernando Martínez Heredia, among others, the "devaluation" of the present culture has its roots in that decade.[23] The crucial date was 1968, when the writers union awarded its major poetry prize to Heberto Padilla's *Fuera del juego*—a title that already pictured the writer "out of the game"—though not without stating that the book was counterrevolutionary. Padilla was arrested in 1971, and forced to read a mea culpa condemned by intellectuals the world over.[24] The literary and cultural atmosphere was considerably chilled after that. The Mariel exodus in 1980 closed this period, after which the state relaxed its cultural (and economic) policies.

The vanguard of the Cuban cultural scene shifted in the 1980s to the visual arts, and major exhibitions in that decade changed the Cuban artistic world.[25] The work that marked the beginning of this decade was Ana Mendieta's, whose renown coincided with the opening of the exhibition Volumen 1 in Havana in 1981. Mendieta was a Cuban-American who traveled to the island and came into contact with young artists who later pushed the boundaries of the permissible throughout the decade. Artists were positioned to be freer agents later in the 1990s, but for authors the collapse of the socialist bloc was disastrous. If most authors saw their book publications assured before 1990, after it there was no paper to publish books or magazines. There was an overall reduction not only in the number of volumes published, but also in the number of pages each could contain. Publishing figures were catastrophic: for a time, the publication of the magazine of the UNEAC (National Union of Cuban Writers and Artists) was transferred to Mexico (in March 1991). That same year, there were 70 percent fewer titles as well as publishing runs. Even these figures are generous, because about fifty titles were reserved for tourist guides and other such work.

In many other ways, though, the situation offered certain possibilities for freer expression. During the early 1990s, younger Cuban writers rendered homage to forgotten, or banned, Cuban authors, and state institutions organized symposia on their work. Cuban and foreign scholars met, although the primary works of many honored writers were nowhere to be found in Cuba. Cuban authors during the 1990s wrote essays on poets such as Lorenzo García Vega—his very personal and iconoclastic *Los años de Orígenes* (The years of Orígenes) (1979) has been mentioned in Cuban magazines, though it is practically unavailable in Cuba. Many Cuban journals in the late 1990s published essays that referred to the work of a notorious anti-Fidelista writer like Guillermo Cabrera Infante, though his name is anathema to Cuban cultural institutions. Cuban literary journals such as *La Gaceta de Cuba* and *Unión* have published essays on diaspora literature.[26] However, opinions that differ from the normative and customary may still be footnoted by a *coletilla* that states how the journal editors do not share the author's opinion.[27] The journal *Encuentro de la cultura cubana*, originating in Madrid since the late 1990s and started by the late Jesús Díaz, underscores the fact that it includes authors who live both in Cuba and abroad—though the magazine circulates in a quasi-underground fashion in Havana, and cannot be bought in any bookstore.[28] The Julian Schnabel biopic *Before Night Falls* (2000), an adaptation of Reinaldo Arenas's memoirs with the same title, played in Havana for a select audience of party members and invited guests, and the magazine *Juventud Rebelde* published a review in May 2001 along with a lengthy article that was also a critique of Arenas, though the film has never played for a broad

Cuban audience. And in 2002, the journal *Temas* published a scathing critique of an essay on José Martí by the Cuban resident Antonio José Ponte and, though it reproduced the original offending essay, it did so only within the context of a directed reading.[29] Whereas in the past the literary circuit did not comment in journals about Cuban writers living abroad, at this point there is a tentative space for them.[30] At least two have been published in the island: Sonia Rivera Valdés, a Cuban author who lives in New York, had her novel *Las historias prohibidas de Marta Veneranda* (*The Forbidden Stories of Marta Veneranda*) published in Cuba in 1997 and was selected by Cuba to participate in the 2002 Guadalajara Book Fair as one of the—lamentably few—Cuban authors living abroad whom the government recognizes. In 2001, Mayra Montero, who lives in Puerto Rico, was honored by having her novel *The Messenger* published in Cuba. Where to place the canon within the broader frameworks of Cuban culture is debated in magazines and pondered in books.[31] Víctor Fowler Calzada, one of the most important Cuban poets living in Havana, published an essay on literature and diaspora titled "Canon, Cuba, transnación," and the latter chapters of his *Rupturas y homenajes* (Ruptures and homages) (1998) are devoted to the question of diaspora and how it affects Cuban letters. Many of these opinions may be actually forms of controlling what has been an inevitable and growing series of exchanges between Cubans living on the island as well as abroad. These encounters had already taken place in the late 1970s at the Círculo de Cultura Cubana, an organization of university professors and artists who wanted to establish contacts with the island, and through the work of *Areíto*, the most radical and controversial journal published by Cuban exiles in the 1970s.[32] In the 1990s, these efforts led to the Stockholm Encounter in 1994, followed by a joint declaration signed by writers living in Cuba and abroad, as well as two volumes published by the Olof Palme International Center.[33] These encounters also produced collections such as Ruth Behar's *Bridges to Cuba*, as well as the work of smaller journals such as *Apuntes Postmodernos/Postmodern Notes*.

Injustices and errors committed during the 1970s are now openly talked about in Cuba, in articles written within state cultural journals such as *Revolución y Cultura* and *Unión*, as well as in the accounts of Cuban writers such as Antón Arrufat's *Virgilio Piñera entre él y yo* (Virgilio Piñera between him and me) (1994) that uncover the ostracism felt by many

during those times. Indeed, the fact that Arrufat won the National Literature Prize in 2000 was a tacit admission and rectification of the suffering
produced during those years.

While the revolution demanded solidarity from its foreign fellow travelers, many of the writers living in Cuba were having a very difficult time.
In the 1990s, writers achieved what seemed impossible before that time:
a kind of pact with the state that allowed them to publish abroad while remaining in Cuba. This was always subject to constraints and to the image
of Cuba that the state wanted to advertise. Many writers abandoned the
island over the course of the decade. Some the best and brightest young
essayists live abroad: Rafael Rojas in Mexico, Iván de la Nuez and Rogelio
Saunders in Spain, Emilio Ichikawa in Miami.[34] Novelists such as Daína
Chaviano, Zoé Valdés, Norberto Fuentes, José Manuel Prieto, and Abilio
Estévez live abroad and have differing political positions on the Cuban
cultural situation. The poets and narrators who started the journal *Dias-
poras* have themselves become a diasporic configuration: of the original
group, only Carlos Aguilera and Pedro Márqués de Armas remained in
Cuba until 2003, but Aguilera won a prestigious scholarship to Austria
in 2001, and after many unsuccessful attempts to obtain a visa, Marqués
de Armas finally relocated to Europe. I mention *Diaporas* in particular—
although the group and the magazine were not as well known as others—
because it has become the living example of what the journal's name
described. Dispersal now seems to be the norm for Cuban artists, while
Cuban art, regardless of the site where it is produced, still tries to understand how to portray, and perhaps reconstruct, a nation divided, with a ruling class that seems determined to hold on to power until the bitter end.

EMBITTERED SUBJECTION

There is always a tension between telling and showing, between putting
the objects on the table and at the same time deriving meaning from
them. In the case of Cuba, the imposition of meaning on every aspect of
life, culture, and its representations problematizes all attempts at explanation. From the outset, the revolution had meaning, cultural objects revealed *something*, phenomena were meant to *represent*.

It is not clear to me whether the private Cuba I inhabit comes as a voluntary or an involuntary process. Like many others, I left Cuba as a child,

though I was raised with the profound consciousness of a Cuban exilic memory. Actually, there was no memory, but rather an invented memory; there was, in fact, no recollection, no epistemological reality. At the same time, the fiction of belonging tempered all narratives constructed at that time. Images were part of a nonfictional account that could cite street names without any degree of lived experience. At the time I first went to Cuba in 1980—*returned* is too strong a word and it does not do justice to the mental process that it entailed—Havana was a city lived on a map, a textual construction, a reference. But it was a reference that was "real" enough for it to allow the paradox of an invented recall.

In essence, this was the Cuban construction involved in exile: the edifice always on the verge of collapse but also continually reinvented. Yet when I tried to use one word in order to describe the "mood" I felt in Cuba in the 1990s, it was a reference to taste and liquid, and not architecture, that I initially came up with. Bitterness was the "mood" that best seemed to encapsulate Cuba then, as the state demanded enormous sacrifices from its citizens, while tampering with a momentous change that seemed to have arrived yet failed to arrive. This frustration and impatience was evident in literature written within and outside the island, and it was represented in the work of new painters and artists such as Kcho (Alexis Leyva Machado), or Carlos Garaicoa, and in performance artists such as Tania Bruguera, who attempted to register the present realities with possibilities lived in the past.[35] Anger, bitterness, and melancholia could be heard in the mellower songs of the Cuban troubadours—they even permeated the nostalgia felt in Wim Wenders's film *Buena Vista Social Club*—and they could be danced with the dizzying pelvic thrusts of the Cuban 1990s beat called *timba*.

This bitterness was predicated on, and even "mellowed" by, a distancing effect. Like the comments by Arturo Arango mentioned earlier, subjects measured past and present and somehow created an alternate self, one that could speak in an *other* voice, going back and forth between illusions and lost illusions, between the preterite and an imperfect subjunctive that measured "what could have been." The bitterness this produced could not be pinpointed exactly—it was a code word that verbalized beings lost *to* time and lost *in* time. Artists over forty could narrate and depict having fought, and won, and lost, and fought again, within a system in place for four decades, while younger artists could only engage those memories in the abstract and ponder in the present what could have been and was not. Bitterness meant constantly measuring the distance between a present time seen as a "degradation" and a recent past represented as "heroic." It was, for me, an aftereffect of the dynamic struggles between the subject and power, but also part of the ambivalent complicity between them both.

This bitterness was predicated on the fact that the webs that link Cuban subjects with power cannot simply be brushed off by stating that Cubans are always at the mercy of the state. This reading, which permeates many segments of the Cuban-American leadership, was always too facile. As the basis for policy decisions taken by the United States, it could never totally account for what has taken place since the revolution. The state, in fact, cannot be explained simply as repressive, but rather as disciplinary. It distributes favors, helps certain individuals succeed and not others, and historically understands its raison d'être as operating for the common and popular good. It funneled strong currents of nationalism that were already present in the republican period from 1903 to 1958, and from a long tradition of Cuban exceptionalism that has been well analyzed by its intellectuals.[36]

It was clear to me that bitterness was the result of a particular dynamic vis-à-vis the state that Judith Butler had already deconstructed, where the power of the state is understood as not being alien to the subject and certainly not external to it.[37] It is the state that allows the subject to constitute itself, that interpellates the subject into being. The state classifies and distinguishes citizens from noncitizens, those who belong and those who do not. It provides its own vision for the future and motivates citizens again and again to emulate heroic figures in every action. If every act has a particular kind of *meaning* for the state, and if every act is seen against the backdrop of what the event could signify in the future, the loss of these points of reference in the early 1990s produced uncanny results. As a reaction, bitterness involves a melancholic way of understanding struggle from the point of view of its future loss. In these terms, it is related to nihilism, defined as more than merely lack of belief, or absence of illusion, but as a distancing effect, one that views events from the point of view of something that has already occurred. However, it seemed to me that, unlike nihilism, there was no real redemptive power to bitterness. It remained within the temporal framework of a relationship with the state and it could not aim toward a "higher" and more distant subject position. The bitter subject, at some level, still retains his or her faith in future liberation. It may see liberation in the past and at the same time lament the fact that liberation was never possible. Bitterness creates a subject "out of joint."

This bitterness is also felt in Miami, of course, but in its temporal dynamics it is related to a death that is constantly repeating itself in the replayed image of the departure. As Gustavo Pérez Firmat puts it in his memoirs: "I have replayed our departure from Cuba in my mind hundreds, perhaps thousands, of times. I have dreamed about it, fantasized about it, and matched memories with my parents and with my brother Pepe who was old enough to remember."[38] That departure is always a replay, a trauma that takes a whole lifetime to absorb. In spite of the fact that the life Pérez Firmat recalls of his late childhood and adolescence in Miami is one lived in the midst of a tight-knit community, the ill will felt toward the home country is never allowed to recede. Explaining why is it that he does not return to Cuba, even as others, including his brother, have returned a number of times, it is clear that for him a return entails understanding the present as a form of usurpation: "I would find it unbearable to set foot in the house, much less talk civilly to the people whom, whatever their specific histories and motives, I cannot help regarding as usurpers."[39] His remark is prescient in terms of the bitterness many Cubans feel. Cuban history since the revolution is a history of departure, but it is also the history of the bitterness felt about the fact of having to leave in the first place.

If it is hard to explain the mechanism that produces bitterness as an aftereffect of the dynamic relationships between the subject and power in contemporary Cuba, it is nevertheless easier to point it out in most Cuban art produced since the early 1990s. A clear example of this can be found in the film *Alicia en el pueblo de maravillas*—a play on words that could be translated as "Alice in the Town of Wonderland"—by Daniel Díaz Torres. *Alicia* was written in 1986, and filmed between 1988 and 1989. It narrates the story of an innocent cultural promoter named Alicia, sent by the government to a Cuban town of unspecified locale. The place is dirty, there is a constant rain that washes away refuse and papers, the town's water is contaminated, and the hotel rooms are in ruins. The townspeople aimlessly repeat revolutionary slogans that they do not believe in. In the restaurant, cutlery is tied to the table in order to prevent its being stolen, but the chains for the cutlery are so short that it is practically impossible to eat.

The town itself is clearly meant to represent Cuba as a whole: everybody suffers from delusional paranoia, and they have all been sent to this purgatory in order to purge some kind of deviance. The town's leader and political paterfamilias is an old man who devotes himself to fantastic projects—the symbol is self-explanatory—and who disappears at the end of the film leaving only a slab of sulfurous mud, which is in turn examined incredulously by Cuban policemen.

It was clear that the film allegorized the economic and political situation in the country at the end of the 1980s, which is why party leaders took offense at its bitter account. Before its official opening, the film was screened for groups of intellectuals and Cuban Institute of Cinematographic Art (ICAIC) functionaries, who reacted indignantly to its critiques. It was rumored that the picture was seen by Fidel and Raúl Castro, who disliked it, but it was nevertheless exhibited in twelve movie theaters in Havana on June 13, 1991, with the state's ideological wing in charge of its dissemination and promotion. The film became a succès de scandale with the party requesting that its militants attend screenings. At the Yara theater in Havana, the audience made two separate queues. One was reserved for party members, and the other for the general public; the ushers were instructed to admit people in equal numbers from both lines. Shouts of "Viva Fidel" and "Viva la Revolución" could be heard at different points while the film was screened, and this created an oppressive atmosphere, heightened by the fact that the air-conditioning system broke down.

After this opening-night fracas, *Alicia* was debated at the UNEAC, with some of its members complaining about the "fascistic" methods used at the theaters. The party formally responded by removing the film from theaters and insisting on the fact that its having been shown at all— for four days—had been a gesture of goodwill. The film chosen to replace *Alicia* was *Alien II*.[40]

The fracas over *Alicia* revealed that artists understood this new period in Cuban history as one permitting more freedom of expression, while it also served as a dress rehearsal for the government's mode of dealing with new expressions of discontent. In the course of the next decade, political censorship relaxed to a certain extent, though it was always subject to governmental and party controls. Still, this kind of bitter account of the present was extremely difficult for the government, because it could not be framed simply as "antirevolutionary," but as disenchanted. A similar conflict ensued with Tomás Gutiérrez Alea's last film, *Guantanamera* (1995). But by the time that happened, it was clearly understood that bitterness and melancholia were going to be the dominant themes of Cuban literature and arts at this point in time.

There are more examples in literature. Leonardo Padura, who lives in Cuba, hit the best-seller lists in Spain with a series of crime novels centered on his own tropical, Cuban, Phillip Marlowe. He is called Mario Conde, a down-and-out Cuban agent who solves gruesome murders and in the process exposes past corruptions and present cover-ups in the higher echelons of the state. Conde is surrounded by a motley assortment of transvestites, maimed survivors of the Angolan wars, owners of clandestine bars, formerly imprisoned writers, and bureaucrats subject to the constant vigilance of a security apparatus created by a system that devours those it places in high positions. Conde roams Havana casting a bitter eye at all that had been and could never be, and the crimes he solves are the jigsaw puzzles of a revolution that went terribly wrong from the moment it decided to demolish the past republic without learning from the republic's achievements and mistakes. The bitter universe in which Mario Conde lives is more than the translation of the acid nonchalance of film noir. It is a melancholia so deep that it can only be redeemed by the human contact of his down-and-out friends, or by the looming possibility of violence.

Padura is but one example of the bitter aesthetics that seems to permeate Cuban literature these days. In one of the stories of *In the Cold of the Malecón* (2000), Antonio José Ponte portrays the encounter between a historian and an astrologer who fail to understand either the past or the future. In another story, Ponte captures the solitude of a Cuban student who returns from a crumbling Soviet Union to his old neighborhood in Havana, only to find that destruction is represented in very literal terms in the demolished Cuban capital. If Padura wants to uncover the past understood as a series of crimes, Ponte is a more subtle, but no less disenchanted, narrator. A man who keeps rearranging the furniture in his house is finally allowed to understand that the changes he makes are just cosmetic: "A true change would be changing the walls. Or giving it all up and leaving the room behind."[41]

This bitter atmosphere seems to permeate many segments of the dismantled and reconfigured social order. Reina María Rodríguez, who hosted a group of poets in her rooftop home (an *azotea*) in Havana during the 1990s, wrote a poem of disenchantment that explored the present while observing a picture of Che Guevara the poet keeps tacked to her wall.[42] It is a minor masterpiece, a discursive text that proceeds from a very concrete event, but that also manages to speak obliquely about pain and lost faith, as when the poet talks as if she lived in a utopia that has already collapsed: "the utopia / of an immense cupola fastened to my head / had fallen" (la utopía / de una bóveda inmensa sujeta a mi cabeza, / había caído). She talks about how the image of the hero has been falsified, and though it still keeps its seductive, luminous power, the poet can see that the image itself will also perish, as the body did before it: "the picture will also die / because of the humidity of the sea, the duration; / the contact, the devotion, the fatal / obsession of repeating so many times that we would be like him."[43]

It is this degraded present that haunts Rodríguez's poem—a statement of nostalgia, but also, within its discursive framework, a bitter settling of accounts between the poet and the image, as in the lines, repeated throughout the text, where she says "(and you, who still demand from me some faith)" (y tú que me exiges todavía alguna fe). Even framed as a parenthetical phrase, the line is a powerful indictment of the structural relationship involved in what is demanded from the subject and what the poet feels she can demand of the figure. It is, perhaps, the most poignant account of disenchantment and bitterness registered in Cuban poetry in the last decade.

SOUVENIRS

Cuban Palimpsests is a book that migrates—from semiotics to history, from history to fiction, from the personal to the political, from the particular to the collective, from past to present, and from the archive to its dispersion. I think the only way to understand Cuba at this point is by migrating in this fashion, taking into account different aspects of a reality that is more than simply a palimpsest of past and present. Stated more clearly, and in a more imagistic fashion, I want to underscore the fact that Cuba has produced exiles, and migrants, but that Cuba itself is also migrating.

This book crystallizes a kind of archaeological journey, but this is not to be understood as an attempt at reclaiming an "exilic" memory for myself.

There are no memories of Cuba other than those that have taken place in the empirical and epistemological context of my visits there; at the same time, it is too much to expect from a book of essays that it produce an act of closure. The book cannot really be a "bridge" and it cannot close off very real differences between one side of the divide and the other. If there is a bridge, I'd rather focus on what moves above it. The idea here, of course, is that this movement, these multiple experiences, and these varied perspectives, will produce a different kind of vision.

I have avoided the temptation to psychoanalyze either in the particular or in general. I have chosen to deal with a collective phenomenon that cannot be reduced to the terrain of the personal. Psychoanalysis can offer many insights into the present Cuban situation, but I think the situation is best apprehended from a collective stance. Melancholia may be the most crucial element in terms of the disenchantment that haunts the survivors of a nation that is, to this date, severed in spite of the fact that many would rather this not be the case.[44] For me, it makes no sense to refer to the Cuban situation without taking into account those Cubans who live outside of the island. In terms of their opinions and beliefs, in terms of how they can read the nation and its literature and culture, one cannot pretend that they have no new perspectives to offer, or nothing new to say, about what happens on the island. To do that is to collaborate in a purely mercantile, economic, and politically self-centered policy. The contacts between Cubans on the island and those abroad have been too numerous to brush off a significant debate.

As a corollary to that statement, any scholar interested in Cuba has to ponder whether one can write a history of the island without understanding that there are at least two histories, and that the history of the revolution can now be comfortably divided into an "official" and a "dissident" view. And what is a present or future historian to do with the fact that there are two distinct memories of the process? A few years ago, while perusing card files at the Casa de las Américas library, I ran across a subject entry for magazines published in the United States. There I found the almost complete collection of the magazine *Mariel*, published in Miami and New York by Reinaldo Arenas, Reinaldo García Ramos, and Roberto Valero—all of whom had left Cuba during the 1980 Mariel exodus, after suffering through the harsh decade of the 1970s. In the institutional memory that Casa de las Américas was invested in creating, this was not a

Cuban magazine published in exile, but simply a journal published in the United States. To compensate for that lack and that loss, we should celebrate the fact that the Cuban Collection at the University of Miami collects all materials pertaining to the cultural production of exile since 1959. That material, at this point, and by its sheer existence, is also part of the Cuban nation.

The collective response to the impasse of the Special Period has been more governmental demands for patriotism and nationalism. But there are also processes of transculturation, as well as constant negotiations within an exilic memory—not simply outside of Cuba, but also within. I want to underscore something: there is an exile of Havana from Miami, but there is also an exile from Havana that manifests itself *within* Havana. Living outside of the island does not necessarily privilege exilic memory. To pursue this point further: there are Cuban exiles *in* Havana, living in very real houses and apartments, and moving here and there in order to make a living, publish a book, or have access to the latest movies. Nostalgia for Cuba does not take place only in Miami.

At the same time, Cuba has to be one of the most oft-quoted countries in the world. Not only just Che Guevara T-shirts, but restaurants, bars, a certain "look" that belongs to the early 1960s and that codifies and reads Cuba in its own particular way—sometimes the minimalist lines of a mid-century modernism that bleeds onto the recall of a Russian constructivist tradition. There is a bar in Amsterdam called Café Havana; there is La Bodeguita del Medio in Berlin, a Café Kuba in Krakow, and salsa saloons in Madrid, Mexico City, and Paris. All of them seek to reproduce the gaze of a country best perceived by the image it creates. They could be called parts of Cuba—sort of like offshore colonies constructed solely of images, where Cuba becomes a privatized construction. And one cannot help but remark on the irony of this fact: for a revolution that always valued collective action versus personal desires, it has now become the last refuge of the disenchanted and the disengaged—the personal construction of entrepreneurs who trade in nostalgia, in exchange for drinks.

History on the Rocks

DOMINO PLAYERS

The Cuban domino game has four players: History, Memory, Representation, and Chance. They have all played their game on the streets of Havana and in a little park off Miami's Calle Ocho, and they have paired off in different teams or played on their own. But collectively they all bear responsibility, in one way or another, for what Cuba is, what it has been, and what it will become. These four players can also be found in the wider Caribbean basin—the region most responsible for the birth of modern European history, the "accidental" islands that prevented Columbus's encounter with the East, and that then supplied sugar on a massive scale for world markets—but in modern times Cuba has been particularly affected by how these four have engaged in the scenarios of the Cold War, and how they have sometimes played their game while holding the world in thrall. A sequence of accidents affected Cuba in a way that found some justification in its history: the change from pleasure island to socialist utopia was effected by the construction of a collective memory of struggle that the revolution deployed in photographs, films, and literature; and at one point the socialist government's incursion into African wars was explained by the common history of slavery and the links forged by neocolonialism. Cuban essays may engage history, memory, representation, and chance at any given point in order to explain Cuba, because the canonical texts that seek to describe in some essential way what it means to be Cuban all seem to position these four players in some way or another.[1]

However, it is actually not an essay or a cultural treatise but a poem written before the revolution that best defines how all these players engaged Cubans during the Special Period. In its long and discursive free verse, Virgilio Piñera's *La isla en peso* (1942)—a title that could be translated as "The Weight of the Island" but that may be more aptly rendered as "Taking the Weight of the Island"—deployed a History that never quite moved, or moved in circular fashion, trapping all subjects, and condemning them to live in a state of amnesia. Piñera wondered at what point Memory could free the insular inhabitant from his or her misery, and what sort of game Representation played at a moment of self-awareness the poet saw as always fleeting, fragile, and impermanent. Piñera sought to uncover something—anything—that could explain how the geographic fatality of Cuba as an island affected its people, aware that this would only represent more pain.

For Piñera, it seemed that memory was always shattered, always destroyed and dutifully recomposed, generation after generation, to the extent that insular inhabitants who took a "step back" and became aware of a particularly Cuban malaise were tormented by the realization that they lived within a "blind" present. The poem's first line invited readers to emulate the poet in a quest that had no definite outcome: "The damned circumstance of water on all sides forces me to sit at the coffee table" (La maldita circunstancia del agua en todas partes me obliga a sentarme en la mesa del café).[2] It's as if Piñera had read history as pure latency, as the empty time before the memory comes back to haunt those survivors who have left their traces on the land. Awareness offers no escape, because it reveals Cubans as beings always haunted by history, and condemned to live within their geographic fatality. But for Piñera this awareness is preferable to living in the blind state of amnesia. Piñera ultimately wants something impossible: a future that could return to the past and change it. And because of this, *La isla en peso* is a poem of self-punishment; for only out of self-punishment—here understood as painful self-awareness—can Cubans create for themselves a memory that will allow them some form of agency. Piñera wants the agency he so insists is lacking in the insular space, but at the same time understands that it is an agency he has always had without knowing. That painful self-awareness is part of the poem's play and part of its confusion: *La isla en peso* is a text of waiting, but it is also a text that waits for something that may have already happened.

Piñera's poem was important for poets in Cuba when they rediscovered it during the early 1990s. It was published again, openly talked about, and commented on. Piñera had been ostracized during the 1970s—his work did not fit within the aesthetics of political literature the revolution wanted to promote, and it was only in the 1990s that he assumed his rightful place in the Cuban canon.[3] At this time, surely the sense that the accumulated weight of history had done nothing to lighten the weight of a particularly Cuban malaise drew writers, performers, and critics to Piñera's text.[4] Its temporal play, focusing on the individual and his or her relationship to insular space *and* to historical time, allowed artists to question the role that History had played in the revolution. It gave them a sense of critical distance at a moment in which the major narrative lines of Cuban history were considered, as a whole, to have led into an impasse, where the domino game was stuck. Cubans could not understand how the future utopia had led to this; they saw the ghosts of the past dashing any hope for the future, and they could only look back to their histories of struggle as one long painful memory that had produced a shattered dream. Like Piñera, they sought to uncover something in the past that would allow them a way out. At the same time, the act of distancing themselves from the present in order to look at the situation objectively produced a painful and hopeless self-awareness.

Consciousness produced the sense of being locked in, geographically and culturally. Piñera's poem offered the lesson of history as a negative consolation that produced more pain. It ran counter to what the revolution had promised from the first: a change in historical paradigms, and the hope that negative self-awareness—that Cuba had never been a developed country, that its progress had been a mirage constructed at the expense of the people, and that it had been historically ill-treated by world powers— would charge subjects into constructing a better future within a generation. More than four decades later, this promise was openly questioned, and Piñera's poem contributed to a critical revision of history and circumstance. If this did not entail shattering the heroic memory of the past, or rewriting History, or changing Representation and taking advantage of Chance, at the very least it forced artists to figure out how the "damned circumstance of water on all sides" that Piñera talked about had produced the mistakes that now trapped them.

ORACULAR HISTORY IN THE FUTURE PERFECT

From the beginning, Fidel Castro justified his struggle by appealing to history. "History will absolve me," he said in a pamphlet that began to circulate in 1954 as the printed version of his self-defense for the Moncada barracks attack. And the three generations of Cubans who have been directly or indirectly affected by that mandate have justified political decisions by repeating those words like a mantra. The speech itself, as historian and cultural critic Rafael Rojas has suggested, belongs to the "oracular" tradition of Cuban history.[5] This tradition is at once apocalyptic and prophetic, and it fashions the citizen of the republic as a tragic hero who can only see his or her destiny as either an enigma or an impossibility.[6] In this speech, Castro carried on his shoulders the weight of the past as well as of the present. From the point of view of an intellectual consciousness, his *History Will Absolve Me* is the account of how one individual survives the legacy of Cuban history. Fidel enacted the voice of all Cubans, lost in a historical maze and trying to make sense of it.

Fidel was not a historian, but his words have been a recurrent refrain—the main theme that appears at the overture to the revolution and that carries the audience all the way to what was anticipated as a final, heroic denouement. Fidel wrote his self-defense while he was in jail (1953–54) waiting to be sentenced for the suicidal attack at the Moncada barracks near Santiago de Cuba. Its jostled temporality—appealing to the future and the past for present action—renders all that happened after the scene of its utterance as the logical outcome of a temporal dislocation. Here, the metanarrative (history) is always counterposed to the subject ("me"). The pamphlet renders Cuban history as the story of one man in his fight with seemingly unmovable structures: "Never has a lawyer had to practice his profession under such difficult conditions," Castro says in the opening lines of *History Will Absolve Me,* "never has such a number of overwhelming irregularities been committed against an accused man."[7]

History always entails a risk, as Walter Benjamin observed: one has to make history, instead of assuming that it always belongs to the past. This idea permeates Castro's text. But, at the same time, as Benjamin noted, history is, and can be, a presence that always fails to arrive, never simply past nor future. It is an image that acts as a guide for our actions, and that guides them in turn.[8] In Fidel's words, "history" also foreshadowed an event that was never going to happen: a time outside of time, a future where "history" could come and judge. As he said in his concluding words, joining his present circumstance to a broader symbolic framework: "I do not fear prison, as I do not fear the fury of the miserable tyrant who took the lives of 70 of my comrades. Condemn me. It does not matter. History will absolve me."[9]

What Fidel presented here was a future that was mostly an image of the present where *that* "future" could be understood as "history." Thus, the future in this pamphlet also beckoned the redeeming force of history as a critical gesture. It mobilized what Slavoj Žižek has called, in another context, the "Stalinist logic" of history: "Actual history occurs, so to speak, on credit; only subsequent development will decide retroactively if the current revolutionary violence will be forgiven, legitimated, or if it will continue to exert a pressure on the shoulders of the present generation as its guilt, as its unsettled debt."[10] Understood in this manner, *History Will Absolve Me* was, and is, a document of debt. It is about all the debts one individual voice speaking for the collective may have to the past, and it talks about the duty living generations have to those who already have come and gone. Fidel fashioned his struggle as the relationship between debtor and creditor, and understood the relationship between the past and present generations as one of sacrifice. As Nietzsche remarked while commenting on this notion of history, "one has to *pay them back* with sacrifices and accomplishments."[11] In this way, the debt constantly grows greater. The debt will be repaid with credit, up until the time when the credit in itself overshadows the amount that was borrowed in the first place.

This sense of debt and duty marked the Cuban Revolution from the moment Fidel Castro gave his self-defense: from then on, the revolution always looked at the present from the point of view of the future. It turned the revolution into an encounter with history—and that encounter always had a messianic and redemptive air about it. It beckoned death and sacrifice, and it played on the religious theme of salvation. And when this oracular tradition became the victorious historical narrative, it became official historiography: it went back to the past in order to seek events in Cuban history that preordained what the present had become. It inscribed all postrevolutionary Cuban subjects as having been born out of violence— not as the result of a pact between different sectors of the social polity but as a result of the breakdown of those pacts. The history written by the revolution, as Rafael Rojas has explained brilliantly, goes back to moments of tension and violence. It does not seek out the long periods of time when the social pact allowed Cubans to carve out their own existence, but rather constructs history as a result of very concrete struggles. Born out of the "oracular tradition" of the republic, Cuban history was then written as a justification for revolutionary work, and it was from then on to be written as prophecy—by definition, outside of time or in a time of its own, ordering and reordering the past and accommodating it to the future.[12]

One of the consequences of this document of debt called *History Will Absolve Me* is the fact that all subjects born after the debt was proclaimed are always forced to go back to the moment of enthusiasm—to the golden age in relation to which every other age is but its degraded image. If distance for Piñera entailed stepping back in order to look at a past that would allow him to understand the present as the point of departure for the future, the act of *stepping back* promoted by Fidel forces us to look at the degraded present from the point of view of the heroic past of struggle. The present, then, will be justified by the repayment of past debt, with the hope for future return—a very different temporal construction from the one offered by Piñera. But, at the same time, being absolved by history in the future entails the awareness that we can never quite pay back the debt that was incurred on our behalf in the first place.

To seek an origin to the ruling psychic mechanism that structures revolutionary discourse in Cuba at this point in time, we have to engage in this temporal shift announced by Fidel. But instead of understanding history as a march toward redemption, here we need to see the older manuscript next to the new. In going back, it will be clear that politics cannot be anticipated by language or rhetoric. It might be that Fidel never clarified that history would absolve him in a future that might never come.

SUSPENDED ANIMATION: HISTORY AND REVOLUTION

Debates on historiography in Cuba serve to strengthen national ideology. In contexts such as that of the besieged Cuban Revolution, separating historical fact from propaganda becomes difficult, because, from the outset, history was too important to remain within the confines of the university. During the 1960s and 1970s, and up to the present, history has been, in fact, popularized by institutional venues dedicated to its production, reproduction, and dissemination. In this way, the Cuban Revolution shares with other modernist projects the belief and the faith that the future needs to build upon the past.

From the beginning, it was clear that one revolutionary narrative began on that triumphal date of January 1, 1959, when the dictator Fulgencio Batista fled. But, during the 1960s and later, that beginning was moved back to July 26, 1954—the date when a group of young rebels led by Fidel Castro attacked the Moncada barracks in eastern Cuba. And already in the 1970s, state historiography moved the intellectual beginnings of the revolution further back. By that time, most every important success, or failure, from the nineteenth century on, anticipated what the revolution always promised and delivered. What Louis Pérez Jr. calls the "national preoccupation with history" served then, as it does now, an official purpose and a public function. The revolution emphasized struggle in order to offer one very partial view of Cuban history, one that extolled sacrifice and that "provided the moral subsidy and, on occasion, the inspiration" that was needed to keep up popular enthusiasm during the transition to socialism.[13]

If the search for origins entailed more historiographical revisions in the past, faced with the question of endings, the revolution has had a hard time *stepping back,* in Piñera's terms. Although the ruling class in Cuba has remained in power for more than four decades, there are markers that have allowed Cubans and others to "structure" that history in different ways. For many, the revolution itself "ended" a number of times: in 1971, when the festive first decade gave way to a bureaucratized regime after the colossal failure of the ten-million-ton sugar harvest; in 1980, when thousands of Cubans left for the United States through the port city of Mariel; or in 1989, when the Soviet Union collapsed. Because, after 1989, the revolution needed to take into account how policies in the past had produced the present collapse, it bracketed periods in its own history (such as the infamous and repressive "quinquenio gris" or "five gray years" from 1971 to 1976), as well as historical discontinuities between that past and the present, in a process of managed revisionism.[14]

Because it could not create a historiography that proclaimed the end of one revolution and the beginning of another, the "Special Period in Times of Peace" actually shifted revolutionary discourse from its preoccupation with time to a focus on space. What this means is that revolutionary images, cultural objects and products, as well as revolutionary ideology, now tend to engage with the outside world strategically. That Fidel himself can move from a business suit during the day to military fatigues at night shows the kind of spatial positionalities that define what critics call the "Cuban condition" at this point. As if concerns with philology and origins in the 1970s had been superseded by a more structural awareness of the different bodies at play in the 1990s, space is now the central category for revolutionary discourse. Even the discourse of "resistance" that marked Cuban political life during the Special Period underscores this; for resistance is a category that detains the onslaught of time—it seeks to freeze time, while the state tries silently to maneuver possible solutions to intractable economic problems.[15]

Resistance as state policy altered the perception of revolutionary time, and it created new images for the island and for Havana. The revolution had memorialized the past as a category that had been superseded, as an object that one could observe at a distance. But when the Special Period opened Cuba to the outside world, it was clear that Havana had been left in a state of suspended animation. For the foreign observer, as well as for many habaneros, walking around central Havana as late as 2002 invited the stroller, or flaneur, to apprehend different temporalities within the same structure—the colonial or nineteenth-century, prerevolutionary capitalist use of the building in the advertising and signs that still remained—neon lights with no neon, or the practically intact counter of what used to be a Woolworth's soda fountain counter—and then also the third stratum: the use that the revolutionary government gave to that structure. This last skin of the building had no relationship with what the building itself had housed in the past, but it allowed the perception of discontinuity to guide all vision. For example, the nineteenth-century house had become a jewelry store during the republic, whereas the revolution decreed that this structure would now be used to repair old television sets. In the meantime, the sign that announced the jewelry store remained in place, and the original use was probably stenciled into the wall. Looking at the city that way, foreign observers found themselves within a palimpsest, thus the kind of temporal and spatial dislocations that are present in many images, including those shot by Wim Wenders in *Buena Vista Social Club*. The visual regime then became important in order to carry on commerce with the outside world, while Cuban historiography set itself out to engage more radical visions of time.

The ideology of history was revised, by openly or privately revisiting the places where it had been codified. This revision entailed not only texts, but also spaces—Havana as a city that could be, fundamentally, read as a book—and events: the literacy campaign, the exile from the port of Mariel. As can be seen in the popular detective tales crafted by Leonardo Padura in the 1990s, origins were not necessarily thought to be exclusive— that is, there was not one moment, or space, totally responsible for the collapse of what was the known world for many Cubans. In the fragmented, but also more open, intellectual thought of the early 1990s, there were many times when the revolution had, depending on the observer, "veered off course" or reacted in a way that had consequences for the future.

One of those events did not happen on the island of Cuba, but it allows us to think about a different island, in the present as well as in the past. By engaging in the narrative that I will present in a moment, I am moving more or less in a backward fashion, as befits the processes of memory that I want to illustrate. Thus, I will set up this scene in the present, move to its constructed representation in film, and then backtrack still further in order to reveal the history that took place at the site that I have chosen now for dissection. This can be seen as an example of historical revisionism within a context in which such revisions became the norm. History and Chance may turn out to have worked in tandem in this case, as we move from the present in order to unveil the past.

CELLULOID DREAMS:
HARLEM, HITCHCOCK, AND FIDEL

On a hot summer night in Harlem the top of the Hotel Theresa looks like an open shell, as if bombed or gutted out, with the letters spelling out its name stenciled on a wall. The top of the building is not dilapidated, but it does suggest decay. That is only the top, of course, and seen from a distance; for one could say that the Hotel Theresa lives on two time zones, each disengaged but also connected to the other as past to present. The top has exposed beams that support a facade where, though half erased by time, the letters "Hotel Theresa" can be read, bringing the past to life, a past that the building hides at street level. If one comes to this corner of 125th Street seeking out a memory, the daily life lived all around it will not allow for contemplation. Harlem now, within the texture of the present, has Dunkin Donuts and Footlocker outlets, and a huge Harlem USA mall with a multiplex near the Church's Fried Chicken. White European tourists take buses on Sunday mornings to hear African American church services that they have heard about in their home countries, and high rents in midtown Manhattan push the upwardly mobile farther up north, displacing the population that resided in the neighborhood for all these years. And they bring with them the first cappuccinos and lattes that many of them sip, improbably dressing as homeboys in order to "blend in" with this crowd. It is certainly a different image from the one that attracts tourists to Havana. History here is not a question of revealing different layers of time, but rather of hiding or forgetting what took place in the past.

For many Cubans, the Hotel Theresa in Harlem is one image out of a collective scrapbook, and it makes sense to talk here about a site that does not really exist except as a symbolic memory (the hotel itself does not exist anymore, though the building still stands), a mental projection of a past. The hotel is not a site of pilgrimage because one has necessarily been there, but rather because one has heard about it, or seen it in pictures—and not

In Harlem, the sign for the Hotel Theresa can still be read on top of the building on 125th Street. Photograph by José Quiroga.

even in pictures, just perhaps in some newsreel documentary way back, where a bearded man, his body half out the window, raised his hand in a salute to people downstairs. It is not part of voluntary or involuntary memory but something else—a place that allows for the perception of an event as if one had lived it.

Faced with the temporal logistics that marked Fidel's *History Will Absolve Me* as a document of debt, it may be useful to reconstruct the concrete site that originated a revolutionary future in "lived"—as opposed to "symbolic"—time. A visit to the Hotel Theresa will allow history to include not only those events that one is *fated* to fulfill, but also those that have been constructed out of strategic choices meant to turn History into a symbolic example. It does not create a less "melancholic" history but it allows us to construct sites of memory where the past can be looked at critically from the point of view of the fictions that have been created for it.

One could say that this site where the Hotel Theresa once stood evokes the memory of a memory—of a time when diaspora had not separated the national entity into two seemingly irreconcilable camps, a time when public and private memory had not been set against each other. It is a dream within a dream—a time before gay liberation and Stonewall, before the civil rights movement and gentrification, before the corporatization of capitalism, before the Great Society and the dismantling of the Great Society, before crack and the AIDS epidemic, before Cubans and Dominicans arrived in a city where Puerto Ricans had already worked for at least two generations in the manufacturing industry, before inner-city kids started wearing Tommy Hilfiger shirts.

An act of memory always has to take into account the disengagement that produces it—the sense of distance from the present that divides the subject in two and holds that moment for the future. It is a disengagement not unlike the one that seems concretely to mark the Hotel Theresa as a physical place, divided between an upper portion that reveals the site and a lower street-level reality that conceals it, as if the building itself personified divided subjects. And the past also needs to be looked at in terms of the fictions it created for itself, the mythic resonances that appear already as fabrications that give an account of the "truth." The echoes of the event perhaps give a better clue as to how to interpret the event than does the event itself.

In Cuban history, the past gets confused with a celluloid dream. It is not only composed of concrete actions but can also be best apprehended in terms of its constructed realities. Let us take as an example how Cold War (and Cuban) history is fleshed out in Alfred Hitchcock's *Topaz* (1969), in one of the central scenes of a film that has been judged by critics to be one of Hitchcock's most confusing. *Topaz* takes place in the early 1960s and while the credits roll it starts with the shots of a May Day military parade in Moscow. At the end of the credits, two sentences appear on the screen:

> Somewhere in this crowd is a high Russian official who disagrees with his country's display of force and what it threatens. Very soon his conscience will force him to attempt an escape while apparently on vacation with his family.

The action moves to Copenhagen, and then the defector is brought to Washington. In Washington, a whole series of complications ensue that will slowly flesh out the intrigue concerning missiles the Soviets want to deploy in Cuba and one André Devereau (Frederick Stafford), a French agent the Americans hire in order to confirm that the deployment is taking place in secret. The French agent, in turn, needs (the plot thickens) the help of an Afro-Caribbean asset. He will pay off a white Cuban government official called Luis Uribe to photograph the papers one evening in Harlem, at the Hotel Theresa, while the Cubans are in New York for a United Nations session. And the core of the movie takes place precisely here.

Plotlines in *Topaz* are consumed, rather than fleshed out. History becomes part of a network of nonevents, and Hitchcock does not allow the viewer to remain in any one space for a long period of time. The Cold War is a kind of diorama: it is a war without an open battle, and it has no beginning and no end. Even the opening shots of the military parade are props to a take that has already begun by the time the film starts, a plot device that merely serves to speed up the action, which ends up in New York City. The scene in Harlem is a spectacle that Hitchcock manufactures for the viewer's entertainment, but it is also one of the possible origins for a plotline that leads all the way up to the missile crisis. Even if Hitchcock's *Topaz* does not begin in Harlem, he pushes up that scene like a condensed dream image that one is then called on to unpack.

The gutted-out impression of the Hotel Theresa at present is only an illusion, of course, because no bomb blasted away at this building, no mass migration left it uninhabited. Like Havana today, four decades after the events depicted in *Topaz*, the ruins themselves inscribe time on the architectural surface. If one recalls the scene in *Topaz* and then moves back (or ahead) to the present, one could say that a war took place here in Harlem—in metaphorical but also in very real terms. The slow bombing out of years of neglect; the sad aftereffect of the Reagan years in the 1980s; the privatization of government, leaving people without a safety net; the ravages of the crack epidemic and of AIDS; the complete and utter disregard, for at least one generation, of inner-city dwellings; the demolition of whole barrios. Havana could also yield similar and juxtaposed scenarios, perhaps in a dialectical exchange: the empty high-class houses turned into schools, the city core abandoned for the sake of developing the countryside, the illegal subdivision of city dwellings to accommodate migrants from the rest of the country, the slow peeling off of paint, the deteriorated infrastructure, the sense of exhaustion born and bred out of a lack of real change. The top of the building that housed the Hotel Theresa in Harlem recalls a history of neglect, but it is also clear that, as happens in Havana, one can also flip it around so that this destruction becomes an emblem for the immense resilience of the place.

The Hotel Theresa is a memory palace, in a way, a symbolic site of what the hero in *Topaz*, André Devereau, tells the Cuban revolutionary Rico Parra: "a damn good show you put out there." The Hotel Theresa affair in New York occurred before the mass exodus, but if we are to see history in terms different from those used in revolutionary historiography, it also sealed diaspora as the only response for the events that took place there. In other words, exile as a fate was already assured by the time Fidel left New York. Just as Hitchcock implicitly points out in *Topaz*, the show at the Hotel Theresa marks a site in the historical moment the director isolates for dissection.[16] It is also the beginning of a particular kind of show that the revolution understood how to play very well. Hitchcock sums up the chaotic sense of controlled improvisation that, ever since then, has been affixed to the revolution as one of its most salient features. The symbolic representation of the revolution and the *revolucionarios* for the West started at the Hotel Theresa in New York. There was nothing fated about it. On the contrary, it was a media event constructed out of Chance.

When Fidel Castro came to New York in 1960 and stayed at the Hotel Theresa, no one could foresee that the fate of Cuba would be sealed for at least the next four decades. In 1960, there were still possibilities for accommodation between the different economic segments that had supported Batista's downfall. One could even turn Dickensian about 1960: it was the best of times and the worst of times, it was the end of the twilight zone where the revolution still had segments of the national bourgeoisie and the middle class supporting it, and the beginning of a different kind of politics. The middle class in Havana cheered the bearded revolutionaries (*barbudos*) and applauded the fair expropriations.

It was Fidel's second visit and it was marred by dispute. The first visit in 1959 was all about the present and the past of the Cuban republic and its newly triumphant revolution. During the second visit, in 1960, Fidel was already an emissary from the future. During the first visit, he did not come officially invited by the U.S. government; he was the private guest of U.S. newspaper editors, who seemed to be more interested in what was going on in Cuba than the U.S. government was.[17] Not unlike the situation today, business interests trumped government inattention. Fidel hired a public relations firm for this first trip, and he brought about seventy people in two airplanes. The firm advised him to smile, to speak English without any degree of embarrassment, to smile yet again at difficult questions, and to project an image of civility, courtesy, and democracy. He was met at the Washington airport by an undersecretary—and immediately Fidel insisted to the press that he was not coming to the United States to ask for money. He charmed the newspaper editors, and spoke at Harvard and Princeton; he met with Henry Luce of *Time,* and he was warmly received, though not officially—except by Vice President Richard Nixon.[18]

That first visit was a political disaster, though a public relations hit. In his account of the rise of the New Left during the 1960s, Van Gosse describes it as "a galloping success, generating a bandwagon that for another fortnight dispelled the gathering storm."[19] But the people in power treated Fidel in a way they would have never treated a sycophantic Batista. According to Louis Pérez Jr., the North Americans "were neither prepared to accept nor willing to acknowledge the depth of Cuban grievances." Nixon recalled later that he had talked to Fidel "like a Dutch uncle" and his interpreter wrote that he had treated Castro "just like a father." It is clear that the Cubans demanded respect, whereas the United States treated Cubans like unruly children who needed a guiding voice in order to deal with their demands in a "mature" fashion.[20]

That is why, in his second visit, Fidel was ready to play ball with the Americans. Fidel and a large entourage arrived in New York for a United Nations meeting on September 18, 1960. Hugh Thomas says the Cuban delegation was originally supposed to stay at the Shelbourne Hotel, in Midtown, but the Cubans complained that the hotel was too expensive and did not fit with their new revolutionary image, so they moved to the Theresa. The official history written outside of Cuba devotes a mere paragraph to the Hotel Theresa visit. The American presidential election was the truly important event for historians, because John F. Kennedy accused the Eisenhower administration of not doing everything in its power to ensure Cuban "freedom." Fidel hastily returned to Cuba on September 28 on a borrowed Soviet airliner.[21]

This cursory treatment by Thomas contrasts with the echoes of this visit in the popular imagination. Van Gosse remarks that it "has lived on in the popular memory, much more than the more decorous visit only seventeen months before."[22] Memory here is what triggers representation and creates solidarity. The Hotel Theresa inaugurated the dissemination of the Cuban Revolution as media spectacle. It produced a sequence of images that would be forever indelible: Foreign Minister Raúl Roa eating a hot dog at the Chock Full O'Nuts, Nikita Khrushchev going uptown to be photographed at the Theresa. Beyond the images themselves, there have always been popular tales surrounding this visit, including the fact that Castro and his entourage caused ten thousand dollars' worth of damage, which included cooking chickens in their room.

The details of that visit to the Hotel Theresa unfold in Carlos Franqui's account, collected in *A Family Portrait with Fidel: A Memoir* (1981), and they are interesting to compare to Hitchcock's presentation in *Topaz*.[23] Both accounts, in turn, deserve to be examined in light of Thomas's historical distance. Franqui fleshes out the different steps of the media spectacle. He explains that the Cubans initially had a safe house—presumably because they were in danger—which then could not be used, and Fidel wanted to turn Manhattan into the mountains of the Sierra Maestra in Cuba, where he had fought his revolutionary war. He asked for a camping permit, first on the grounds of the UN and then in Central Park, but it was denied. Franqui does not even talk about the classy Shelbourne

Hotel, but explains how the owner of the Theresa offered a whole floor to the Cuban delegation. And the Cubans accepted the offer, though the Theresa was then known as a hotel where one paid by the hour. Ramiro Valdés, one of Fidel's most trusted men, was the one concerned with the bad publicity this move could generate, because the hotel was full of whores. The whores, meanwhile, refused to leave the premises, insisting that they were also Fidelistas and that they could offer their services to the cause of revolution.

The performance and the media spectacle worked. It helps to put things in context by recalling also how Harlem in the early 1960s was full of things to come. It had seen the Harlem Renaissance and was about to be swept by the Black Panthers and the civil rights struggle of Martin Luther King Jr. and by Malcolm X. Fidel's visit in many ways was the prelude of things to come, and he made sure to meet Malcolm within an hour of his arrival, in a meeting photographed by Carl Nesfield.[24] Cubans opted to forgo the racial politics the island had traditionally played with the United States (white Cuban men trying to talk to white Americans), and they created an alliance between Cubans and African Americans, which remained solid throughout the years. The allegiance was at that time already cemented by Richard Gibson, the main public leader of the Fair Play for Cuba Committee, a group that injected a black element into its politics and that had been organized in the spring of 1960.[25] This African American alliance had happened because Gibson in 1961 was the executive secretary not only of the Fair Play for Cuba Committee, but also of the New York–based Liberation Committee for Africa. Moreover, Gibson participated in the famous July 4, 1960, issue of *Lunes de Revolución*—the literary supplement of Franqui's newspaper *Revolución*—titled "Los negros en U.S.A." that introduced Cubans to African American voices such as LeRoi Jones, Langston Hughes, and James Baldwin.[26] He was very successful in explaining solidarity for Cuba along racial lines, and his efforts bore fruit in the Hotel Theresa affair.

The media spectacle was always understood as a question of images, of representation. Carlos Franqui recalls that there was a reception at the Theresa at which the Harlem intelligentsia met with the Cuban delegation. Hanging around the Hotel Theresa were LeRoi Jones—who had been invited by Gibson to join a delegation of black writers visiting Cuba, resulting in the transformative experience represented by his piece *Cuba*

Fidel at the Hotel Theresa was the center of a media spectacle. Photograph by I. C. Rapoport. Reprinted with permission of the photographer.

Libre—and James Baldwin. Allen Ginsberg was there, and he defended to all the *comandantes* the use of pot as a revolutionary drug. "What does the Cuban Revolution think about marijuana?" he asked security chief Ramiro Valdés.[27] In 1965, Ginsberg went to Cuba and was kicked out for daring to say that the revolutionaries were quite sexy.[28] And from the very bitter space where Franqui is obliged to speak, after fighting for the revolution and having been in charge of its propaganda and then after falling from grace—after all these things, from Rome, where he was living in the early 1980s, Franqui added, taking a jab at the racial politics involved: sure, they were staying in Harlem and they were feted by the African American intelligentsia, but all of the delegation, with the exception of Juan Almeida, was male and white.[29]

Franqui always understood a lesson that the Cuban Revolution learned very well and has used throughout: the battle over Cuba had to be waged first of all on the media front. One may think that the media construction was already present at the time when *History Will Absolve Me* was penned— it was, after all, a media event that turned Fidel into a famous figure. But bitter Franqui remembered the scene in 1981 as if he had already been the premonitory image for Juan Uribe, the white Cuban gentleman in *Topaz* who betrays the revolutionaries at the Hotel Theresa. Franqui was, in fact, the architect of the revolution as a brilliant, creative mess of a media show. His bitterness arises from his backward glance at an event that to a large extent he helped create, but whose symbolic ramifications overwhelmed him: by playing the race card, Fidel was already showing himself an adept manipulator of the media image, which was already an issue when the *revolucionarios* were waging their war at the Sierra Maestra. Back then, even Che Guevara had recalled that "the presence of a foreign journalist, American for preference, was more important for us than a military victory."[30]

It was understood that Fidel had to play with the gringos, he had to up their ante at their own game. And he could do that only from an uncanny but very Cuban sense of class privilege, combined with the heroic romance of the revolution and his own belief in the fact that he had fought an epic war that more closely resembled, in fact, "a political campaign in a tyranny, with the campaigner being defended by armed men" (Thomas, *Cuba*, 1038). For Cubans, Castro was an immediate source of identification. He was a liberator and a savior in a political and religious manner, in a country where "politics, magic and religion are neighboring provinces, sometimes without boundary lines" (ibid.). He had panache and charisma, and it certainly helped that he was coded as "white" for the population at large. Because he was not a member of the struggling middle class, he had not gone to a Cuban military training facility, and did not have the experience of going up the ladder of military service—which meant, in Cuba, either turning into a bureaucrat or into part of the repressive machine. (Cuban soldiers did not really see combat: they spent their time in the barracks until the next military coup.) For many, there was something to trust about Fidel—he was part of a wealthy class, a disaffected member of the bourgeoisie—and there was something *modern* about his athletic demeanor. He spoke clearly, back then, without the Latin American penchant for the rhetorical flair. The fact is, there was something so *American* about him— American in that Cuban way of being American that one can see nowadays in the Miami middle-class neighborhoods of Kendall or Hialeah.[31]

The military fatigues were certainly an important element in the construction of the media event at the Hotel Theresa, in terms of what the military uniform exposed: a lack of respect for proper authority and for the proper rules of the game. The charismatic personality of Fidel played with a sense of class and even patrician pride. Only a creature of the Cuban republic, with all of its contradictions, could have assumed the sense of deservedness that Castro brought to the table. Fidel showed them, in the words of Van Gosse, "how political the hip could be, given half a chance"[32] and it was certainly the best example of "hipness" until the Sandinistas came along, and appealed to London bands such as The Clash. Even Hitchcock treats those revolutionaries with a certain element of respect—they were, after all, simply a rare breed of white people. Rico Parra, the green-eyed monster who represents the revolutionary class as a whole, is a man beholden to his ideals. He is cold and ruthless, but he inspires awe because of the strong masculinity he exudes in every scene. Parra is not exactly endearing, but the element of controlled chaos that he seems to be surrounded by is darkly colorful. He looks around his hotel room at the Theresa for an important document, and he finds it greased up by the remnants of a half-eaten hamburger on top of a desk. The cinematic gaze is vintage Hitchcock: the Cuban revolutionaries are managing a government but they are, in effect, grown-up kids who eat hamburgers and who want nothing more than to play ball.

Hitchcock also chose to zoom in on that small detail—the hamburger soiling the paper work of government—to point out what has been called the "ties of singular intimacy" between Cuba and the United States.[33] In retrospect, there was nothing more frightening for Americans than encountering one of their own who spoke in a different language. If Fidel had been a shade darker, Eisenhower and Nixon would have treated him with condescension. If Fidel had been a bit less educated, less tied to the formal bourgeoisie in power, they would have packaged him as an object made for export. But he was not a paradigm that the United States was prepared to accept; he did not fit into the traditional roster for the "Latin race." As Pérez puts it, "In growing numbers Cubans were arriving at the realization that emulation could not produce authenticity, that North Americans could not deal with them on any terms other than instrumental ones— without a past, without a future . . . They were learning that 'Cuban' was defined simply as the North Americans' exotic and tropical Other."[34]

The fact that the world was divided into cardboard cutout figures did not bode well for the coming problems that the empire was to encounter in the 1960s. Fidel was the American product packaged as a believer in democracy, but never giving an inch to a sense of (national, cultural, even class and patrician) pride. That pride would have been manageable had Fidel come from the South, but it was untenable for the kind of neocolonial compact that the United States had with Cuba. Cuba was an overseas province that made a lot of money, it had the largest number of TVs per capita in Latin America, and it was in the midst of a consumer frenzy for anything that was made in the USA.

Getting out of the Shelbourne and camping at the Hotel Theresa signaled clearly that the revolution had not been fought in Congress, and that the Cuban political class had been discredited. In fact, the revolution tuned in and dropped out, and those echoes were felt throughout the 1960s in the United States. Beards and long hair, riots against the staid bourgeois morality of the shopping malls and the obliged conformity of Levittown. The New Left learned from the Cuban Revolution—it didn't care too much for the Shelbourne either, and thought it could be more comfortable at the Theresa. It argued for pot as a revolutionary drug and then for free love, and its politics of engineered "happenings" was not very different from the "happening" that took place at the Hotel Theresa.

That trip to New York and the United Nations in 1960 reconfigured the dynamics of the Cuban situation for the next four decades. It cemented the alliance between Cuba and blacks, and it gave the revolution a sense of style constructed by a sophisticated media apparatus. The extent to which this represented a threat can be seen in the historical narrative that was being played out in other quarters at that time. While Fidel was in New York, Kennedy put the issue of Cuba squarely within the presidential election. The CIA was training mercenaries in an operation that already, in September 1960, was heading for trouble because of disputes that plagued it from the onset. Back in Cuba, the trip highlighted the growing isolation of the American embassy building. In the meantime—and this is part of Hitchcock's plot in *Topaz*—there were rebels in the Escambray mountains fighting against the increasingly disturbing direction of the revolution itself. In October, right after Fidel's visit, Eisenhower announced a ban on exports to Cuba, and the Cubans retaliated by confiscating more and more property in Havana and elsewhere. The American ambassador was recalled that October and he never returned. In January, Fidel argued for a general mobilization in Cuba, on the grounds that Eisenhower was planning an invasion. He demanded that the embassy reduce its staff to eighteen. Eisenhower broke diplomatic relations, and the rest is part of a history that does not need to be recalled or explained here. While the New Left gained voice and strength in the United States, Cuba and the United States had already broken diplomatic relations and would not resume them.

The Hotel Theresa affair is an *event* forever affixed to a *space*. It interjected itself into a concrete site and changed it in a radical way. This concern with the space in which the event in itself is inscribed was a source of inquiry for Michel Foucault, who argued that the category of space was as crucial for understanding the twentieth century as the category of time was for the nineteenth.[35] The act of apprehending, in one particular site, the different layerings of time, simultaneously, was the radical consequence of the change from philology—as the study of the origin of words—to Saussurean linguistics, and then to structuralism. This validation of space, and of placement, marked a different way of understanding history and political action. This was an effect of the compression of time felt during the socialist collapse of 1989, for the present became an expanded category that included all of the memorialized past.[36] One has to understand that this epistemic shift, as Foucault reminds us, is not immune to disciplinary control. Sites memorialized are also created by the state in order to foster particular visions of the past, and to legitimize their own hegemony over history. Even though sites such as these were complicit within broader structures of power, they also hold the possibility of allowing us to create an alternate history.

As Foucault defined them, heterotopias could be understood as sites where an alternate history took, or even takes, place.[37] They are not disconnected from other sites of struggle, and they also illuminate how subjects understand and deal with relations of power. These relations are never clear-cut, as any reader of Foucault knows. They are bisected or engaged in other struggles, both within subjects and among them. Heterotopias illuminate, in a more complex light, the underlying struggles for power. In these terms, the Hotel Theresa serves as a site where official memory takes place, but it can also be flipped around to be an emblem from a future foretold. It is as if Fidel himself knew that chance and savvy media manipulation made this the moment and the place that would define his revolution vis-à-vis U.S. racial politics and world media attention. That is why he visited the hotel forty-five years later, in October 1995, trading the suit and tie that he wore at that time to his meetings Midtown for the military fatigues that he had sported on his 1960 visit. Now, as then, there were notables present, some old and some new: Charles Rangel and José Serrano from the Bronx, Angela Davis, Amiri Baraka (LeRoi Jones), and Leonard Jeffries. There were people there who recalled that earlier time, and there were crowds that came to hear the Cuban revolutionary talk about injustice and racism and Third World debt.

Yet something felt different: this visit was not intended to agitate the establishment, and it was not meant to beckon the downtrodden with the romantic vision of a future free of poverty. The return was melancholic, in a way, simply because it was, above all, a return; because, in the linear vision of history the revolution had constructed, from a glorious past to a glorious future, the time scale here was askew. If the visit in 1960 was all about the future, this visit was all about the past. The first one was about building coalitions and seducing the American media; this one engaged different kinds of capitalists and allowed the media to participate in the act of memorializing the past within the present. Back then, Fidel wanted the world to be different; at this point, it was certainly a different world. It was a world that in 1995 received Fidel as part of a living museum, though he himself was struggling against the sense of defeat implied by the measures taken in order to forestall the popular revolts of 1994, taking place barely a year before this second visit to the Hotel Theresa. Hence, the return of the past involved repeating all the slogans, replaying all the exhortations, insisting that the revolution was not over, that the struggle still needed to go on. In 1991, the Hotel Theresa was designated a Harlem landmark, now called the Theresa Towers Office Building. And in 2002 there was a fund-raising reception attended by a very different cast of characters—Gov. George Pataki, Mayor Michael Bloomberg, and others—seeking to open a Harlem Republican Club at the site. Over and beyond demands for historical accuracy, memory gets rewritten by the state and manipulated at will.

CODA: THE PURSUIT OF FREEDOM

A city like Havana may now open up the diverse historical strata involved in its composition. But at the beginning of the 1970s, utopian enthusiasm was yielding to the ordered narratives of history. Those external to the revolution thought they could accomplish this sense of affective distance demanded by history, but they were trumped by an inability to understand properly how the tenor of things had thoroughly changed in a decade. They also stepped back, in a way, and apprehended Cuba as a space with a sense of purpose, but this purpose produced questions, and those questions had no definite answers. The best place to see this is in the conclusion to British historian Hugh Thomas's monumental *Cuba: The Pursuit of Freedom* (1971), one of the most complete histories of the island, undertaken precisely as a result of the spectacular changes brought about by the revolution. It is, in many ways, a very British account of modern Cuba (its point of origin is, in fact, the British invasion of 1762), but it will allow us to see how "stepping back" produced a melancholic and painful self-awareness within the revolution.[38]

Completed in 1971, Thomas's project was always perceived from the point of view of the present, from the twilight realm where the old Cuba of the frivolous pursuits changed its skin and became the utilitarian moral example of Third World struggles. One of the last sections of the book was titled "The Pursuit of Freedom," in order to return to the line of thought that structured the work as a whole and that used that same "pursuit of freedom" as its subtitle. And it should be noted that one of the last plates of that monumental history has a view of Havana in 1962 that is haunting

even today, when fundamentally nothing has changed in that skyline.
Thomas began that section with a totalizing comment, meant to allow
him to establish a distance from the narrative of history itself: "Cuba in
the 1960s has thus presented a tragedy for a large minority of her citizens,
especially for the many of them who, through no fault of their own but
because of the accumulation of social history, seemed previously too frivolous for drama" (1483).

Back when Thomas's book was written, history was conceived with the
pedagogical certainty of its liberating force—a certainty that was also
shared by the Cuban revolutionary government. But this is where the
similarities end, for Thomas at that point in the book had to give an
assessment of what the present was like to a foreign ("impartial") observer,
and what the past could teach the present. It is in this context that he
develops a statement on the relationship between history and political circumstance, or between the pursuit of a historical "truth" and the political
consequences involved in the "pursuit of freedom." These two categories
were already at conflict in this revolutionary society: "For a historian, the
good life is a society where Truth is not abused and where the study of
history, even recent history, can be pursued without interference" (1484).
The freedom to pursue the possible lessons of history should certainly be
one of the aims of a new society. It is precisely at the root of this tension
between utopia and history, between the "pursuit of freedom" promised
by utopia and the "pursuit of truth" that involves the historian, that one
can feel the bittersweet aftereffects of the revolution, which can be found
throughout Thomas's work. The most obvious tensions are to be found
when utopia is linked to politics, and when economic justice entails the
loss of free inquiry and personal freedom. At this point, and as a result
of these dialectical oppositions, Cuba becomes a moral example: "[t]he
Cuban Revolution, therefore, gives a lesson in politics" (1483). This we can
also see as the return of a timeless question: whether the end justifies the
means, and whether the pursuit of truth needs to be sacrificed in order for
the "pursuit of freedom" to have meaning.

The question was answered negatively by Thomas, but not without
grappling first of all with its implications. What is interesting about
Thomas's project is precisely this attempt to deal with the aftermath of
a historical period—the first decade of the revolution—that had come to
a close. Thomas understood at that point in time that the question about

ends and means could not be solved in the present time in which his history was written, and thus the "lesson" of history could not be learned. But, at the same time, the conflicts between majority and minority rule could already be seen as a step in this direction, and his nuanced assessment foretells a political line that will appear again and again over the course of the next decades: "Castro has done many things which have been popular even if they have been unjust to minorities or even if they have been at least partly designed to achieve popularity"(1484). Thomas calls it what it is—a dictatorship—but at the same time cautions that history reveals this to be a system created purely within the Cuban tradition, that it is, in some way, a logical extension of Cuban history: of Cuban desires for a leader of epic stature, and of Cubans' many claims to be taken seriously as participants on the world stage. Fundamentally, says Thomas, Castro created "a strong, ruthless, but original and popular despotism, with many remarkable social reforms to its credit and which, whatever label is given to it, represents a serious challenge to liberal society" (1492). Hence, the moral example that he talked about hinges on the relationship of the mass to the individual, of collective history—broadly understood and in broad strokes—versus the discrete and accidental history of the Cuban nation.

That none of these contradictions can be resolved is part of a situation that Thomas would surely call "traumatic"; for the "challenge to liberal society" that he speaks of is the distorted mirror that creates the tropical blend of fascism and socialism that beckons that same liberal society's fascination. There is a drama here insofar as Thomas is at a loss to understand his own situation, and as he tries to comprehend it by creating spatial relationships and a subject at a loss to understand them:

> The history of Cuba since the late eighteenth century, when the country began to produce sugar on a lavish scale for the world market, has been like the history of the world seen through the eyes of a child: an invention in Silesia, a plague in Africa, a war or a prosperous time in England or in France—these apparently unconnected events beyond Cuba's control have determined the lives of Cubans who, despite their tropical innocence, were the only links between them. (1493)

Cubans, then, are those who can never make sense of their situation, because their history exceeds individual bounds and can only be apprehended by connecting the dots at a distance foreclosed by the fact of living *through* history. It is a history that can never be merely contained, but whose sense of duty creates the narrative of the "pursuit of freedom" as its overarching purpose. Cubans' ability or inability to confront the consequences of events taking place in faraway locales gives them a sense of "chosenness" while being engaged in the "pursuit of freedom." Thomas's Cuba is the history of that sense of exceptionality, understood as the collective revolutionary will to ascertain what that mandate means.

Cubans, for Thomas, had been thrust upon a present that was not entirely their own, and had been forced to confront *history* as a consequence of their *political* decisions. The difficulties involved in engaging with this confrontation account for the melancholic tenor of Thomas's later chapters. The stakes had been raised. What was at stake in the revolution was not merely the history of an island nation, but the response to five centuries of colonial exploitation. At the point where history became a category that could be lived in a state of self-awareness, in the present, history itself turned Cuba into a *symbol.* Its inhabitants were entrusted with a mission, and it was a mission that defined Cuban exceptionality.

Generations after this theoretical move was accomplished, Cubans are still grappling with the relationship between facts and their symbolic meaning, between the concrete instances of life and the abstract notions of Cuba they themselves have constructed. Accomplishing the move from time to space in this manner, History became a visual: it was a structure, a picture, an image.

Espionage and Identity

IDENTITY SNATCHERS

Curious things happen in an immigrant city when people think they are being silently watched by agents coming from the country the immigrants have left. The usual scenarios that structure immigrant tales here are given a different twist. When one is dealing with the specter, or possibility, of spies in one's midst, one is dealing with an alternate reality. This reality is populated by delivery-van drivers who barely deliver a thing, doctors who know nothing about medicine—unclear, confused biographies, full of holes, full of information that doesn't add up and makes no sense, and opposed to the authenticities that are always involved in immigrant identity formation. There is a void in this scenario, a kind of silence where loose ends do not structure a narrative tale that proceeds from beginning to end, from escape out of oppression to immigrant success. What is important in the scenario of espionage is pretending, posing, assuming false identities. In espionage, what distinguishes one side from the other is revealed as a series of performative gestures, opinions that are given operatically, categorically, to excess; biographies that are fully constructed in order to achieve maximum effect. Espionage and identity are dialectical categories; the former allows for the uncomfortable possibility that identity frameworks may ultimately be reduced to acts of cultural and political transvestism, that all identity is actually imitation and that the authenticity that accounts for the original is the void, the hole, at the center of the narrative.

Political espionage as an element of the identitarian narrative may partly explain the "difference" and the "passion" that consumes Cubans in the United States—or perhaps it is *that* difference and passion that created the need for espionage in the first place. Whichever way it is, this variation on the identitarian framework also creates an equally tangled temporality, where events pile up one after the other, producing an action narrative where time itself seems to stand still. Even if there are now two generations of Cubans born outside of the island, and even if those who originally left Cuba after 1959 cannot be said to have ever had unanimous political ideas and beliefs, the narrative of espionage locks them into fixed positions, within parameters that seem to have been created decades ago and never outgrown. From a macrostructural perspective, this immobility is everywhere: on the one hand, a government ruled by the same man since 1959, and, on the other, a loose network of minority organizations with no visible or unified leader—this in spite of the fact that exile organizations have never really represented what the majority of Cuban exiles believe in, and that changes from below in Cuba reconfigure people's perceptions that time brings about no change.

Espionage is one of the results of the internationalization of Cuban affairs: it is at once the symptom and the effect of extraterritorial concerns and global symbolic networks where the Cuban state has positioned itself. The revolutionary government in Cuba sustained its power by inserting itself in a Cold War that was always a struggle between Americans and Russians. But the revolutionaries also needed internal cohesion, and consolidated power by infiltrating unions, political organizations, and established networks of civil society. The situation, in the first years, was extremely volatile in a country that had sustained such close ties to the United States. Surveillance was validated in political as well as artistic terms. The detective novel, and espionage tales, were encouraged by the government literary institutions and its broad networks of prizes during the 1970s, and these in many ways validated other revolutionary decisions as far as aesthetics was concerned.[1] That subjects could be either *for* or *against* the revolutionary project already led directly to identities performed within social situations, and to beliefs and convictions held in secrecy or out in the open. This constant concern with beliefs, actions, and language was given an official imprimatur as early as 1960, when mass surveillance was codified by creation of the dreaded Comités de Defensa de la Revolución

(Committees for the Defense of the Revolution), which canvassed and reported on citizen actions in every city block throughout the country. Even as late as 1991, Senel Paz structured the tale that became the film *Strawberry and Chocolate* by focusing on surveillance, espionage, and betrayal directed at its main character: the suffering homosexual Diego. The constant appearance of this topic, so popular in the 1990s in the novels of Leonardo Padura, suggests that, to understand Cuban identity within the present Cuban condition, espionage needs to be seen as an integral theme.

The Cuban identity in question also leads from the internal surveillance of espionage to the way Cuba is positioned in broader global narratives. In the James Bond film *Die Another Day* (2002), the action brackets Cuba as a station between Hong Kong and London. In Cuba, North Korean agents assume new identities in order to infiltrate the West, taking advantage of the fact that the Cubans have the equipment necessary to change the body and the skin of former spies, so that they can be once again spies but with new identities. Because identity in Bond films is based on what can be seen, the characters' inner soul is left untouched. That Cuba in the film can deliver a new body with the same authentic soul is related to the broader, symbolic image of the country as a whole: the island where communism imperfectly sheds its skin while remaining true to its own nature.

The premise of this Bond film is that death is not contingent upon identity. If identities could change, then death could always be postponed, or could have happened already and happen again in the future. At the same time, as bodies are transformed, identity becomes such a flexible and mutable construct that memory is left as the only constant that structures time. Previous wrongs can always be remembered in spite of identity changes, but that does not necessarily mean that the mistakes can be corrected, because there is a temporality to all lived narratives. One mind and two bodies, one of which has been prosthetically engineered by a Cuban state that is itself morphing as a way station for identities in a postcommunist world, allows viewers to understand the inexorability of time, as well as its repetition. Just as there will always be *another* day, each day will be an other, different and the same. The film's formula self-consciously produces recall as Halle Berry's striking appearance at a beach in Cuba allows viewers to recall Ursula Andress's knockout presentation in an early film of what is, in fact, a series with somewhat formulaic structures. A serious statement is being made about Cuba and geopolitical contexts in *Die Another Day*—as long as one keeps in mind that this is all part of a James Bond film that is ultimately supposed to be fun thanks to its martinis and its constructed sense of ironic distance.

One of the appeals of the Bond series is precisely the fact that at some level one can only talk about spies by talking about cartoons. This is why it is instructive to go back momentarily to the Cuban cartoonist Antonio Prohías's work, for it is arguably the best account of what it meant to be living in this atmosphere at the height of the Cold War, and of surveillance as a metaphor of how an old society sheds its skin and becomes a new one. If whatever Cuba means at this point for global symbolic capital is represented in the James Bond film, something of the Cuban condition can already be read in the pages of Prohías's famous comic strip.

For thirty years, Prohías's *Spy vs. Spy* strips at *Mad* magazine traced the defining madcap chase of the Cold War.[2] The strip was one of the magazine's most consistent features, and it stands as one of the most striking and coherent bodies of work produced by a Cuban exile. For Prohías—as well as for Stanley Kubrick in *Dr. Strangelove*—the Cold War could only produce an ironic work of art. *Spy vs. Spy* was a parody of what the Cold War meant, but it also gave its readers an idea of how it felt to be stuck between two superpowers—the weary worldview of what Prohías thought was Cuban civil society's impotence.

The compulsive saga of the black spy and the white spy did not need context, or drama, to be perfectly understood by the audience. The black spy and the white spy were identical except for their colors. At some points they could even exchange costumes in order to fool the other in seemingly endless permutations. Nothing changed in this universe, fixed as it was by rigid laws beyond the control of its subjects. They each could only have, individually and for a brief instant, the illusion that things would change, that a victor would finally emerge in the give-and-take of random actions. The illusion itself was brief, because their world was ruled by speed and repetition. Prohías's universe was simple, but there was nothing simplistic about it. The fact that the trick always returned to hit the trickster allowed for the economy of the strip to depend on that circularity. Because there was not one subject but two, and because they were travesties of each other, both received at different times what they had originally intended for the other. In other words, the "gift" they planted for the other returned

MAD #88, July 1964

Cuban exile Antonio Prohías's *Spy vs. Spy* cartoons depict the futile games of the Cold War. *Spy vs. Spy*™ and copyright 1964 E. C. Publications, Inc. All rights reserved. Used with permission.

to the original giver, in order to remind him of the damage in the future that the other intended to provoke in the past. From one frame to the next, the familiar was also uncanny, as the reader was exposed to ever more complicated frameworks that revealed how the spies' subconscious was defined solely by the desire to trump the other's ploy. The complex operations that Prohías drew in his series of tableaux engaged all these elements into one combustive, yet always ultimately stable, stew.

Spy vs. Spy was a commentary on its Cold War times, but its silent frames create a dense, allusive network of considerable philosophical and political complexity. The Roadrunner always held the moral superiority vis-à-vis a coyote that became a desperate lover of booby traps. In *Spy vs. Spy*, black and white spies were observed with a sense of distance by the reader, who looked "down" at their games as futile permutations seductive only because of the baroque elegance of the traps they set for each other. Aware of the moral pitfalls of his own position, Prohías at one point attempted to resolve the moral neutrality of this universe by creating a third character: a female spy dressed in gray who appeared in the strip from September 1962 to December 1965. In an interview, Prohías explained that "The lady Spy represented neutrality . . . She was clever and she never lost" (*Spy vs. Spy*, 47). Prohías allowed the woman to be always victorious in what was described then as a chivalric gesture, one that now seems sexist. But the female spy changed the permutations of plot. The spies fell in love with her, and they behaved differently when she was around. The game became too contrived; the outcome was predictable with a third character, in a way that did not fit the dialectical relationship the spies had to each other. So Prohías allowed the female spy to disappear, and returned to the same bitter game played by the two opposing and ridiculous forces—in part because the pleasure of the game was all in the permutations of plot, and not in its resolution.

The strip was the response to Prohías's experience with infiltration and espionage in the early years of the Cuban Revolution, and this illuminates the traumatic context in which the first exiles arrived in Miami. Prohías was seventeen when he began studying at Havana's San Alejandro Academy, where most of Cuba's important painters are still trained. He became a cartoonist and started working in Havana newspapers at a time—the mid-1950s—when the city could boast of having eighteen well-established dailies.[3] The Batista dictatorship was fighting the revolutionary army in the mountains of the Sierra Maestra, while Prohías was drawing cartoons with titles like "El hombre siniestro" or "La mujer siniestra." *Sinister* was here equated to something elusive, unexplainable, even uncanny. According to Marta Rosa Pizarro, Prohías's daughter, these cartoons reflected the "sour mood" of the time, when "people were on edge, expecting catastrophe at every corner" (*Spy vs. Spy*, 22). The catastrophes were the events themselves, and were outside of the frames, for no historical or social referent was found in drawings without words. Its characters were mostly middle-class and urban, but the tricks depicted and that they played on each other could only be described as sinister—provided one understood the word as a cognate for nasty, cruel, picaresque, or bawdy. The characters were not fixed. Unlike the cartoon spies, the characters were not masked, although the joke that they played on each other often consisted of unmasking. Hence, the use of *sinister* as a way of defining an act that has a hidden motive beyond the reach of common explanation. Sinister is gratuitous, though it is suspected that character is a motive for the actions, or at least that a plan has been devised at some point.

It is not difficult to see how the sinister context led to the focus on espionage, considering the events in Prohías's life after the revolution and the madcap turn of events that followed it. After 1959, his story becomes emblematic of the processes that accompanied the revolutionary takeover and that are traumatically remembered in Miami to this day. That year, Prohías was president of the association of Cuban cartoonists, and he started drawing Fidel as a communist. Fabiola Santiago recalls that Prohías drew a cartoon of Fidel surrounded by "brown-nosers, who doted on his every word," which prompted Fidel to work a crowd assembled in front of the presidental palace "into a frenzy" demanding that the cartoonist face a firing squad (ibid., 15). Prohías was accused of being a CIA operative, was asked to resign from his position at the Cuban Cartoonists Association, and his cartoons were subjected to lengthy *coletillas*—explanations, disclaimers, or statements of editorial policy that were common at the time, and that chilled the political atmosphere in many Cuban newspapers. According to Santiago, at one point Prohías's fellow workers at the newspaper *El Mundo* organized "a trial by his peers" and he was condemned as a reactionary. Having lost his options as a cartoonist in Cuba, he left on May 1, 1960, and took a job at a clothing factory in Queens, while working on a portfolio of new materials by night. After his family received threats in Cuba, he sent for them to come to the United States and then, with his daughter as interpreter (he spoke no English), walked into the editorial offices of *Mad* magazine, where he was immediately hired to create the *Spy vs. Spy* strip.

Prohías's biographical tale of espionage and betrayal in Cuba and success abroad is one of many told in Miami, a city that still clings to the notion that it was founded by Fidel's "betrayal" of the revolution. Prohías's lack of English language skills may have accounted for the silence of his cartoons, though he clarified that drawing was "a language in itself" (ibid., 8).[4] Whereas *Mad*'s adolescent-geared prankster humor struck both a verbal and a visual punch, Prohías's cartoons were always strangely silent. They were the one silent feature in an otherwise very verbal magazine. The strips deployed three different codes, and only one of them used words in the title. The author's byline ("By Prohías") was written in Morse code, and there were from four to six frames, and occasionally eight. The first two frames generally set up the situation, and somewhere between the third and fourth, the opposing situation developed, with predictable results. The reader who followed the frame-by-frame account many times had to go back in order to understand how everything was not what it had seemed at the beginning.

There was no overt reference to the ongoing conflicts between Cuba and the United States in *Spy vs. Spy*, perhaps because the lead time for the drawings to appear was about eight months. But it is important also to see this absence as a deliberate gesture that avoided the particulars of Prohías's own situation, as he excised from the strips all references to the country of his birth. Stripped from their roots, and from all linkages to culture and identity, the spies belonged to a moral universe that had no center, that provided no specific commentary other than parody, and that was predictable to the very end. There was, in fact, nothing to *get* other than the pure repetition of the strip itself. If Hitchcock in *Topaz* read the Cold War as a web that covered the whole world, Prohías reduced it to its minimal elements—pure repetition, pure compulsion. The sign writes itself over and over again, with no meaning attached to the black or white colors of this scenario. This was not the good guy versus the bad guy, but two interchangeably dangerous, absurd, and clutzy types.

Part of the brilliance came from the convoluted memory that the strip effectively deployed, but that only served to underscore the spies' failures.

The spies were constantly on the lookout for each other's tricks, and this was sometimes signaled by the fact that they thought each could anticipate what the other would do. But this anticipation, built on the memory bank of what happened before and could happen again, was of no use in preventing the fatality of the situation. Memory as one of the themes of this spy chase is also illustrated in more detail in the extraordinarily complicated eight pages of the instruction manual that accompanied a board game based on Prohías's cartoon, called *Mad Magazine Spy vs. Spy,* and produced in 1986 by Milton Bradley.[5] "A word or two about your mission," the instructions read with typical understatement. The spies are supposed to build a "network of tunnels to the bombs" and then return them safely to home base, which is, of course, a manhole. Tunnels are built one at a time toward the bombs, the spies try to reach the bombs, and then when they bring them home, they follow further instructions that are found under the bombs themselves. This would be an easy cut-and-chase game for two to four players, except that the instructions add that these spies are known "for botched-up missions," and the scenarios in this game are true to that pattern. Opponents at any time may block the tunnels, and they "can use your tunnels to try to grab bombs before you can." Even if one player avoids that and stlll gets to the bomb at the end of the chase, "a roll of the bomb die can blow you right home without the bomb!" In other words, it is practically impossible to win in this game—all sorts of traps are laid out precisely to ensure that all players *lose.*

The game in itself, like the cartoon strip, was an allegory of the Cuban situation even if there were no overt references to it: the botched-up struggle that had no victors, whose origin was unknown, and whose denouement could only be the comic destruction of self and other. The cartoons were devoid of hatred and its concomitant emotions. Because the spies were not portrayed as working for opposing ideologies, there was no background information and no biography that could explain how they saw themselves as individuals. This created the effect of there being a "void" at the center of identity, because identity was merely predicated on the colors of their cloaks. It is not that the spies were indifferent to each other—they actually relished their game, and always played it with gusto. The moments of sentimentality in some of the cartoons are reserved for moments when there is a possibility that the game itself may end. Repetition accounts for the absence of resentment, because acts that backfire could always be responded to with other acts. There is no time to sit and think of causes and consequences, because the cartoon temporality does not allow those moments of self-reflection. Even though, in the historical time of exile, the spy game had produced much suffering, in Prohías's translation into the madcap chase, it was a fight beyond country and ideology—a fight that had no origin and no conclusion, except a sense of mission that the spies undertook without giving a thought to what they did. Within the context of betrayal and banishment lived by Prohías and his peers, this was a very Cuban way of understanding the memory of destruction as something that could always hold the future at bay. And it makes sense, that when Prohías died of cancer in February 1998, the only thing that could be remembered of him where those silent drawings that seemed like a visual representation of internal strife at work within one solitary Cuban—one who was accused of espionage in a trial of his peers, who then betrayed him and forced him to leave the context where he created his art.

BOTCHED-UP MISSIONS

The line between the cartoon world and the confusing deployments of identity that sustain espionage is relatively clear-cut. Espionage hinges on time, and on turning the question of "seeing" into a problem. If the voyeur gives a narrative tale to events that may be disconnected, the spy presumes that the narrative exists and turns every act into evidence. Because it is linked to surveillance and observation, espionage is also related to memory, understood as the ability to manage situations in which identity changes. The Cuban state uses espionage to rekindle the memory of its struggles for subsistence, because the memory of surveillance compresses history—it has the effect of rendering it closer to the present than it would otherwise be.

There is always a manipulation of archives and files when it comes to espionage, because so much observation creates the illusion that time stands still. In the Wasp Network spy case that uncovered Cuban citizens spying in Miami from 1998 to 2001, *El Nuevo Herald* confirmed the impression of a detained temporality: "Castroist Espionage in Miami" (Espionaje castrista en Miami) was the title of the archive kept in the newspaper Web portal. The case was indeed the most important evidence of Cubans meddling in Miami affairs, but the archive itself was unwieldy:

it summed up more than one hundred pages of information, and it covered material ranging from the important developments of the case to its more banal and daily minutiae. Because it was a memory created solely in Spanish, it points to the relative insularity of the Cuban community in that city—the impression that there is a parallel universe in an urban enclave where identities are contingent on political positions, and where both are staked out more insistently than in any other city. Because identity is predicated on memory, the *Miami Herald* and *El Nuevo Herald* created two distinct memories for the city itself—part of the problem that haunts Miami to this day.

Responding to the memory archive in Cuban Miami, the Cuban state has organized a wide network of Web sites and solidarity committees in order to promote a broader vision of what it calls the continuing terrorism network that originates in Miami and threatens the revolution. The specific event that triggers this memory is the case of the Wasp Network, which is known in Cuba as the case of the Five Heroes serving time in U.S. jail for spying on Miami exile operations. There are Web sites in English and Spanish, "Free the Five" T-shirts, a full archive of U.S. media coverage of the case, links to other official Cuban sites such as *Trabajadores, Prensa Latina, Radio Rebelde, Radio Reloj,* and the official newspaper *Granma.* In addition, there is merchandise: political buttons, and a poster that shows an outstretched hand with a Cuban flag, with the five names inscribed on all five fingers. There are solidarity committees in the U.S. in cites such as Los Angeles, Denver, Miami, Chicago, and Philadelphia, and an international web with chapters in Spain, Austria, Turkey, the United Kingdom, and elsewhere. There is a CD for sale, titled *Regresaré* (I will return), with musical versions of the poems of one of the Heroes, Antonio Guerrero, sung in the troubadour style of the Nueva Trova, which has been popular since in the 1970s. Clicking on the pictures of each of the Heroes allows access to information on their lives, their unjust sentences, their jails (including the address where they can receive correspondence), and their life stories with pictures and family correspondence.

This is a universe of words and images that breaks with insularity by creating virtual communities joined by memory of past wrongs. It establishes links by means of language and visual immediacy, understood as the only modes in which historical reality can be apprehended and insularity defied. Prohías's silent treatment eluded insularity by also eluding language.

It highlighted the silence of the spies, their nonverbal codes, the reticence to communicate, their preference for deeds instead of words. If, for Prohías, secrecy and silence could only be rendered in ink by means of silent drawings, in *El Nuevo Herald* the spy chase becomes an ideological morality tale that accounts for Miami's difference and particularity, and in the Cuban Web archives the same ideological morality tale produces consensus and transnational collective rage.

There is a Cuban history to espionage, but to look for a linear narrative is a fruitless task. One link leads to the other in a kind of decentered net that includes the most dissimilar characters in the most far-flung locales. The United States was inciting open rebellion in Cuba by 1962, and there were at least 612 attempts on Fidel Castro's life from 1959 to 1993. These included, famously, diving suits with a fungus that would produce a disabling skin disease and, in 1963, seashells that would explode upon contact while Castro was skin-diving.[6] These complicated maneuvers could be the stuff of parody if we were at a sufficient historical remove from them. The U.S. government (and Cuba's in turn) still keeps alive the memory of the Cold War as a kind of ideological "recall moment" that justifies present actions in dissimilar contexts and cultures.

During the Cold War, Cuba was at the center of a wide net of information gathering. In 1964, the Soviet Union opened the listening station at Lourdes, for which it paid the Cuban government up until 2002, when the Russians themselves, without prior consultation, closed it without much fanfare or ceremony. This was an important moment in the United States and in Cuba, where Fidel protested loudly. At one point, the Lourdes satellite dishes could intercept data from more than a hundred satellites relaying communications within the United States and between the United States and Europe.

The closing down of the Lourdes facility may have been the end of the last vestige of the Cold War and of Eastern European presence in Cuba, but in the broader political situation radar and electronic equipment were always only the tip of the iceberg for more mundane information gathering that took place at other levels. Although the U.S. diplomatic presence in Havana consists solely of the Cuban Interests Section opened in 1977, it was always clear that this entity was also in charge of monitoring Cuban developments. Even then, in the 1970s, the Cubans anticipated that a good number of the diplomats stationed there would be CIA agents. From the start, they were easy to spot: the CIA segregated them on the second floor of the building, and cemented the windows in a way that made the floor look like a bunker. It was clear to the Cubans that spies were placed there, and thus they monitored their activities constantly. As part of the intelligence protocol between the two countries (espionage does have its codes of conduct), Cuba agreed not to conduct espionage at its Interests Section in Washington, and to limit its information gathering to its UN mission. But this bilateral protocol has always been complicated by the fact that both countries keep a close watch on Cuban-American organizations in Miami. And it is well known that many of these have been successfully infiltrated not only by the FBI, but also by the Cuban government.

One does not know if, like all narratives of ethnicity, the spy chase begins in Cuba and then continues in Miami, or whether espionage is a home-grown diasporic creation. There is a narrative arc, but it goes from one place to the other, and it links subjects in a way that they themselves can only explain by having recourse to terms such as "honor" and *patria* (fatherland), or by mobilizing a repertoire of images where besieged masculinity begets acts of necessity. Struggles in Cuba had repercussions in the Miami exile, but secrets concerning Washington's financing of exile operations grew as more moderate organizations left the city and moved elsewhere. The secrecy in which exile politics and affect were initially bred contrasted with the spectacular, very visible achievements of the revolution. In Cuba there were mass rallies and popular mobilizations that were recorded and photographed, and speeches published and reprinted throughout the world as examples of solidarity, cohesion, and consensus. For a number of decades, Miami did not offer massive and collective displays of solidarity; in fact, escaping from compulsory solidarity and mass rallies was one of the reasons why the Cuban population of Miami left the island. Collective events are rare in Miami, and this is why the repeated accusation from the Cuban state of a "Miami mafia," with all its implications of secrecy and silence, strikes a sensitive chord. Power and popular consensus—even if coerced—were visible in Cuba; division among exiles and between them and Washington tinged the whole situation in different tones.

Like a traumatized subject that needs to reorganize its own sense of affect, Miami after 1959 became a well-organized city. It was something of a joke to say that not only did Fidel mobilize Cuba by creating a wide net of popular organizations, neighborhood blocks, and worker brigades, he also managed to organize most of Miami—or at least to tap into the compulsive needs of the population to speak in some sort of collective voice. As María Cristina García recalls, a popular joke made the rounds in Miami during the 1960s: "if you put two Cubans in a room with a political problem to solve, they would come up with three organizations."[7] There were so many organizations that the departments of state and justice could not keep track of them all, and Cubans themselves joked about the "industria de la revolución" that created organized factions wherever Cubans settled.

Divisions produced botched-up missions, in terms of the actions to take versus the victorious Cuban state in power. This *versus,* which repeats the title of Prohías's *Spy vs. Spy,* should be understood as opposition as well as return, as befits its etymological origin that also accounts for verse, as the return and recall from one line to the next. All of Miami was invested in opposition and return, at the most primary level. As early as 1963, there were already at least four provisional governments in Miami.[8] The Junta Revolucionaria de Liberación Nacional (Revolutionary Junta for National Liberation), for example, tried to launch another invasion after the Bay of Pigs and it failed. The Asociación de Magistrados Cubanos en el Exilio (Association of Cuban Magistrates in Exile) went so far as to create a government in exile, and the Junta Revolucionaria Cubana set off from Puerto Rico on an invasion, though they were intercepted by a British destroyer in the Bahamas. At one point, there were attempts to organize the organizations themselves, as in the far-ranging plan devised by José "Pepín" Bosch of the Bacardí Rum Company, who polled more than seventy-five thousand exiles to choose the leaders of a new government. The referendum yielded a number of names from different organizations—one from the Cuban Families Committee, one from the Federation of Telephone Workers in Exile, one from the Association of Public and Private Accountants in Exile, and one from a group called Juventud Cubana, led by a Cuban exile named Jorge Mas Canosa, a veteran of the Bay of Pigs.

On the island, intelligence and counterintelligence were extraordinarily effective as a bureaucratic apparatus that could count on the loyalty of its members. In 1961, the Cuban government created the DGI (Dirección General de Inteligencia), as a branch of the Cuban ministry of the interior, responsible for foreign intelligence collection. The intelligence bureaucracy was a response to the constant spying by the United States on the island. The Cuban government set up agents in Miami, and the United States had Cuban assets in Cuba. Between 1978 and 1987, the Cuban Ministry of the Interior claimed that there were 151 U.S.-financed spies in Cuba, and that most of them were Cubans, or of Cuban ancestry. But in 1987 it was revealed that one of the CIA's top assets in Cuba, with the code name Mateo, actually worked for the DGI in Havana. This information was provided by two DGI agents who defected in the 1980s, Antonio Rodríguez and Florentino Aspillaga Lombard. The first stated that "all the Cuban assets the CIA had managed to recruit during the previous 26 years were in fact DGI plants" and the second went so far as to state that the DGI "had succeeded in turning every single one of the 38 assets the CIA had recruited in Cuba since 1961."[9] It was not hard for the CIA to conclude that everything it knew about Cuba up until that point was actually DGI disinformation.

These were anything but botched-up missions. The DGI planted agents in Miami who passed as members of the Cuban community and infiltrated important exile organizations that did not necessarily have sophisticated systems for detecting espionage within.[10] Between 1970 and 1979, a Cuban defector insisted that the city was full of Cuban spies. According to Orlando Castro Hidalgo, who fled to Luxemburg in 1969, taking his family with him and obtaining U.S. asylum, there were at one point about 150 intelligence agents in the city—the number itself the object of speculation, though the fact that Miami was a city under surveillance did not go undetected. Cuba's espionage apparatus was one of the most sophisticated in the Western Hemisphere, composing at one point more than ten thousand spies, according to some sources. From the opposite side, the U.S. Department of Defense moved all of its attachés from Havana to military installations in South Florida, while the United States Information Agency also kept officers in Havana.[11] According to E. Howard Hunt, Cuban intelligence in the early 1960s had about two hundred agents monitoring all exile activities.[12]

The threat and the reality of espionage were part of a broader context of political strife created out of the internal dynamics of revolutionary acts that tolerated no dissent and that provided no conciliation with enemies or dissidents, whether within or outside the insular territory. Although the two sides were defined by geography and politics, the reality belies the spy chase that clearly pits a black and a white spy against each other as simply opponents manipulated by hidden powers. From the distance that Prohías saw the scenarios he had created, the situation for Cubans on both sides of the political divide was neither simple nor clear-cut, especially during the 1970s.

The decade was a particularly notorious, bloody historical period for the population of Greater Cuba, which includes the United States. Cubans on the island were living through what many there call the "repressive five years" ("el quinquenio gris"), while violence in Miami reached ever more dizzying heights. In Miami during the 1970s and 1980s, terrorism was the response to anyone who would depart from the "Patria o Muerte" (Fatherland or death) struggle that *el exilio* waged with itself and with the Cuban government.[13] From 1973 to 1976, while Cuba was sending troops to fight in Africa, more than one hundred bombs exploded in the Miami area.[14] In 1976, exiles exploded a bomb at the Cuban mission to the United Nations, attempted to kidnap the Cuban consul in Mérida, Mexico, and detonated a bomb at the Cubana Airlines office in Panama. Radical exile organizations also planted a bomb in a Cuban jet after it left Barbados, killing all seventy-three passengers. These acts were not in response to any specific measure the revolution had enacted but the work of disenchanted and politically volatile Cubans. They were not legitimate responses in a situation of war, but the work of remnants of U.S. sponsored terrorism against the Cuban state. In fact, the Cuban exiles were so effective that the Chilean state police under Augusto Pinochet hired them to kill Chilean ambassador Orlando Letelier in Washington. And three of the Watergate burglars—Bernard Barker, Virgilio González, and Eugenio Martínez— were Cuban exiles who had a relationship with the CIA.[15]

The story continued into the 1980s, though its compulsive repetition at times seemed to exhaust itself into increasingly parodic scenarios. The FBI identified at least twenty Cuban spies who took advantage of the 1980 Mariel exodus to enter Florida. The boat lift included Spanish-speaking agents from the FBI's counterintelligence section, who developed physical and psychological profiles of Cuban spies—just as it had done with airplane hijackers—in order to recognize and pick them out from among the thousands of Cubans who were then arriving on the Florida coast. Rumors circulating in Miami at the time insisted that Castro had not only emptied his prisons, but had also taken advantage of the mass exodus to plant agents in the Cuban community. In spite of the mistrust toward "Marielitos" on the part of many in the exile community, Francisco Ávila, who was employed as a tile workman (*instalador de losas*), admitted to being a double agent who had worked for the FBI and for Cuba up until 1992. His implausible case is dramatic and instructive: he was the military chief for the exile organization Alpha 66, one of the best-known and most feared exile paramilitary groups. He confessed that the Castro government gave him cash in order to finance three exile expeditions into Cuban territory. These agents were of such concern that a prominent member of the Cuban-American community, Joe Carollo, Miami city commissioner, declared on April 25, 1983, "I'm extremely sure that there are Miami police officers working for Communist Cuba." He said that his information was provided by turncoat agents of the infamous Cuban Central Intelligence Directorate (DGI).

THE STING OF THE WASP: PART I

In February 2001, five Cuban spies from the Red Avispa (which has been translated as Bee Web, though a more precise translation would be the Wasp Network, or the Web of the Wasp) were charged in the United States with espionage. According to the charges, the Wasp Network monitored the Southern Command in Florida, the naval base of Boca Chica in Key West, and the McDill Air Force Base in Tampa. It infiltrated exile groups, and it built up files on enemies of the revolution and its leader, Fidel Castro. Its activities ranged far and wide into the Cuban-American community. By the time they were condemned, the five spies had been identified as Fernando González Llort, born in Havana in 1963, an international relations specialist; René González Sehwerert, born in Chicago of Cuban parents in 1956, a flight instructor and aviation specialist; Antonio Guerrero Rodríguez, born in Miami of Cuban parents in 1958, a civil engineer and a poet; Gerardo Hernández Nordelo, born in Havana in 1965, an international relations specialist but also a cartoonist and the supposed leader of the group; and Ramón Labañino Salazar, born in Havana in 1963, an economist. Their stories were pieced together from notes, letters, affidavits, interviews, and in the biographies that circulated in Cuba after their arrest and during their trial.[16] They have also been given wide publicity by the huge campaign that the Cuban state produced, which echoed the very successful Elián González popular mobilizations. Their trial ended on June 9, 2001; it lasted six months, and the jury deliberated for five days before returning guilty verdicts. The prosecutor's case, according to newspaper accounts, was based on "two thousand pages of decrypted information peppered with communist jargon," presented as evidence that the fourteen-member spy network was committing illegal acts. The Cuban case—the defense mounted nationally and internationally by revolution-ary media—is that the spies were protecting U.S. and Cuban interests by spying on Cuban-American terrorist organizations bent on provoking a political conflict between the United States and Cuba. In fact, Cuba insisted that it had shared all of its information with the U.S. government, going so far as to claim that in June 1998, barely three months before the suspects were arrested, the Cuban security agency (Seguridad del Estado) had given the FBI some 230 pages of information on terrorist operations against Cuba, along with five videocassettes with news reports on these actions selected from Cuban television, and eight audiocassettes of con-versations among terrorists. In drafting its campaign for popular consen-sus, the Cuban state used this information to prove U.S. governmental hypocrisy, while at the same time insisting that no actions were being com-mitted against its neighbor. According to its scenario, cooperation from the Cuban state met with U.S. betrayal because of the close ties between the government and the "Miami mafia."

In initial accounts in U.S. newspapers, notably the *Miami Herald* and *El Nuevo Herald,* the Wasp Network case supposedly started with a stolen computer recovered at a police station, though this narrative of origins was never again mentioned in later accounts of the case. The computer was taken to a police precinct and a desk cop turned the computer on. As the police officer waited for the hard drive to boot, and as the contents of the computer were scanned, an officer noticed there were some interesting files. Something read by someone, a code name that hid a transaction—something out there turned those files into *evidence,* into elements of a future puzzle. Those computer files proved crucial to the case, and, as one of the jurors commented later, it was amazing that the spies had kept this stuff.

The district attorney examined the files before calling a press confer-ence, and on September 12, 1998, the FBI announced it had uncovered the biggest Cuban spy ring operating within the United States since Fidel

Castro took power in Cuba in 1959. There were ten people in total, members of what at that point was named the Red Avispa. Three of them were charged with conspiring against national defense; seven others were accused of acting as Cuban agents without having previously informed U.S. authorities—in principle, the government needs to be made aware of any agents from governments intending to monitor activities of their transnational or diasporic subjects. That the members of the Wasp Network had failed to do so was problemmatic for U.S. authorities—although the Cuban state insisted that the United States knew all along of their presence in Miami. Some of those arrested—Nilo Hernández and his wife Linda, Joseph Santos and his wife Amarilys Silverio, and Alejandro Alonso—agreed to collaborate with the authorities in exchange for reduced sentences. Over the course of the next couple of years, as arrests were made, and as the DA built a more complete picture of the tangled tale, its vast and tentacular body implicated others—a Cuban-American businessman, an exile leader, a diplomat from the island, several U.S. political figures—and it got linked to other cases that had happened both earlier and later. Three cases stand out in particular.

The first, the one that had the most direct link to the Wasp Network, took place in December 1999, when the United States ordered the expulsion of three Cuban diplomats, a first secretary and two aggregates of the Cuban permanent mission to the United Nations, for "activities incompatible with their posts."[17] The expulsion resulted from information gathered with the cooperation of two spies captured in the Wasp Network and who received reduced sentences: Amarylis Silverio Santos and Joseph Santos.

The second case is not directly related to the Wasp Network but it was also included in the memory archives of the case as a particularly damaging corollary to it. It involved a senior analyst for Cuba at the Defense Intelligence Agency called Ana Belén Montes, who received a twenty-five-year term followed by five years of parole. Montes had worked at the DIA since 1985, and seven years later was assigned to analyze Cuban affairs. As a senior analyst, she had access to classified information. When the U.S. authorities raided her apartment after the arrest, they found two computers, a shortwave radio, tape recorders, five passports, and foreign currency.

The third case—chronologically placed between the other two—is more complex, and involved a high-ranking Cuban-American Immigration and

Naturalization Service officer, Jorge Faget, who was arrested on February 18, 2000, when the FBI, doing a routine surveillance of Cuban government officials, realized that one of the Cubans under investigation was meeting with a senior INS officer. They started tracking Faget in December 1998 to determine whether he was a Cuban "asset." The FBI set a trap. Héctor Pesquera, a special agent of the Miami FBI office, deliberately set out to test whether Faget could keep a secret; he told Faget that a consular officer assigned to the Cuban Interests Section in Washington wanted to defect. Faget claimed he knew the vice consul of the Cuban Interests Section, José Imperatori, only from a previous dinner in Miami, although the truth was that he had met him more than once.[18] Twelve minutes after Pesquera gave Faget the piece of news, Faget passed that information to a Cuban-born businessman in New York named Pedro Font, and the FBI recorded the call.

The case was known as operation "False Blue Cuban Spy," a parodic take on "true blue" as a symbol of patriotism. According to INS district director Bob Wallis, the case "speaks to the heart of public trust."[19] Faget was accused of serious crimes under the Espionage Act: revealing classified information to an unauthorized person and meeting without authorization with Cuban officials believed to be intelligence operatives. Not unlike the Wasp Network, a confused element of affection and politics was involved in this case. Both Faget and Font came to the United States as teenagers, both were sons of officers who served in the Batista army, and they were friends. Faget, in fact, was the son of Mariano Faget Sr., who had been one of Batista's *caza-comunistas,* a hunter of communists, and the one who ran Batista's Office of Anti-Communist Repression. But Font had contacts at the Cuban Interests Section in Washington and he was well connected there.[20]

The FBI insisted that Imperatori be removed from the Cuban Interests Section and returned to Cuba, alleging that he was a spy. Imperatori wanted to clear his name and requested a trial in his own defense. But the FBI demanded that Imperatori leave the country. Imperatori at that point claimed that his honor had been violated: he resigned his consular job and thus lost his diplomatic immunity. He retained former Baltimore mayor and Yale graduate Kurt Schmoke as part of his defense team. Imperatori wanted to prove his innocence beyond any doubt; he wanted to publicly clarify that at no point was he involved in espionage.[21] What had started as a simple transaction between intelligence agencies became a roving soap opera. Imperatori said he would "not resist arrest, not even if I am handcuffed and jailed . . . My truth will be my shield." He sent his wife and his three-year-old son to Havana, and he locked himself in his apartment, intending to stay there "until I have been absolutely cleared of the accusation brought against me."[22] Imperatori went to Ottawa on a transit visa valid for two days, taking advantage of a courtesy the Canadian government offers Cuban diplomats who are accredited in the United States. But the visa expired, and the Canadian authorities demanded that he leave. On March 1, 2000, the Canadian police surrounded the Cuban embassy in Ottawa and forced Imperatori to leave the country. He went back to Cuba, where he now resides.

THE STING OF THE WASP: PART II

It is a well-known fact of exile politics that an event in Miami triggers the memory of a chain of events in the past. The event does not rewrite history, but it adds a piece to some hidden puzzle where history becomes defined.[23] The arrests of the spies in the Wasp Network took the Miami Cuban community by surprise, not only because of the extent of the network, but also because of the fact that the alleged spies had been posing as responsible members of the Cuban-American community, at times mingling with some very prominent people. The members of the network held jobs in mechanic shops, Internet agencies, and doctors' offices—the very fabric of what makes Little Havana, or Miami itself, run. Amarylis Silverio, accused as a spy, was the receptionist for the Miami clinic of Dr. Rafael Peñalver. Her supervisor, quoted in *El Nuevo Herald*, confirmed that "Amarylis was a good employee . . . punctual, she never had conflicts with her coworkers and, on the contrary, everybody appreciated her." Another had connections even higher up: René González Sehwerert at one point asked for the aid of Ileana Ros-Lehtinen (R-Florida) and Bob Menéndez (D-New Jersey) to bring his wife and his adolescent daughter from Cuba, and they facilitated their entry with immigration authorities without knowing that he was an agent.[24] The FBI itself tried to recruit González Sehwerert as an informant in the fall of 1996.

The identities of the spies were the first mystery that needed to be resolved, and no one knew for sure who these Cubans were until December

2000, when defense attorneys revealed their identities, and then more fully at the end of the trial, in June 2001, when the Cuban government published complete accounts of their lives. The names of two of the accused, Rubén Campa and Luis Medina, were fake, appropriated from death certificates of babies who died in California in the late 1960s. The authorities referred to Medina for some time as "John Doe" because federal agents could not determine his identity until, at some point, he was identified as Ramón Lavañino Salazar, who had even obtained a U.S. passport and registered with the Selective Service under his assumed name. Rubén Campa's real name was Fernando González Llort. The FBI found thirty-one death certificates among his belongings, along with a business card identifying him as a desktop publisher. Medina (Lavañino Salazar) presented himself as a shoe salesman.

The ringleader's name (Gerardo Hernández Nordelo) was another mystery, and it was the most important one because, according to prosecutors, he gave Cuba the detailed flight plan of the Brothers to the Rescue, who were intercepted by Cuban authorities and had one of their planes downed in 1996.[25] He was known as a freelance graphic designer for advertising agencies (although the building manager saw him working with an "old lousy computer") and he was called Gerardo Hernández by the DA. At the beginning, his lawyer insisted on calling him by what he said was his real name, Manuel Viramontes, though the DA replied that Viramontes was an alias and that within the group, he was known as Giro or Giraldo. Viramontes was Hernández's assumed name, and his fake identity was that of a Puerto Rican single man, with an ex-wife living in Mexico. In May 1999, Gerardo Hernández Nordelo was formally accused of conspiring to commit murder, by virtue of the fact that in 1998 he was linked to the downing of the Brothers to the Rescue plane on February 24, 1996.

Although the question of identity is a common thread in all espionage cases, in this case it touched on questions of citizenship in a particular way. Two of the accused spies, Antonio Guerrero Rodríguez and René González Sehwerert, were U.S.-born, and the latter posed as an ardent anti-Castro activist even as he was on Castro's payroll. Gail Epstein Nieves, reporting for the *Miami Herald* on December 15, 2001, said that "González was so convincing in his patriotic fervor that even after his arrest . . . exile leaders hesitated to believe that their cocky, sharp-tongued friend was indeed a Cuban spy in their midst." The ones who cooperated illustrate the complex histories of Cubans within the United States. For example, Joseph Santos (known as Mario in the group) was born in New Jersey to Cuban parents who later returned to Cuba. He became a university professor in electrical engineering and was recruited by the DGI in April 1984. Linda Hernández (who took the name Judith) was born in New York in 1957 and went to Cuba with her family when she turned one. She married Nilo Hernández in 1977, and came to the United States in 1983. Nilo Hernández (known as Manolo) became a U.S. citizen in 1988. Their son, now a teenager, lives with his maternal grandmother—Linda's mother—who took her to Cuba in 1958.

Most of the spies entered the United States in the 1990s, possibly taking advantage of the fact that the Cuban Adjustment Act of 1996 gives Cubans who arrive in the United States the opportunity to become residents after one year and one day in the country. Antonio Guerrero Rodríguez is married to a U.S. citizen, Maggy Bécquer, who found out that he was a spy after his arrest, and who Cuban authorities insist has been fully "supportive" of him during his case. Most were born after the revolution, and belong to the same generational cohort. The oldest, René González Sehwerert, was born in Chicago in 1956, and the youngest (the accused ringleader, Gerardo Hernández Nordelo) was born in Havana in 1965. These are all members of the first revolutionary generation, and their sentimental biographies reproduced on Cuban Web sites are meant to elicit identificatory responses. They are presented as loving sons, husbands, and parents, and there is profuse information about every school they attended and their performance at them. They are the best students, and their social ascent comes by virtue of sacrifice and hard work, not capital or connections. They are Communist Party militants, some of them volunteered for military service in Angola, and they are all white—Gerardo's mother is a Spaniard who emigrated to Cuba in 1950, and Sehwerert is the son of a U.S. white mother.

The Heroes lived austere lives—something highly valued by the Cuban state in order to show how selfless sacrifice produces heroism. But there are other ways of reading this austerity, because the Wasp Network case also uncovered sharp contrasts in terms of the class background. In spite of the wealth and power of the Cuban-American community, there was nothing classy about the Web of the Wasp. None of the accused had fancy cars and none belonged to the dry martini James Bond world of intrigue.

Although the FBI classified them as an 8.5 out of a possible 10 on the level of sophistication, they had old radios and they had money problems. The head of the spy ring paid his rent late, and another spy held two jobs to make ends meet. Incredibly, they used beepers to get in touch with each other.[26]

This class register gives a good idea of what the spies were looking at and informing on—at what Cuba thought, or thinks, is the real center of power for these kinds of operations. These were not members of the elite fighting in court over trademark issues (Havana Club rum, Cohiba cigars, or Bacardí), and they did not mingle with the people who appear in the pages of *Cigar Aficionado* dedicated to the allure of high-class living in Cuba or in the advertisements found in the Havana-based magazine *Opus Habana* for spectacular golf courses next to the beach. They did not frequent the fancy parties at Key Biscayne, where the apartments have real art and the butlers dress in impeccable tuxedos, but the auto mechanic shop where they fix old Chevys, certainly not Mercedes. By no means do those auto mechanics and family doctors in Little Havana qualify as members of the "Cuban mafia." The "Cuban mafia" has money, but it just hands out a check to the Cuban American National Foundation. That was the brilliance of Jorge Mas Canosa—accepting checks that allowed the foundation to hire working-class people from Little Havana who felt betrayed by the revolution.

The Cuban spies were told to mingle, hence there was nothing ostentatious about them. They were essentially spying on middle- or working-class Cubans who themselves seek jobs and influence. These people are, for the most part, not privy to the legal battles of restitution of lost property, and they barely have money to invest in the stock market. They are not trafficking in stolen goods and they are not holding classy fund-raisers in South Beach. As a matter of fact, they tend to be more recent migrants rather than older, more established émigrés. The three cases that were more or less offshoots of the Five Spies legal saga—Jorge Faget, Ana Belén Montes, and José Imperatori—seem to take place in a parallel universe to the Wasp Network's. There were fancy restaurants and high positions and secrets involved in those three; the Wasp Network seemed to have been a duller affair. Even the portraits that have emerged from the Cuban press and its propaganda highlight the sheer normality of their picture-perfect lives, with wives and children, grandmothers and parents. Faget and Ana

Belén Montes were successful within a capitalist structure, whereas the spies came from contexts in which material difficulties are still felt. As a lesson about the intersection of politics and class, the people the Wasp Network were in charge of represent the real threat to the regime: fringe elements who hold long-standing grudges against the Cuban state, and who have not completely assimilated to the way politics and influence are managed in the United States.

Havana authorities have complained about the swiftness of the verdict in this case, though it was understood from the outset that no member of the jury could be Cuban, or related to Cubans. In a moving tribute titled "Un sol que no se apaga," translated as "A Sun That Will Never Burn Out," on one of the many Web pages produced in Cuba and dedicated to their fate, Ricardo Alarcón Quesada, president of the Cuban National Assembly, insists that jury intimidation explains how fast the jury reached its verdict without seeking any counsel from the judge. Alarcón has insisted (as did the defense throughout) that a new trial take place outside of Miami. Punishment was meted out swiftly, indeed. Gerardo (they are known by their first names in the Cuban media) as the ringleader was given the harshest sentence: two life sentences plus fifteen years in prison. Ramón got life plus eighteen years, Antonio life plus ten years, Fernando nineteen years, and René fifteen years.[27]

The Cuban government has mounted an international campaign to free the Cuban "heroes."

The Five Fallen Comrades are the closest thing to celebrities within the culture of revolutionary spectacle. They were granted the highest honor the Cuban government can confer upon its citizens, "Heroes of the Republic of Cuba"; their mothers were given the Order of Mariana Grajales, an award named for the mother of independence hero Antonio Maceo y Grajales; and their wives were given the Ana Betancourt award, named for a woman who supported and inspired Cubans in their fight for independence from Spain. The year 2002 was officially declared the "Year of the Heroic Prisoners of the Empire." The Cuban government also mobilized its networks of solidarity abroad in order to turn the Five Fallen Comrades into heroes, each with their own biography. T-shirts and buttons were printed, letter-writing campaigns fostered, Web sites launched.

RED ALERT

When the Cuban state mobilized collective memory in order to rescue the Fallen Comrades, it was arguing for its own continuities, in spite of the cosmetic changes it had suffered since the collapse of the Soviet bloc. And it held on to this identity, as it had done in the past, precisely by resurrecting statements it had already made regarding the history of crimes committed by Cuban exiles.[28] Time and time again, the defense, each one of the Five, members of the Cuban state, and its propaganda apparatus insisted on resurrecting history. Even the statements written by the Five bear an echo of Fidel's time in prison, when he penned *History Will Absolve Me*. Even if this comparison is not explicitly made in the literature devoted to the case, the insistence on the harsh prison conditions in the United States and the ill-treatment that some of them allege to have received is accompanied by a defense tactic that broadened historical reference while localizing it in the "Cuban mafia" in Miami. In fact, in many ways their defense was also an accusation of Miami—a strident and hyperbolic picture of the city as buried in layers of hidden meanings and unfathomable actions. The Cuban state and the five spies themselves insisted that no espionage had been directed against the United States, but rather at Cuban exile operations.[29] In so doing, they sought to address directly the power structure in Washington, DC, claiming that the Cuban state was actually cooperating with Washington and the FBI in monitoring and keeping track of renegade exile Cubans. The tactic avoided recognizing that what was ultimately involved was an internal dispute between Cubans. For the Cuban state, internal disputes in extraterritorial locales need to be addressed to the highest power, not to the diasporic community.

The spies assumed the identity of dead people who were thought to be living beings by a state that issued, among other documents, driver's licenses: dead people come back to life in order to commit crimes in bodies that already had proper names registered under a different state. The state may not care if you can justify what you did as long as it can read your identity as one that has only one story, with a definite beginning and end. In this sense, the state wants a clearly defined narrative from the bodies that it can name. In other words, it cannot read identity as a tactical decision, and even as a necessary fiction, to be deployed at particular instances and for very specific goals. Upon these bodies the state deploys the narrative of espionage in order to wreak havoc with the relationship between names, bodies, and histories.

Revisiting the history of the revolution as one long spy narrative branching out onto a grid allows us to see in the dynamics between Cuba and the United States something other than a history marked by lack of communication. The states have been in constant contact for more than four decades in their own particular silent language, with its own codes. In political terms, as any reader of John Le Carré can confirm, uncovering espionage is a way for states to engage in a conversation—sometimes silent. Historical events aside, espionage is like murmured conversation, always at the level of rumor, or innuendo, but it is still a code-switching, message-sharing experience, best apprehended with a thorough knowledge of linguistics. Positionality, relation, and structure are as important in this linguistic constellation as are gender, speech act, and the arbitrary nature of the sign. Context allows us to understand this partially at best—the fact that these narratives take place at this particular historical juncture is not coincidental, but to a certain extent is as fabricated and contrived as Prohías's spy chases. With the major rationale for punitive measures gone, only the U.S. government is officially invested in keeping the trade embargo in place (preventing direct commerce between the two countries). In the meantime, and at a different level, the embargo is being chipped away slowly, "from below," by congressional delegations, business interests, and ordinary citizens. The spy cases can only reap ideological benefits for the Cuban state. The more right-wing elements of the Cuban exile community in the United States are weakened to a certain extent, and portrayed as recalcitrant and disconnected from the broader American public; internal cohesion with mass mobilizations of citizens protesting the memory of terrorism are conducive to a return to revolutionary origin—though they belie the growing network of contacts and family links that have always taken place, and more so now, when remittances and travel from the United States have been possible since the 1990s. More stringent rules enacted by the Bush administration in 2004, however, tipped the balance again in favor of the extreme right wing, by insisting on further restrictions for travel by Cuban-Americans.

The U.S. motives are harder to decipher, and cannot be simply dismissed as conferring benefits to the Cuban exile population who dominate the Florida electoral trophy. The U.S. state insisted that no espionage by foreign governments could be tolerated on U.S. territory, and it insists that justice has been meted out in accordance with the law. It might even be conjectured that the spies are a cover-up, spoken about in a code that only a few in higher echelons of power can decipher. Certainly, the U.S. faith in the law was upheld in the Elián González case, and the World Trade Center attacks occurred just as Judge Joan Lenard was about to render a ruling—she then postponed her ruling until December 2001. The atmosphere was not conducive to U.S. leniency on the question of espionage. As if to underscore this point, the Five were taken to prisons in different and faraway parts of the country: California, Texas, Colorado, Pennsylvania, and Minnesota. The prisoners are able to send and receive letters, and some of those they have written have been published in Cuban newspapers. One of the Five, Antonio Guerrero Rodríguez, is a poet and has published a collection curiously titled *Desde mi altura* (From my height); Gerardo Hernández Nordelo is completing an edited collection of essays in Cuba. It is clear that the Five are subjects of an intense war of propaganda that can only be explained in the legal universe where "law-abiding" procedural "rightness" trumps affect and mass mobilization.

In Cuba, the endless television commentary about the case informed the population about the particularities of the U.S. justice system—a civics lesson that Cubans also received as they followed the Elián González saga. Cuban television also, predictably, uncovered the financial dealings that make or break presidential and congressional elections, it continued demonizing what it calls the "Miami mafia," and insisted once again that they were not part of the "nation"—the nation understood as a shared belief in the consensus created by the revolution. Cuba and the United States surely exchanged information as to the state of the Cuban population on both sides of the Florida Straits, and gauged the degree of contacts that exist between these two communities. Such contacts have been on the rise for more than a decade, and some segments of the Cuban exile population have shown themselves to be more open to discussion and accommodation.

It was precisely to that segment of the Cuban population that the carefully worded decision of the federal appeals court in Atlanta addressed itself, when in August 2005 it threw out the convictions and sentences of the five accused Cuban spies. The court felt compelled to add that "the reversal of these convictions will be unpopular and offensive to many citizens," even as they agreed with the defense that, although none of the jurors was Cuban, prejudice against Fidel Castro and the Cuban government is strong in Miami, and the trial should have taken place someplace else. For José Basulto and other right-wing segments of the Cuban-American community, the decision was extremely disappointing, and it rekindled the traumatic history of reversals that had apparently peaked with the Elián González case. The judges further insisted in couching their decision in the ideological tone of civic patriotism in order to avoid inflaming the passions of the already "passionate" Cubans: "the court is equally mindful that those same citizens cherish and support the freedoms they enjoy in this country that are unavailable to residents of Cuba." The Cuban American National Foundation reacted to the paternalistic tone of the court with righteous, and nationalistic, indignation, calling the decision "an insult" to the Cuban community in Miami. The Cuban government immediately called the decision an important victory in its struggle against the "Miami mafia."

The spy cases are ritualistic events that deploy their own code in order to keep lines of communication open. They may even allow us to think that there is something compulsive in communication—that even when nothing is being said, something always *has* to be said. Beyond language, as a system of verbal signs, Prohías insisted on the very real communication taking place in a pictorial code. Espionage does not reveal isolated events, but rather stacks up meaning in a chain—displacing meaning ultimately to reveal only its own modes of operation, its own constitutive laws. There is not one identity, but rather the constant shedding of the skin of identity, leaving behind an empty shell: a *cubanía* of performance and not an essential form of being Cuban. Ultimately, and after more than four decades of this struggle, Cuban identity may best be apprehended as a *Mad Magazine* comic strip, a cat-and-mouse chase, a cartoon work drawn by a penniless Cuban exile named Antonio Prohías, in which identity pursues essence, and we are always trumped by the fact that essence in itself is but the elusive theatricality of the chase.

A Cuban Love Affair
with the Image

Pictures of contemporary Cuba are not pictures of a war, even if they portray Havana as a city in ruins. The ruins in Havana produce extraordinary aesthetic effects—collapse somehow allows the city to levitate in pictures. Hardship in Cuba during the 1990s could not be conveyed in an image, and even in 1993 and 1994 when the situation turned critical, photographs always seemed to demand qualifiers that in turn led to policy debates about how historical events had brought about the changes experienced by habaneros. In the context of affirmative nationality and with the return of revolutionary patriotism, visuality—what should and could be seen—was the medium of paramount importance. The gaze, the look, the evidence, and their process of elaboration were causes of national concern. In the fourth decade of revolution, the question as to how the Cuban state and the Cuban nation needed to be represented—and how these representations engaged citizens' own self-understanding—affected perceptions beyond those of the nation. In Cuba, there was always the need for discourse to supplement the image, as if those pictures *demanded* captions that explained what was visible in relation to what was missing. There were no atrocities in the ruined city, and thus no need to shock viewers. This was *dignified* poverty, the poverty of resistance. Cuba entered the world's perennial market for images in the 1990s as an impoverished country, yet one where poverty could always be rendered in aesthetic terms. And it is a poverty that can be felt in real time, as some of the images obviously worked on the allure of the mysterious island.[1] Images exposed different layers of history in the city walls, and this gave the illusion that the poverty itself could be *narrated*.

There are historical reasons for these kinds of images. Although Cuba was one of the central domino pieces of the Cold War, the island became the Cold War's quintessential example by the way in which pictures implicitly noted the absence of a horror that was lived elsewhere. Any encounter with the photojournalism of the Central American civil wars of the 1980s will reveal what is missing in Cuban photographs. The destruction wrought by ammunition or heavy artillery cannot be found in Cuba and, contrary to what happened in the Southern Cone, memories of the disappeared are not part of a collective and social trauma. There have been executions and probably torture, but nothing comparable to the scale elsewhere and, more important, little information as to their having ever taken place. This comes as a surprise when one considers the extent to which all proxy wars in Latin America have been fought with Cuba on the minds of those who have died and perished. In the moving diorama of Latin American history of the past several decades, photographic images of Cuba are striking because they seem to note the absence of conflict.

It could be argued that this absence is actually a form of surfeit. There are no pictures of Cuban soldiers maimed in the Angolan wars, and no photographer captured families suffering as their bodies were brought back to grieving relatives. In the absence of that kind of tragedy, we find instead the melodrama of crumbling buildings, as if what happened in Cuba were not an event, but rather a slow unfolding that could only be captured by means of structural metaphors. Susan Sontag's comment that "sheared off buildings are almost as eloquent as bodies in the street" is relevant to Havana.[2] Contemporary photographic accounts attempt to let history speak by capturing decay in a single image, and this trade-off between the temporal and the static allows for particular effects—viewers do not question poverty and ruins as resulting from governmental policies, but rather apprehend them as a metaphor for *something*. Conversely, it is as if the sheer historical density of the present can only be captured by its temporal effects on walls and structures where history is peeled off like onion skin.

In the photographic register of imperial U.S. domination Cuba was both ancient and new, and as such the island was depicted in the collection *Our*

Islands and Their People—a work commissioned after the Cuban-Spanish-American War in order to present these territories to their new colonial masters.[3] The albums were engineered constructions themselves, combining military might and academic expertise, and buttressed by an archive of images that included people, bridges, streets, animals, flora and fauna, scenes from daily life, panoramic vistas, and commercial prospects. As an archive, it allowed for past and present to be joined under the possessive colonial gaze. Unspoiled and so fully inscribed within what was then called the Spanish Main, the pictures were the evidence of an island surrounded by text, with captions that guided the viewer. Because this was an understanding for the benefit of empire, evidence was an integral part of the project. It permitted the entrepreneur to travel, the citizen to feel empathy, and the bureaucrat to feel like a king, and it created bonds of solidarity with the imperial project that had been born out of the invasion. Inextricably bound to evidence, the Image was necessary for the imperial project, if Cuba and the other colonies were to fulfill the needs of imperial subjects who understood themselves as harbingers of progress. By creating and fostering this community bound to islands seen as possessions, ideology did something more than just relate image to truth; it also called for the production of imaginary projects: texts of desire and want.

HAVANA: 1933

Photography about Cuba has always engaged narrative. It seems as if no picture has been taken there without being subjected to reflections of a "writerly" sort. Context seems to overwhelm the image, creating circuits of meaning over and beyond the photographed object itself. An example from the present may give a clearer sense of this. In the late 1990s, there were photographers who approached tourists in front of what used to be the Capitol building in Havana. They took pictures for a dollar on what seemed to be an old camera mounted on a tripod. The ambiance they tried to reproduce was that of the late 1920s or early 1930s. There was no reason for this pretense at antiqueness except to underscore an unwritten rule that demands that Havana be stuck in time: those old cameras somehow correspond to the old Chevys on the streets. On closer inspection, the picture show is all deceit. That old camera turns out to be nothing but a wooden box that hides a Polaroid inside. This is a game of implicit and explicit "realness" that overwhelms the shot with context, and it fits with the fact that these pictures are being taken in front of a capitol building that is not at all the seat of government—a building not used as a capitol after the revolution. The image taken by the fake photographic apparatus is a fake device at all levels. The relationship between image and evidence—or between what the picture says and how it is produced—is part of a game, and the monetary transaction between the tourist and the photographer depends on it. The shot itself is nothing except when one talks about the narrative surrounding it, which may range from comments as to how one got to Cuba (if the tourist is a U.S. citizen), to sociological narratives about how people make money in Cuba nowadays (signifying the resilience or resourcefulness of the population and so on). It is not that one needs the context in order to understand the image, but the image in itself is nothing without the context that surrounds it. A great deal of what Cuban images after the end of the Cold War advertise to the global market uses the same mechanism: Cuba as an entity is predicated on the revolution and its symbolic capital as providing the historical narrative. It is a narrative in which the national and the foreign gaze collide, in which investment in a symbol becomes transnational.

Context and image—what the image shows and what surrounds it—are emblematic of representations of the island, and are present in one of the most important visual essays on Havana, shot by Walker Evans before the fall of the Machado dictatorship in 1933. The Havana collection is important for its influence over time, although Evans did not come into contact with Cuban photographers, nor did he start a school of visual artists in Havana. Its influence is partly owing to the coherence of the project, but also to the literate feel that Evans brought to his work. His images have always been part of the narrative of Cuban photography—they have been claimed by those subjects whom they sought to capture. Evans's relationship to later photographers is organic, for Cubans saw in his images a mix of aesthetics and politics that they wanted their own work to convey.

Before traveling to Cuba, Evans roamed the streets of New York in the late 1920s and early 1930s with a Leica and a roll film camera. He cultivated a dandyish pose within the bohemian lifestyle he enjoyed in New York and, before that, in a year spent in Paris around 1926–27, supported by his family. He was drawn to the model of the Flaubertian pure writer, and reviewed Atget's photographs of Paris for the magazine *Hound & Horn* in 1931. As shown by his penchant for Atget, it is clear that Evans was looking for an object—one could say he was looking for a *city*—that he could approach. His pictures have a literary "feel" to them and it seems that he decided—at great psychological cost—not to be a writer. He was surrounded by a writerly milieu in New York—Lincoln Kirstein, Hart Crane, and Ben Shahn, who was one of the artists assisting Diego Rivera in his ill-fated Rockefeller Center commission—while also working at a brokerage firm. His projects were associated with architecture: *The Bridge* (1930), with his friend Hart Crane, and a 1931 series on Victorian houses in New England and New York State.

One of the first important elements in Evans's pictures concerned their reality effect, produced as a result of his engagement with modernism and politics. Evans only tampered with the image by cropping it out of the negative, and editing the picture until he got the exact object he wanted. His was a kind of grammatical correction, akin to pruning the sentence of unnecessary adjectives. There *was* a political framework to his images. He was not a "political" photographer, though the overly aestheticized stance of the 1920s was already leading him into political commitment. Part of the reason for this change had to do with the growing contact between North and South, represented most forcefully when, in 1931 and 1932, the Mexican muralist Diego Rivera traveled around the United States. In 1933, Rivera worked on his famous commission for Rockefeller Center in New York, and Evans met him there through Ben Shahn. There, Evans followed his work enthusiastically, and often went to see the mural as it was painted, before it was destroyed—on orders by Rockefeller himself—because it depicted Lenin.[4]

Evans's project was part of a *book:* the project was called *The Crime of Cuba,* it was written by Carleton Beals, and denounced U.S. complicity with the despotic Machado dictatorship. In 1931, students at the University of Havana were resisting the strong-arm tactics of the dictator, and journalists, political activists, and union leaders were killed in the savage repression that ensued. Repression bred more agitation in a vicious cycle that ultimately ended with the fall of the government on August 12, 1933, a U.S. invasion, and the ascent of Carlos Manuel de Céspedes. When Evans landed in Havana in May 1933, the tropical paradise was turning into a tropical nightmare. "I did land in Havana in the midst of a Revolution," Evans recalled in an interview.[5] That revolution is what he was supposed to capture there.

Evans had met Carleton Beals just once, and Evans had appeared "sullen and scowling, even a bit truculent," imposing his conditions for the project: he wanted to be allowed to submit twice the number of pictures, sixty-four prints, with the understanding that thirty-two of these would be used.[6] He also wanted complete freedom of choice as to the images reproduced, as well as the right to establish the sequence in which they would appear. He insisted that the pictures be placed at the end, not at the beginning, of the work, as a kind of self-contained appendix.

There was a tension, even then, between text and image. Evans wanted a sort of aleatory relationship. He would stick to the project, but he also wanted an independent *space*. Although Evans most probably had not read the book before he went to Havana in the spring of 1933, Beals must have explained clearly his political take on Cuba. Beals had been there the previous year—in the winter of 1932—and had written the book during the summer of 1933.[7] Lippincott's contract with Evans allowed for a two-week stay in Havana, though Evans spent three. By that third week he was penniless, though he had the good fortune of running into Ernest Hemingway, and Hemingway paid for Evans's last week in Havana out of his own pocket.

Evans's took two cameras to Cuba, a medium-format $2\frac{1}{2} \times 4\frac{1}{4}$ camera for handheld shots, and a $6\frac{1}{2} \times 8\frac{1}{2}$ view camera with a tripod.[8] He used those two cameras interchangeably. He kept about four hundred negatives from his trip, though only thirty-one pictures were published in Beals's book, three of them culled from Havana newspaper files (Evans liked to appropriate, in pre-postmodern fashion). In Havana, Evans pushed back and observed, though one feels that his encounters are not necessarily fortuitous, and there is no apologizing for moments that have a more obvious aesthetic or "artistic" touch. His photographic text depends on this trade-off between deliberate choice and chance, turning Havana into a compact space of tension—compact also in terms of the range of the city Evans photographed, which were the spaces the photographer could walk to: Old Havana and the Parque Central, or, on the other side of the bay, the small streets in Regla. At the very far end, perhaps Vedado, or a couple of excursions to the countryside. It is a Havana as compact as the crowd of celebrants Evans photographed on the capitol steps surrounding an open convertible with the Cuban flag on its chassis.

Beals's book was scandalous in a way Evans's pictures were not.[9] Beals's book was a dissection of Cuba in historical, social, and economic terms. Throughout, Beals shows his knowledge of Cuban literary discourse, and he sees himself as an intermediary between the Cuban literate classes, their projects for social renewal, and their relationship to U.S. imperialist domination. It was like many other texts that would follow it, all the way up to the revolution, in which the U.S. visitor assumes a position of defending the population against the interests of the United States. Evans placed himself at some point between the shot and the printed image, and this claim to authorship is registered in his Cuba pictures. In one of the pictures that he took of a barber giving a man a haircut, we can see the hat of the photographer, looking down at the viewer of his handheld camera. It is barely visible in many prints, but it is there.

This inscription shows us the place of authorship in these photographs, as well as the site of human solidarity. The choice of subject already speaks to Evans's loyalties with the working class. It is not solidarity with a project, or with a political program, but with the anonymity of the man in the street who is a tradesman doing his job. This is not a torn-down, beaten-up barbershop in the middle of nowhere, still resilient and surviving in spite of the difficulties of the times, but rather a busy and prosperous shop. This whole scene is not predicated on this being a "special" barbershop, but rather (and this is underscored by the very interruption in the trades-man at his job) one that has been found by a Baudelairean flaneur strolling down the street and looking in. Evans did not want to lay a heavy hand on political programs, but rather to work at the intersection of contingency and singularity.

The photographs seem to be about dialectical exchanges: people and architecture, construction and utensils. Evans photographed the exterior of a movie house with its painted announcements, with men lounging around under the columns and on the street; he took shots of the city as a whole, photographing the Plaza Vieja from above, and other photographs of people looking out of windows, clothes hanging on worn-down balconies, a young black Cuban in a white linen dress and smoking a cigarette. Evans captured buildings in order to give an illusion of permanence, but this permanence would then be traded off dialectically with the utensils he shot, meant to show the things one uses in order to build things, or destroy things, or merely keep things going—a candy vendor with a makeshift stick where sweets can be displayed, a pushcart with rags and brooms, a poor wooden kitchen, and a woman peeling a pineapple on top of a wooden table. He balanced his compositions in order to unsettle. Things were somewhat off-kilter, and this was part of his commentary on

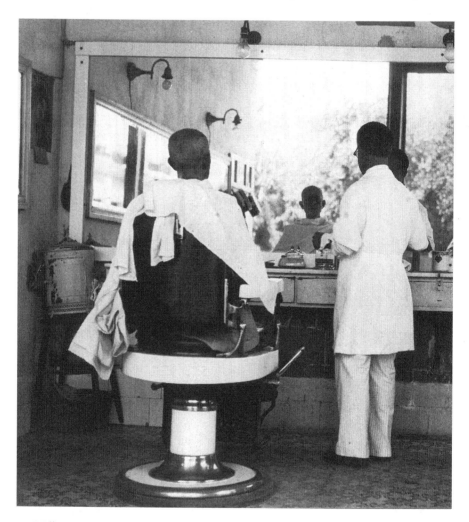

Walker Evans (American, 1903–75), "Havana Barbershop." Courtesy of the J. Paul Getty Museum, Los Angeles.

the mood of the place—the woman stops cutting the pineapple in order to look at the camera; two men look at the photographer from inside an empty store, while a woman stands in the corner. Evans's direct gaze on poverty is not necessarily meant to arouse viewers' solidarity, but to show how hard it is to read it. Poverty turns people into visible ciphers—there is a kind of invisible code to poverty, a mystery that he seeks to decipher. He pushes back and zooms in. This was a method he would perfect in a later photographic essay, the most important one of his career: a study of poverty coauthored with James Agee and titled *Let Us Now Praise Famous Men* (1941).

Evans underscores the fact that there is something that cannot be *seen*, in spite of the intrusion of the photographic image. This is dramatically highlighted in the pictures he takes of people asleep. It is as if, in his own way, he wanted to strike a balance between Marx and Freud, between the proletariat and the dream (or nightmare) of capitalism. If images after 1959

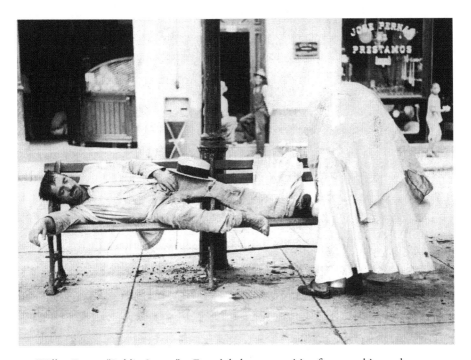

Walker Evans, "Public Square"—Evans's habaneros waiting for something to happen. Courtesy of the J. Paul Getty Museum, Los Angeles.

rendered all actions, perceptions, and situations capable of being explained by having recourse to the links between the nation and the state, here sleepers sleep just as beggars beg, cooks prepare food, or barbers cut hair. The sleepers are mostly poor; their bodies are contorted on park benches. Evans understood at some level—he had studied Atget, after all—that photography aims to capture the memory of the event. But the fact that the object photographed has no memory of it turns the photographic image into the depiction of an unreadable subject. The viewer cannot penetrate their dream. There is no memory here for the object photographed, except the absent memory of sleep.

Did Evans aim to capture the "dream" of revolution? At some point, he did join image and context in order to produce the text of want and desire, the imaginary text that resulted out of the image and its overdetermination by context. Escaping the revolution or dreaming while it happens under a blazing sun or under a precarious shade at noon is more than an act of ennui. Were these subjects dreaming of their own liberation, or are they just muted examples of abject poverty? It would be more accurate to say that this is waiting time as absent memory. Not the stillness of eternity but the stillness of something about to happen, perhaps best captured in the picture of the two men, one in front of the other, in the Parque Central. One of them waits for something, looking out for something else while the other, behind him, sleeps. Sleeping and then waiting for something—that combination was the dialectical tension Evans wanted, and it is constantly captured in his photographs.[10]

Waiting, sleeping—people expecting something that will not happen but always could. More than seventy years after Evans's pictures, after Machado begat Batista, Batista begat Fidel, and Fidel begat the triumphant march of the people's revolution; after the Soviet subsidies and then after the fall of the Berlin Wall; after the "Período especial" (the "Special Period in Times of Peace"), a contemporary Cuban narrator perhaps summed up best what these pictures meant, in a different time but in the same place. "She pointed toward the door with the hand holding her cigarette," explains Antonio José Ponte in his collection of stories *In the Cold of the Malecón*. "Surely he too had prepared himself for something that wasn't going to happen."[11] The Machado dictatorship fell, but events immediately rendered it an aborted revolution, one that would only be completed nearly thirty years later, in 1959.

REVOLUTION: 1971

To think of Evans's effects on later Cuban photographers as organic in nature implies adopting a vision attuned to the historical narrative of the revolution—for the Cuban Revolution of 1959 looked for continuities, as it sought to fulfill the deferred dreams that could not be brought to fruition the moment Machado fell. Evans is important to the history of struggle as the one who is capable of representing both the desire for the future and the specificity of the present. This notion of organicity and continuity pertained not only to the relationship the revolution had to the Cuban past, but also to the relationship between what is captured in the photographic image and reality itself, and what it was able to express about the nation and the state.

The kind of photo reportage anticipated in Evans's pictures was not in opposition to art; in terms of these two categories, the relationship was always, to a certain degree, dialectical. The merging of the two turned photography into one of the most important media for the revolution,

Walker Evans, "Parque Central II"—Evans's other Havana. Courtesy of the J. Paul Getty Museum, Los Angeles.

The romance of the *barbudo* circled the globe: Fidel lighting cigar with Zippo lighter. Photograph by I. C. Rapoport. Reprinted with permission of the photographer.

and the state relied on it to document revolutionary changes in the press, in government buildings and institutes, and in museums. Since *History Will Absolve Me,* Fidel's self-defense for the Moncada barracks attack in 1953, the state knew that history needed to be documented in order to become a living presence, as well as to reinforce the historical import of all decisions taken since the very early years of the revolutionary process. In this sense, there was certainly a coincidence of purposes, "a process that needed to document its passage into history, and a series of photographers who wanted to capture those moments—moments that would never again be repeated."[12] In these terms, photographers captured the nation, and in many cases did so at the service of the state, so that a collusion of interests could take place.

This exchange between history and contingency can be seen clearly in *Fidel's Cuba,* subtitled *A Revolution in Pictures.* The pictures are by Osvaldo Salas, one of the better-known postrevolutionary photographers. The captions are by his son, Roberto Salas, who is also a photographer and who contributes a few pictures of his own. The book is arranged more or less in chronological order, with the images serving as props toward the reminiscences of the son. Much is made of the fact that the photographs capture reality, in spite of the fact that the lines between photo reportage and art are intentionally blurred because their aim is to humanize power, to render power *aesthetically.* Thus, important revolutionary figures—Fidel himself, or El Che—are apprehended in moments of scripted intimacy, as when Fidel speaks with peasants in the Sierra Maestra, or with students at the university, or when he is cutting sugar cane and relaxing in a hammock. The scripted or planned nature of these encounters is explained by Che Guevara's biographer Jon Lee Anderson, who says that Fidel displayed "an awareness of the power of the graphic image" that many other heroes of the revolution did not know how to manipulate.[13] Most of the moments in Fidel's life have been photographed, Anderson explains, and he has encouraged the presence of photographers at every moment. Che Guevara, on the other hand, was more reticent around the camera: "He was moody, capable of playing to the camera one moment and resenting its intrusion the next."[14] In an interesting psychological tidbit, Anderson notes that perhaps this was because El Che had been an aficionado photographer and somehow "understood the power of the medium."[15]

As an exemplary photographic object, *Fidel's Cuba* deploys the past as lived experience with a very clear genealogical narrative. The son (Roberto) completes the work of the father (Osvaldo) by means of words. At the same time, the history of the revolution is assumed as an organic whole: it starts with Fidel in New York trying to convince exiles in the 1950s to support his revolution; it follows a chronological line up to the Bay of Pigs; and the last chapter is dedicated to people, reflecting what historians of photography in Cuba after 1959 like to call the new emphasis on the heroicity of the ordinary. Throughout this journey, the observer realizes what others have already commented on: few ruling classes have been as photogenic as the Cuban *comandantes;* they were, from the beginning, the most aesthetically self-conscious political *nomenklatura* in Latin American history.

Although there has been much debate about what early Cuban revolutionary photography owes to images taken during the Mexican and the Russian revolutions, the debt to the world of advertising is much clearer. The great photographers of the revolution, such as Constantino Arias, Raúl Corrales, and Alberto "Korda" Díaz Gutiérrez, worked on assignment for magazines, and they documented the life of the bourgeoisie. They had a deep commitment to their surroundings, and they knew the work of Evans and other American photographers from the 1930s. There was a school of photoreportage in Cuba, and the country had a market for action-picture accounts of contemporary events before the revolution, particularly in magazines such as *Bohemia* and, later, *Revolución.* The early tradition of Cuban revolutionary photography is indebted to this aesthetics, which in turn was indebted to the world of advertising and fashion—in spite of later attempts to deny it, when the government closed the last vestiges of semiprivate nightlife in the late 1960s. During the first decade of the revolution, photojournalists slowly disentangled themselves from the purely documentary function of their trade, and other aesthetics available to them came from the world of media, broadly understood. This accounts for the difference in subject matter before and immediately after the revolution. Whereas Evans refused to photograph famous people, Cuban photographers turned their revolutionaries into iconic images.[16] They were like new celebrities that the people could identify with, subjected to a "star treatment" that only photography could offer. In Korda's picture of the defiant gaze of Che Guevara we can see the most-reproduced publicity shot of the late twentieth century. The heroism that the shot wants to capture is indebted to advertising in a way that becomes perversely clear in more recent years, as the picture itself has been used for all sorts of capitalist images.[17]

The link between advertising and revolution perversely blurs the distinction between political star treatment and mass rallies. Although these seem to be opposing categories, in the early images of the revolution, as well as in later, more overtly political shots, we see them as related representations. There was revolutionary glamour and it was created by photographers, but later on there was also nobility of purpose, which endowed many subjects with glamorous appeal. This was by no means the sole register for a much broader and more complex archive of photographic images, but it is important to note the way in which they sold, appealed, beckoned, and allowed for the self-representation of noble hardship to be inscribed with the state's political ideology.

The realm of the visual transformed the revolution by structuring iconic sequences.[18] Events coalesced into a common narrative reflecting productive achievements and the mass concentrations in Cuban political mass rallies.[19] The photographic project, as well as the filmic one, was fully dependent on the state, which, after the 1960s, became the most important client for the photographers, buying pictures in order to place them in hospitals, schools, factories, public administration buildings, and embassies. Thus, the lens was always focused on changes taking place in Cuba, and images were part of a general project of "uplift." Photography was not seen simply as "reportage"—in the sense that one understood this term later on, in the 1970s and 1980s, during the Central American wars—but it was also not "art" in the bourgeois sense of the term. It circulated at the threshold, it moved back and forth within the circuit of the professional look and the artistic gaze. The photograph had a duty to perform: it was a document and, as such, it contained a certain kind of *knowledge* that would be used to produce more *knowledge* in turn. From the point of view of the state, and from the point of view of the nation, which these intellectual workers belonged to, the common producer of language was photography.

Professional and state-commissioned photographers during the 1970s visited workers in their factories and peasants on their farms. They aimed to portray people as they went about their daily lives, whether working or in moments of repose.[20] This prompted others also to follow their lead and the state's emphasis on education and self-improvement provided a good context for the medium. Miguel Castro Muñiz speaks of the great impetus given to Cuban photography by a burgeoning *aficionado* movement in the 1970s, when stores sold large quantities of cameras, film, and photographic matériel imported from the Soviet Union at very affordable prices—although these cameras were better known for their optics than for their mechanical systems.[21] The *aficionado* movement put the means of production into the hands of the people, and this was understood as a way of democratizing art, by setting in motion the endless reproducibility of revolutionary life. Instead of the extraordinary heroism of the revolutionary leaders during the early days of the revolution, the subjects were workers, farmers, students, and common people.

History was an ongoing process that moved in accelerated revolutionary speed, one that only stopped for the brief instant of the shot. If Evans's photographs captured the dream that people were waiting to live by placing it at the center of the viewer's gaze, in the 1970s reality was depicted in the photographs and they also reflected what was happening throughout the country as a result of the new laws enacted by the people, in the great strides of the educational system, in the pursuit of happiness that now seemed possible for all and not just for the lucky few. There are organic continuities in these pictures that were absent in the dialectical tensions that Evans wanted to portray. After the revolution, nation and state are seen as one rather than as dialectical opposites. In addition, the disruptions caused by history, understood as the fated march toward a future predicated on the fragility of the present, give even the most propagandistic pictures taken during the revolution an air of melancholy. The pictures of the heroes of the revolution, in their larger-than-life formats, beckoned viewers to be mobilized toward a permanent resurrection. The pictures of El Che, of Camilo Cienfuegos, of Fidel playing baseball, were always anticipated obituaries. At times, they cast their subjects in tones of lyrical masculinity. They see themselves as if from the point of view of the negative, projecting themselves onto a future. For a brief instant, they make the viewer ponder the contrast and the context of an experiment ennobled by conflicts with its neighbor, the most powerful nation on earth. This was a different context from that of Evans, one that represented total annihilation as being possible at any time. Without this context, the photographs become, in the present, embarrassing images of sentiment for a past that refuses to die, and that prefers the living death that the image provides.

The ostensible permanence of the icon remained acting in historical time for decades. By the 1990s it was starting to become an empty signifier. The image was then thrown into a totally different mode of production and reproduction, one that understood its iconicity as the point of departure for the production of a trinket. The context still lives on, and the text is carried by the image in order to provide it with a sense of being. The owner can recall, or advertise, but the icon itself seems exhausted from the wealth of its significations. During the Special Period of the 1990s, and after tourism became one of the ways the Cuban state guaranteed its survival in a world that had totally changed, those same photographs were reproduced on T-shirts, key chains, and coffee mugs. They became posters and postcards. They were reproduced everywhere in CD booklets, laminated into tabletops, turned into revolutionary mementos devoid of their ephemeral sense of purposeful photoreportage. They now add to the folklore of the "Havana" bars cloned in cities like Paris, Amsterdam, Madrid, and, yes, even Miami. The images assume, with relative dignity or not, the fact that what is left is not necessarily the signifier itself, but the signified: Cuba as the "elusive nation" that only photography can represent in a snapshot. This is why, by the Special Period, photography was mourning something the text still sought to celebrate.

HAVANA: 1994

There is a dialectical interplay in recent photography on Havana: while the city itself crumbles, it also seems to levitate in pictures. The more ruined and collapsed the city looks, the more it seems to defy gravity with the same sense of melancholic height that Wim Wenders used to such sublime effect in *Wings of Desire*. Ruins are the central motif in this scenario. This "morbid fascination with the destruction the city," as Emma Álvarez-Tabío Albo describes foreigners' gaze on Havana, turns out to be another part of the "service" economy that has always thrived within the urban fabric. Within this framework, Havana is now—as it always has been—where the foreign voyeur finds his or her desires met by the city in itself.[22] At the same time, the city is the intermediary for the fulfillment of those desires, commercial traffic in objects—sugar, rum, wood, silk, and so on—turning into traffic in symbolic referents.

In books that serve as visual aids to the city, photographs seek to ascertain Cuba's "mystery," but the mystery is predicated and inscribed on the glamour that those early iconic heroic images once had. The past is always present in these photography collections, adding luster to the most insignificant moments that can be captured on film for posterity. The Cuban photography movement that flourished in the 1970s captured the population assuming the tasks and the challenges that history demanded. But the more recent crop of photography books depends on the structural unfolding of a historical text under the eyes of the disciplined gaze of architects. Havana becomes a monumental dream constructed over the span of generations that add their layer of historical space upon the city. The city becomes the laboratory for registering time, and this seduces a subject as a *viewer,* not as a participant, as was the case in the 1970s.

In the 1990s, Cuban images entered once again the networks of commercial photography as a result of a collaboration between Cuban officials and foreign observers. Although these were not state-sponsored projects, they did depend on the support of the state. Permits had to be secured, and equipment had to be moved. This does not mean that the state dictated projects, but one can presume that the glossier the product, and the more complex the logistics for its production, the more they depended on Cuban connections. The books produced fall into distinct categories, but not on a chronological continuum; they shared the space of representation as if Havana and the revolution needed to be presented from multiple angles. The first to appear were architectural and historical volumes, such as *Havana* (1994), edited by Nancy Stout and Jorge Rigau and published by Rizzoli; or the special 1996 issue of the *Journal of Decorative and Propaganda Arts* dedicated to Havana during the republican years.[23] Then there are picture books on the island in general, such as *Cuba* (1997), edited by Rachel Carley, with photographs by Andrea Brizzi, and *Havana: Portrait of a City,* with text by Juliet Barclay and photographs by Martin Charles, which predated all of these, and was published in England in 1993.[24]

These books began to appear during the Special Period, most after 1994, which marked perhaps the most difficult year, with riots in Havana in August followed by the *balsero* crisis. It is not too farfetched to think that the mere fact of opening the city for its representation onto other spaces was the object of much internal debate about the place of historical contingency and the limits of photoreportage concerning Havana's crumbling architecture. For example, in Stout and Rigau's *Havana,* architecture provided a broader temporal framework that avoided talking too directly about the contentious political issues of the time. In spite of the fact that the city is always seen from the point of view of its inhabitants—as a city built, constructed, and lived in by people—Cubans are not necessarily represented, but their buildings are. In Barclay's *Havana: Portrait of a City,* there is no revolutionary mecca, and very little poverty or social malaise. There are carefully selected pictures of the few city streets that had been rebuilt at that time, and a history of the city that ends with its being called "the most brilliant metropolis of the Caribbean"—this, precisely at a time when social hardship allowed residents electricity only a couple of hours at a time. In Stout and Rigau's *Havana,* Stout, in her introduction, thanks urban planners such as Mario Coyula, architects such as Eduardo Rodrí-guez, and scholars such as Emma Álvarez-Tabío Albo, Roberto Segre, and Lohaina Aruca, names that reappear in other books at the time. Stout also mentions officials at the Ministerio de Relaciones Exteriores, and help from the Cuban Interests Section in Washington, DC. This team of guides into the formal depiction of the city may not have had any bearing in terms of content, but it does point to the need for a collaboration between foreign-ers and their hosts, who are called upon to provide expertise.

It is not clear who makes the concessions in terms of representation, and at what point the decision was made not to dwell too much on habaneros' daily lives. Like *Our Islands and Their People,* the audience for this project was external to the territorial boundaries of the state, though homegrown intellectuals provide a validation and authenticity that the earlier project lacked. Because these books were not commissioned by foreign states, but rather by corporative editorial concerns, the inscription of the present shapes them by means of a sales pitch. For example, commenting on the Casa de Don Mateo Pedroso, on Calle Cuba near Cuarteles, Juliet Barclay states that "the house still has tremendous feeling of luxury and a pro-nounced air of the Arabian Nights . . . Now there are craft shops in the entresol and by the patio there are a bookshop and a bar. There can be no more soothing way to pass a day than to spend it in the quiet of the Casa Pedroso, soaking up poetry and rum."[25] The "feeling" that the author wants to convey, and the image that the pictures portray, are not merely bourgeois, but aristocratic. It is important to distinguish between one and the other: the past in Barclay's book is not capitalist or mercantilist, with their negative connotations and their ideologies of enrichment. The impli-cation is that aristocrats have always been rich—they are not made rich by virtue of commerce. Thus, wealth, sensuality, and pleasure have origins that are beyond historical contingencies.

By making their appeal to aesthetics, or hedonism, the books de-emphasize the mercantile presence in Havana and the city's position within the capitalist exchange for goods and images. Whereas in the past the pleasures of the self were obtained at the cost of much social suffering, present-day visitors need not feel guilty at their pleasure, because the social project guarantees the absence of past inequities. Hence, the collaboration with the Cuban intellectual community guarantees the participation of sub-alterns who are able to guarantee these claims. This does not mean that governmental constraints necessarily affected what was portrayed in the volumes, and it does not detract from the serious architectural scholarship that is present in some of them. But it is important to see them as the product of new configurations of capital and the state within a context different from that of the 1960s or 1970s.[26] They belong to a world in which possibilities in the future have ceased to become the merchandise, and where concrete achievements allow us to gaze upon the present and the past. In other words, photographs of the revolution and within the revolution always beckoned the observer, always sold an image. In the past, this image was fragile because the project was always on the verge of not being realized; in the present, the fragility of the cityscape, and of its buildings, is predicated on the fact that the *past* itself may be lost and should be maintained.

Ideological concerns were contingent on the financial realities of the 1990s. The reason for these books' appearance can be traced to the government's desire to pursue tourism as a way of earning hard currency. The Cuban government built on the 1982 UNESCO designation of Havana as a World Historical Site and began to repair the crumbling buildings of the old city. The Office of the Historian of the City, headed to this day by Eusebio Leal (who also wrote *La Habana: ciudad antigua* [1988]), set itself the task of revamping the colonial structures in order to make them amenable to a tourist economy. In the 1990s, the state engaged in mixed-company financing through its state-owned company Habaguanex in order to accomplish the herculean task. But what the government had in mind was a tourism different from the kind found in other Caribbean cities. This was to be "literate" tourism, building on the educational and social achievements of the revolution. In 1994, the government founded Paradiso:

Turismo Cultural (taking its name from José Lezama Lima's difficult, baroque masterpiece), a branch of ARTex, S.A., in order to market Cuban culture for the needs of the tourist visitor. Its Web site claims that "It is not Paradiso's interest to create a culture for tourism but to insert tourism into our country's cultural life, thus offering the visitor the opportunity to learn about more than five centuries of history that have made up the Cuban people's identity."[27] These guided and specialized tours are contingent on cultural offers already programmed at different points in the city—thus, the emphasis on the fact that visitors partake of the governmental cultural project for all, and not necessarily of spectacles produced for them. To know Cuba through its culture allows for the opportunity (as stated in the brochures) of "living the Cuban way inside of you," because, although being Cuban is predicated on the very concrete site where the government and its people coexist, it is also a "way of being" that taps into subjects' innate sensuality and pleasure. The combination of tourism and education is what accounts for the aristocratic flair of Barclay's book, which has a foreword by historian of the city Eusebio Leal Spengler and an introduction by Francisco de Borbón y Escasany, Duke of Seville. The old city invited these curious combinations, where old money and socialism could go hand in hand.[28] Guided by the text that framed them, the accounts intended to "save" the city. The mixture of text and images—the images always subservient to the text that accompanied them—underscored architecture. As the revolution traded oracular time for its own particular mappings, Havana became a city of spaces.

The first picture books focused on Old Havana, because that was the area of the city that needed to be rebuilt for the tourist economy, as well as the area that allowed the observer the most compact vision of the city as a whole. At the same time, these books created a totality that habaneros at times found hard—if not somewhat impossible—to understand. The lack of fuel and the resulting constraints on public transportation in the 1990s prevented for them the kinds of journeys that the visitor photographers were able to undertake. Given the difficulties they faced, habaneros' perception of the city turned necessarily into a more local and condensed affair, with people unable to get from one neighborhood to the other, or undergoing hardships to make those trips. The urban fabric itself changed, as did the way of living it—partly because class was predicated to a certain extent on place of habitation. Thus, a person living in Vedado, close to the historical center of the city, found it very hard to go to Arroyo Naranjo farther out; and residents of the old part of the city almost never ventured out to fashionable neighborhoods like Cubanacán, where the old bourgeoisie built houses that are now used by embassies and foreign personnel. Such excursions could only be contemplated by foreigners, who could travel from place to place and take in the city as the totality that they presented to the foreign voyeur.

The gaze upon the city from the outside colluded with the work of Cuban intellectuals—especially architects—who were among those able to engage in the inside/outside focus that these projects demanded. The passion for the city colluded with the taxonomical and archival work done by Cuban architects such as Eduardo Luis Rodríguez, spurred to act by the strength of their convictions and by a deeply felt sense of national pride. The collusion was not predicated on money, but on nationalism and intellectual and professional responsibility that at times ran counter to perceived government projects. Rodríguez, for example, argued that although the government was fully committed to Old Havana, it could not afford to abandon the modern city, even if, or rather because, its eclecticism revealed the very Cuban style of the republic and of its bourgeoisie. The city that was being reconstructed, he and others explained, offered only a partial view of what Havana had been: not simply the military bastion of the Americas (with all the symbolic repercussions the notion had for revolutionary discourse), but also an "open" and eclectic city. An architect by training, Rodríguez recounts in *The Havana Guide* how Cuban higher education in architecture around 1980 did not validate twentieth-century work but, on the contrary, denigrated it as "instances of inefficient architecture, devoid of social consciousness, that had been produced by and for the dominant bourgeoisie."[29] Contrary to the pedagogical and political aims of their formal training, Rodríguez and others of his generation saw modern architecture as formally and functionally interesting, and they set out to document and catalog existing structures in order to preserve a heritage that the 1990s atmosphere of foreign investment and capital speculation threatened with destruction.

How Rodríguez addressed the question of ownership demonstrates what a radical undertaking this was. Because many of the structures of the republican period in question were private residences and not state-sponsored projects, this entailed, in some measure, reconstructing the network that linked the former bourgeoisie to its architects. As Rodríguez explains it, "[t]he near complete loss, after 1959, of the personal records of the architects whose projects are included here, compounded by the fact that most opted to go abroad for temporary exiles (which soon became permanent relocations), caused immense difficulty and delays in the completion of this book."[30] Rodríguez had to reconstruct an archive that took him to the United States, Puerto Rico, Spain, and France. He searched for pictures, maps, and people. It was a delicate operation, because attempts to safeguard memory were linked to the contentious political issue of property and ownership—one of the political and economic sources of tension between the United States and Cuba. According to international practice, the works had to be labeled according to their original name or use. Thus, the city that Rodríguez reconstructed is an image frozen in time of a bourgeoisie that abandoned its structures only to yield them to a new ruling class that lives in what are now areas of limited access. Rodríguez needs to add that the names of the original owners used in common architectural practice "does not imply the present state of ownership or use of the buildings, which, in almost every case, has changed since their construction."[31]

There was always a political rationale behind images produced for foreign consumption. These were part of an ideological memory project, because what needed to be saved from the period before the revolution was also related to the kind of text that the revolution wanted to create for the prerevolutionary past. Picture books illustrated a particular notion of history, and an ideological framework. This is why it is not surprising that books concerned with architectural preservation were followed later in the decade by other kinds of photography books, which organized history according to their own particular teleology. In many cases, these other books depicted traveling exhibits that took advantage of the fact that Cuba was now opening itself up to different publics. Produced with the help of Cuban intermediaries who positioned themselves as cultural guides and facilitators, they signaled an island that had become a product for capitalist consumption by means of culture, broadly defined. Culture itself was the element that allowed them to negotiate between the sense of national dignity sustained by the revolution and the needs of the market for all things Cuban. Cultural authorities memorialized their own past in exhibits such as Cuba: 100 años de fotografía, or the more recent exhibit at the Los Angeles County Museum of Art (April 15–July 1, 2001) titled Cuban

Photography after the Revolution, whose book of that title has a foreword by Wim Wenders—who captured the particular texture of Havana in his film *Buena Vista Social Club*—and essays by Tim B. Wride and Cristina Vives.[32] These initial forays into the world market for images opened up the space for a third kind of book: accounts such as *Havana in My Heart: 75 Years of Cuban Photography,* edited by Gareth Jenkins, or *Six Days in Havana* by James Michener.[33]

All these visual accounts turned Cuba, and Havana in particular, into an iconic presence. The revolution, the city, and the country as a whole were the property of the people, while Cuba itself and all its referential and possible sources of dispersion were souvenirs close to the heart of the nostalgic traveler. Not all travelers to Cuba could be classified as nostalgic, though the images lent themselves to the construction of the city as the space where past and future perfect colluded. It was a particular nostalgia, completely different from the one that can be seen in exile publications, or from the images that adorn Cuban restaurants in Miami and that get marketed there on calendars or address books. The pictures in Miami are glossy color reproductions that most of the time offer no claim to authorship. Those photographs are not only somewhat frozen in time, but they index a particular building, street, or landscape, and not the affect that they may produce. Photography books such as Jenkins's or Michener's, on the other hand, deal in a sort of anticipatory nostalgia communicated by the combination of site, political project, and a present understood as being on the verge of decay. Lost property in exile publications is equated to lost dreams of a city in 1959 at the apex of capitalist modernity. A similar utopia is registered in contemporary photography books, except that this one is predicated on the utopian dreams registered in ruins. Context is important for nostalgia in the recent books in ways that differ from the way dreams are manipulated in exile publications.

Text and context produce the dialectical tensions found throughout the four parts of Gareth Jenkins's *Havana in My Heart.* "Street Scene," "Revolution," "Everyday and Ritual," and "Artists and Performers"—all these sections correspond to a particular relationship between the quotidian and the historical, between the present time, unregistered by history, and historical time. There are many references to literate and aesthetic discourse, both in the text itself and in the quotes that Jenkins has selected (from Graham Greene, José Martí, or Federico García Lorca), as well as in the color-coordinated pages in sky blue and brown. The book is a hybrid: an aesthetics of history as well as an aesthetics of everyday life. There are classic pictures from Korda, Osvaldo Salas, and María Eugena Haya (Marucha) next to pictures from the *Bohemia* archives of the 1950s, or work by more modern photographers. Jenkins adds captions to most of the pictures, explaining the context of the image, or guiding the reader to an important aspect that he or she may have missed. A 1987 picture by Sergio Romero of an apartment building covered with flags that hang from every balcony prompts Jenkins to ponder, "Why is it that Cuba is so full of potent symbols?" He is referring to the heroic pictures of the revolution, but also to a broader field—in Havana, the "iconography goes much deeper" and objects are held together "by some strange alchemy" that includes people in their daily lives, street scenes, and the national flag itself. Jenkins is rhapsodic about the flag: "Under the tropical sun, softened by salt sea breezes, infused with life from the infectious smiles on street faces, everything is transformed into an icon" (26). The flag is "Simple, unforgettable, and proudly flourished by islanders celebrating independence from 'la Yuma,' the Monster to the North, and by their hostile cousins across the Florida Straits who also claim to represent the nation" (ibid.). But the simplicity of the flag belies some strange forms of historical understanding that confuse the nation with the state. Family ties are reduced to accidental people ("cousins"), who are in turn disenfranchised: they do not belong to the nation because of the hostility they feel toward the state.

Jenkins's *Havana in My Heart* is not really a memoir built out of his own experiences in Cuba, but rather a kind of collective archive that is also a memory bank where past and present are juxtaposed. There is solidarity with the revolutionary process, but at the same time the author does not pretend to "belong." He manipulates his own distance by reporting popular tales as he brings all historical events to the present moment. This amplified present can be seen in a photograph by Sergio Romero taken in 1984 of a woman making a phone call in Havana. The accompanying text explains that, "In the early days of the Revolution, many services were provided free, including telephone calls" (43). The picture serves as the excuse for a statement that repeats a "received" knowledge. The lonely woman in the picture, who may certainly look somewhat distressed to a different observer, is transformed by Jenkins's quasi-ethnographic comments: in those early days, queues would form in order to make telephone calls, where "everyone would take a great interest in the conversation, joining in the discussion of family problems, expressions of love, and so on" (ibid.). Not only are the Cubans oblivious to a northern sense of decorum, but the private act of having a telephone conversation is turned into a public example of how the revolution demolished bourgeois notions of privacy.

There is also a sense of dislocation predicated on time. In Jenkins's book, a picture by Constantino Arias of the Paseo del Prado in the 1950s lit up at night and with tables outside is accompanied by text that places it in a different time frame: "A vibrant night life is returning to the streets of the old town. Prado, the elegant boulevard that runs from the Castillo de la Punta, at the mouth of the harbor, past the Central Park and the Capitolio, is being restored to its former glory" (38). Viewers do not get a picture of the present; instead, the picture of the past helps them imagine, in the present, what the future might be. The sense of dislocation involved in these image–text dynamics distances the object from the one who performs the gaze: the text is dedicated to a foreign observer, who morphs into the role of the investor, symbolic or real. Because of its symbolic value, investment in the potential capital of the city is equated with investment in the revolution as a symbol. This is why the first point these books have to make concerns the question of sentimental or affective solidarity with the project. Once this solidarity is gained, they can engage in the creation of a present-past.

Even as past and present layer each other over the same space, it is clear that the future does not intend to be simply an image of the past. If one reads the city as a cultural text, time is trumped by words. The text one creates for the image codifies it within the circumstances of its production. Something is detaining time, and it is not the city itself—though exactly what is it that accounts for this eternal present is never mentioned in the books. Whether the text accounts for this effect, or whether the images themselves do the trick, can be source of endless argument. Emma Álvarez-Tabío Albo believes it is the result of the fact that the capital of a revolutionary state seems paradoxically involved in a grandiose attempt to detain time; in other words, the modern impulse involved in any revolutionary gesture stands in contrast to repeated viewings of arrested time. This entails thinking that the city itself absorbs state policies that render it susceptible to being viewed in these terms, as if the city had no impulse of its own, and as if there were no other collaborators in ensuring that Havana is precisely rendered in this mode. As an outside viewer, Jenkins is fully complicit with this ideological construction, and he feels obliged to participate in the myth that the city can be read as a cultural text. As such, there is a tension between revolution and recuperation. Revolution is equated to culture, and both together relish the constant gaze of the city *on* the city.

The pictures incarnate present into past and vice versa; hence, their unlimited textuality. The text in itself always reads the pictures as evidence of an "original" time. It is a sort of preindustrial fantasy captured photographically and engaging in essentialist views of culture: the revolution is hard work, but it also entails a sense of fun and adventure. Jenkins puts it best: "it was, after all, a very Latin and a very Caribbean revolution, and one during which its participants never ceased to crack jokes about its shortcomings" (69). Photography, then, aims to capture this Cuban "character," which is in turn exemplified in the revolution that the Cubans created. Pictures are evidence of essential Cuban traits, while photography short-circuits the tensions between the nation and the state. It glues one to the other in an indissoluble link, and creates an illusory "openness" for the act of reading: even if the city contains an air of mystery, it is a mystery that is capable of being deciphered. In *Cuban Photography after the Revolution,* Tim B. Wride explains that "[t]o walk in a Cuban city is to be inexorably a part of the vitality, rhythm, and sensuality of the place. Omnipresent music (a mixture of everything from traditional Caribbean sounds to the latest Madonna single) somehow harmonizes with blaring TVs and the friendly shouts that have replaced long disconnected doorbells."[34] The text and the pictures want to capture an instant of time, because this vitality is also modern—it is busy assaulting the viewer with a wide variety of codes. Some of these codes, of course, are completely fictive, a trade-off between desire, want, and reality, as if the tactile and physical encounters with the city always implied an idea. Wim Wenders understood that Cuba was better thought of as a "state of mind" and "a country of dreamers." The visual register he produced in film also defined the way in which Cuba was represented to the outside world. There was color and juxtaposition, formal compositions that went from the discrete and particular to the architecture of empty hallways at sunset that we traverse in order to see some of the musicians interviewed. Construction surrounds these individuals in Wenders's *Buena Vista Social Club,* and in the more recent silent visual poem to the city, *Suite Havana,* directed by

Fernando Pérez. When Wim Wenders sees Cubans, he says that "Even if some of their dreams might have turned to nightmares / they don't seem prepared to give up dreaming altogether" (ibid., 10). This could also serve as the motto for *Suite Havana*.

During the first years of the revolution, exceptionality was always inscribed as part of the political background to Cuba's struggle with the power of the United States. A different kind of exceptionality is in place now: one that creates the impression that time has stood still. From that present that includes all times, photography and text confer a new meaning in time and space. Cubans are there for us to read in them traces of a besieged cultural discourse. They are props: they give a building a sense of scale. Always living as a function of the structures that surround them, and ultimately impervious and "unknowing" with regard to the history of these structures that they can only conceive from within their daily use, Cubans are children of light within the poetics of the ruins that all these books manipulate. They can be innocent, yet with the resilience of experience; they are not victims of circumstance, but rather products of it; they talk and gesticulate as if surrounded by light that is partly, but not totally, conferred by the collective situation in which they find themselves. They generally exist as a function of the structures that surround them, and that is part of their appeal for a viewer, who is the friendly voyeur in a situation that demands solidarity and empathy. Moving from the receiver of the discourse to the subject presented in it, Cubans act out a role that allows them to be like those native inhabitants who live next to archaeological monuments. The exceptionality of their circumstance allows the photographer to see them as illuminated by a particular kind of glow, emanating from within the social experiment of which they are a part. They can be perceived with a certain nostalgia, and we can feel this nostalgia because, ultimately, in these books, Cuba is part of all of those who feel it.

IMMORTAL CUBA

The city seems to float in photography books published in the 1990s. This is the way Havana defies time, by allowing itself to pretend that it exists outside of concrete space. It is an effect produced by nostalgia projecting itself upon timelessness, and it is found in the revolutionary project, as well as in exile. The revolution produced nostalgic narratives manifested in countless stories of the guerrillas in the Sierra Maestra in the 1950s, in the iconography created around the first *guerrilleros,* and in heroic achievements such as the literacy campaign. But the aristocracy also has claims on nostalgia and it can see Havana as a work of art that it conceived for itself and for future generations.

María Luisa Lobo Montalvo, author of *Havana: History and Architecture of a Romantic City,* was the daughter and heir to one of the most important and influential men of the Cuban republic, the great sugar magnate Julio Lobo, who collaborated briefly with the revolutionary government and then left the island. Tasteful and elegant, Lobo Montalvo's book was written from the point of view of power and money, and at times the rarefied air of one who looks at things from above. Even the cover underscores this gaze: a composite of Havana cupolas, with plaster angels high above the ground. It is a city that seems about to levitate, that seeks immortality.

In his preface, British historian Hugh Thomas explains the sad tale of María Luisa, who died in Miami in 1998, and who conceived the book as a way of linking herself to Havana forever—a kind of memoir that speaks of a different reality but that also erases the present for the sake of a future narrative. The book can also be seen as a kind of mausoleum. There, María Luisa's love for her city can be inextricably linked to her own narrative of childhood and loss. She contributed the text, compiled the pictures, and prefaced the book with an introduction titled "My Faraway, Lost World." It is an exemplary text in many ways, and wants to engage a very Romantic narrative of loss and reconciliation in which Cuban aristocracy is called on to make peace with History and collaborate in rebuilding the City of Memory and turn it once again into the City of Light. As the aristocratic counterpoint to Carleton Beals's *The Crime of Cuba,* money and investment here can only be engaged by appealing to a different kind of sentiment: the sense of responsibility that old Cuban families of tradition and wealth have toward the *patria* over and beyond what particular governments may have done.

Lobo Montalvo's *Havana* is the final piece in Cuba's love affair with the image in the twentieth century. It is a love affair that plays on time and space, past and present, that is predicated on history and on the desire to find a suitable angle from which to represent the city. The street is full of meaning, and every gesture acquires an inordinate symbolic importance because *patria* and history are here looked at from the point of view of eternity. Contingency is historical, but love of the fatherland (*patria*) renders it beyond time. In her book, the claims of experience are trumped by the metaphysics of nationality. She deals with both, though the accent is on what binds Cuba to Greater Cuba. Although her introduction is not the first aristocratic memoir in Cuban history, at times it has the effect of an appeal to all sensible Cubans promoted by the aristocracy for the sake of the common good. But the fact that the text appears after more than four decades of revolutionary social engineering turns it into a very particular kind of exemplary narrative, in which continuities and eternal values reappear.

Her introduction is more than a valuable piece of social history, but even if it were only that, it still gives an idea of how some segments of the sugar aristocracy have conceived their national mission at least since the early twentieth century. The book was a "labor of love," as she says, a deeply personal memoir that is also a collective vision of a lost world: "I have always marveled at our Cuban world: my own, with all its peculiarities, and the essences of an everlasting, immortal Cuba."[35] Immortal Cuba begins with a childhood trip to El Wajay, outside of Havana, where the family's summer home was located. The world of the countryside allowed for constant contacts with nature, and serves as a counterpoint to her life in the city. As the narrative comes back to Havana, the freedom that Lobo Montalvo felt in many of her family plantations turns to awe at the city itself—its fabulous courtyards, the mansions along the Quinta Avenida in Miramar. There is wonder and surprise at every turn, as the text moves to the house in Varadero, and then displaces itself in order to give an account of how María Luisa as a child perceived the sugar harvests. There are magnificent pictures of canefields, nineteenth-century Cuban landscapes, and the gazebos and urns that graced the avenues of Miramar. The prose registers emotion with none of the strident nationalism of a revolutionary rally. Here we have a simple, graceful, bourgeois *cubanía* defined as intimacy. There is a socioeconomic background to this intimacy, but it manages to portray itself from the point of view of eternity, where elegance is understood as the perfect detail: "I smell Guerlain's Eau de Cologne Imperiale, which all the men in my family used; and my mother's jasmine-scented Joy" (29). The author talks about how she searches in vain until she finds, in London, the fragrance of a particular kind of night jasmine she used to smell during her childhood. In the end, she says, "My romantic vision of Cuba, and of Havana in particular, is marked by memory, by the distance that separated us for many years, by the yearning for childhood and youth and, of course, the nostalgia that clings to any world so abruptly abolished . . . I am homesick for my childhood and for a far-away world, lost in the distance" (31).

The aristocratic nature of this memoir might jar readers who are accustomed to an entirely different kind of Cuban narrative. When the revolution talked about aristocracy and added text to images of wealth, it conditioned responses to the past with the certainty that the signifiers of the "good life" needed to be juxtaposed to the invisible suffering of the population. The past was not allowed to speak in its own words; the revolution insisted that the real Cuba was always to be found in a long tradition of struggle against power and wealth, with the Cuban bourgeoisie just an irresponsible intermediary in the world sugar markets. But in Lobo Montalvo's text and book one can see the kind of affect that produced in one member of the national bourgeoisie a sentimental *cubanía* that is not, in retrospect, very different in terms of *affect* from the sentimental appeal of revolutionary images. The exquisite fragility entailed in the search for a long-gone aroma can be equally perceived in the sentimental strength of the fragile island and in a song by the troubadour Silvio Rodríguez, or Carlos Varela.

The book is arranged chronologically and it focuses on buildings, especially those that reflect social class or standing. As readers and viewers get closer to structures built in the twentieth century, there is a wealth of details coming from the aristocratic social milieu that Lobo Montalvo knew best—for example, the fact that Plácido Domingo's parents sang at the Teatro Martí in Havana or that Lilita, one of the daughters of the Abreu family, corresponded intimately with Jean Giraudoux and St.-John Perse (173). The tone of the book is not intended to offend anyone, for Lobo Montalvo presents aristocracy as inoffensive—an aesthetic and mercantile one that is ready to collaborate for the good of all Cubans. Exile is relegated to the epilogue, where Lobo Montalvo comments on the persistence of *lo cubano* in Miami, renewed by successive waves of migration. These appeals to Miami are also part of a mission which she entrusts to the national bourgeoisie: "The revival of Havana will be one of the most important tasks facing the Cuban people, in a certain future: a future of healing its wounds, restoring its damaged spaces . . . delivered from the dingy sadness that has obscured its countenance for so long" (305).

If the pictures taken at the beginning of the revolutionary process aimed to engage viewers with the fragility of utopia, Lobo Montalvo turns tragedy into contemplation. Pictures in her book illustrate that long-gone and faraway space where all Cubans could conceivably participate in a national project of remembrance. Personal wealth is linked to memory and to the life of the nation to such an extent that the last picture of the introduction comes as a sentimental surprise. That Julio Lobo's amazing fortune allowed him to possess the most complete collection of Napoleon-ica, with original, priceless pieces placed in a historically accurate—to the most minute detail—space, is not simply a source of familial pride, but, a *Cuban* achievement.[36] As the aristocracy claims its own rights of possession over the city the revolution partly sells as its achievement, Lobo Montalvo's claim is not without merit, to the horror and surprise of many.

The acknowledgments, written by her children after her death, include a roster of figures that illustrates the immense prestige the sugar aristoc-racy still has, as it has summoned warring factions of the Cuban political landscape into collaborating with each other. The institutions and people named as having supported the project encompass the full spectrum of national reconciliation: Florida International University as well as the Bib-lioteca Nacional José Martí in Cuba; the City Historian's Office and Jorge Viera of National Trust Bank; Eliseo Diego, the renowned Cuban poet, who died in Cuba, as well as Giulio Blanc, who published literary maga-zines during the 1980s. What is most impressive about this roster is the common denominator that selects members of a circuit bonded by both money and capital, as well as by humanist and aesthetic values that are, presumably, beyond political differences.

These are hopes for a return, and for a solution to what is perceived as a *national* problem that extends beyond one of the thorniest national political divides of the second part of the twentieth century. In the end, the relationship that exists between the nation and the state in the images is also present in terms of the affective links between the nation and the family. The revolution has succeeded in creating and crafting new forms of social polity and new ways of understanding history, but at its twilight moment, when it reflects on itself from the temporal structures of mem-ory that it has invoked, it cannot forestall the different social actors that memory compels to tell their tale and talk about the past. Lobo Montalvo's *Havana* is not a collection of images with signatures, but rather a book on history and buildings.

Within this literate enclosure, the old bourgeoisie and the revolutionary classes have joined hands in creating a monument to a space and a city. The same structural armature that created photography books on Cuba after the collapse of the Soviet bloc may be found here, except that the book addresses its publics as members of a national family bonded by a sense of culture and common historical memory beyond the insular space. For Cubans who have not been to the island in many decades, the pictures allow for the past to come back to life. The pictures are all taken in the present, but they also try to hide the visible ravages of time. This is not the dirty Havana documented in the work of the contemporary Cuban novelist Pedro Juan Gutiérrez, and it is not the revolutionary, sentimental Havana where iconic images abound. It is not even the Havana where popular music inflects revolutionary slogans, where there are spaces full of mystery, and where the city as it is lived by its inhabitants changes the structural interiors of buildings in accord with the new uses that those buildings are put to. It is a Havana captured as an *eternal* city, conceived as an ongoing national project. It is a city conceived, finally, as a narrative, in spite of all the images.

Migrations of the Book

THE BOOK AND THE LETTERED CITY

The revolution understood the power of the visual image, but above all it valued the importance of the written word. Cultural change was also part of the mission entrusted to what Ángel Rama called Latin America's "city of letters," and in the Cuban Revolution these *letrados* looked back at other moments of mass transformation in the region.[1] One could argue that to a certain extent the book was even overvalued, for the photographic image was associated with the present, and with a fleeting vision of time, whereas words created the illusion of permanence and history. Books exceeded in symbolic value what they were materially worth. The lettered city wanted to destroy the walls that separated its creations from its citizens, and it did so by means of publishing presses and collections, and by massively producing books. The revolution had in mind a national and a revolutionary *book:* produced in Cuba, its contents written in Cuba or translated in Cuba and designed with a specific Cuban "look." The book became the object that could reveal utopian desires to re-create life in the form of art. But, like the image, it could not exist outside of ideology, and it soon became entangled in the history of its contents: it could be criticized, withdrawn from circulation, or even banned. Or, as in the case of Heberto Padilla's *Fuera del juego* (Out of the game) in 1968, it could be given a prize, and then published with a specific warning about the antirevolutionary nature of its contents. Or it could exist in the future tense, as a novel that could never be a book, as was the case with Reinaldo

Arenas's manuscripts, which were confiscated again and again by unknown hands.

Predicated as it always was on the fact that the symbolic value of the book exceeded the specific value it materially represented, the revolution tried to produce a cohesive literary project. It initially steered clear of socialist realism but it also could not give in to the expression of doubts about the process, nor to petit bourgeois melancholia. The project allowed for experimentation within certain parameters clearly established as early as 1961, in Fidel Castro's famously cryptic, open-ended, ambiguous assertion that everything "within" the revolution could be tolerated, though no tolerance would exist "against" the revolution. Like the sentiments of *History Will Absolve Me*, these words seemed to try to measure the distance between the future act and the present by means of open-ended statements. Over the years, their interpretation would be contingent on particular situations—as very narrow parameters at times, or as a broader, more tolerant framework in others. The words themselves gave a certain cohesiveness to intellectual production at a moment of war, and they justified cultural policy for more than thirty years. But they could only give the illusion of a cohesive project that, in retrospect, was nowhere to be found beyond in what revolutionary institutions intended to create. There were too many disputes since the early years of revolutionary triumph for one to believe in the real existence of that unanimous project. Perhaps it was all a work of fiction, an illusion that advertised how the whole country more or less thought the same way, read the same books, and agreed with the norms of a consensus, with its predictable sources of tension and ruptures.

What happened to the book after the collapse of the Soviet Union and the loss of subsidies for the Cuban book-publishing industry? The book at this point is an object that also exists as a material palimpsest of what it was. There was a fetishism of the book at the origin of the revolution that was very different from the fetish of the 1990s. In an early novel such as Daura Olema's *Maestra voluntaria* (Volunteer teacher) (1961), literacy is capable of changing the sense of the real.[2] Olema's novel was a celebration of readership, but it also exalted the literacy campaign—the state, its ideology, the mobilized collective will. Toward the end of the novel, after the main character Vilma and her *compañeros* have ascended the Pico Turquino (Cuba's highest mountain) three times, in a physically demanding show of strength and sacrifice, Vilma herself echoes the words of a camp leader who explains that the real winner in all these struggles is "the Revolution, because the liberty of a people is in direct relationship to its culture."[3] The book in *Maestra voluntaria* equated literacy with being liberated from the shackles of the past, while at the same time offering very clear ideological guidelines for instruction, as in the episode when Vilma is offered *Fundamentos del socialismo en Cuba* as a book that reflects the government's projects for the future.

Thirty years later, in Senel Paz's *El lobo, el bosque, y el hombre nuevo,* (The wolf, the forest, and the new man), the story that served as the basis for *Strawberry and Chocolate* (1994), the book retains its value as a fetish, though it is one that signifies forbidden knowledge: Diego and David meet over banned books, such as those by Mario Vargas Llosa. The book retains the possibility of commenting on the situation, but its value is inversely proportional to its availability. Whereas the book in *Maestra voluntaria* is valuable because of its ubiquity (it is given as a present), in Senel Paz's story its absence accounts for its importance. Overdetermined from the start, the relationship between the revolution and the book is also the story of Cuban culture at this time.[4]

DISPLACEMENTS OF THE BOOK

In 2001, there were three bookstores on the ground floor of the Palacio del Segundo Cabo, where the Cuban Book Institute (Instituto Cubano del Libro) is located. To the left of the entrance, most of the ground floor had been taken over by the Mondadori bookstore. Owned by a Spanish-Italian publishing concern, the shop rivaled some of the best in Spain. There were pricey editions of the classics and the latest best-sellers from Spain and Latin America. Mondadori sold tourist guides for Cuba and Havana there, but its main trade was literature, and not the kind of books that the average tourist reads on the beach: Gabriel García Márquez and Carlos Fuentes, but also such Europeans as Saramago, Cervantes, Kafka, Dante, and Beckett. The bookstore was impeccably designed, with wooden cases and air conditioning. There were three attendants in the back, probably to make sure that none of that stock got shoplifted. There were no Cuban customers at the Mondadori bookstore—at least none who live on the island—because all customers have to pay in dollars, and the dollar price for a book is still steep for the average Cuban citizen.

The second and the third bookstores on the ground floor of the Palacio had Cuban books, published in Cuba. One bookstore sold the books in dollars, while the other sold the same book in Cuban pesos. Although there was considerable overlap between the two, the dollar bookstore generally had more titles. A customer would probably find the same books in each place—the same edition, in many cases—but there was a considerable difference in price. A book in the dollar section of the bookstore might cost three dollars, while the same book in the peso bookstore sold for the equivalent of twenty-five cents. Technically, citizens from another country were not supposed to have access to pesos in order to buy the cheaper book. But a bibliophile soon finds out that it may be difficult to find a particular book in Cuban pesos, but not in dollars, or vice versa. This was owing to another peculiarity of the Cuban book industry during the late 1990s: if the state published a thousand copies of a book, part of the edition was slated to be sold in pesos, while another part was sold in dollars. The proportions were not necessarily the same for every book, though one thing was certain: the peso copies disappeared almost immediately. Authors got some copies, others bought copies for friends or relatives, and still others bought the book in pesos in order to resell it in dollars, in the kiosks full of old tomes found right outside the Palacio, in the Plaza de Armas.[5]

Like many other sites in Havana, this circuit points out the way different economic realms coexist in one space. Ever since the legalization of the dollar in 1994, Havana has lived in different economic zones; generally the "dollar" zone is marked by the availability of products that may not be found in the peso circuit. What is peculiar to the book trade is that in many cases the same object changes its economic citizenship according to the different site in which it is placed. The cost of producing the book may be constant, but the category of economic value—which is contingent on citizenship—changes depending on the buyer. These policies have effects over and beyond the clear-cut understanding the state wants to have in terms of the producers and the consumers or readers of the book. Many times, what gets offered for public consumption is not the book, but rather the opinion and the debate around the book. In other words, the book may never appear in Cuban bookstores, yet it could still make its presence felt in the Cuban literary world, for there are books reviewed in Cuban literary magazines that could never be published on the island.[6] Take the case of a review by Juan Valdés Paz in the Cuban journal *Temas:*

Cultura-Ideología-Sociedad titled "All Is according to the Color of the Glass with Which One Looks."[7] It is a commentary on Jorge Castañeda's biography of Che Guevara, *La vida en rojo* (which has been translated as *Compañero: The Life and Death of Che Guevara*).[8] Given the importance of its subject matter, it is clear why the book deserves to be reviewed in a Cuban context. But the importance of the review is directly related to the symbolic value of the book in itself.

One could argue that Castañeda's book is not only a biography, but also a melancholic account written by a disenchanted member of the 1960s generation. Castañeda, who was Mexico's minister of foreign relations until 2002, has had a rocky relationship with the Cuban government, and it is fair to say that his political writings, from *Utopia Unarmed* (1993) to *Compañero,* are not well regarded in official Cuban circles.[9] In his review, Valdés Paz praises Castañeda's serious attempts to come to terms with the historical figure of El Che, but also calls his book more of an "interpretation" than a biography in the strict sense of the word. He mentions his dislike of Fidel (Castañeda's *antifidelismo*) and remarks that he relies too heavily on psychological interpretations, without understanding the sociohistorical conditions that motivated Che and his generational cohorts. Faced with a Che that Castañeda portrays as "ambivalent" in his later relationship with the revolution, Valdés Paz insists that, on the contrary, he always voluntarily subordinated himself to the revolution's main directives. Angrily, he also insists that the revolution never betrayed Che while he was in Bolivia, contrary to Castañeda's conjectures, which he calls "an act of political defamation with academic trappings."[10]

Opinion in Havana circulates more than cultural products. Castañeda's *Compañero* is an example of an important debate occurring at many levels within the Latin American left, yet the interesting fact in this regard is that Cuban readers are informed of a debate without necessarily having access to the book in which it takes place. The review may signal the fact that the book itself has been circulating within that segment of the Cuban public that does have access to these materials, and the insistence on having the "right" line of thought points to the possibile existence of different opinions within the lettered city. But it is also symptomatic of an attempt to control these opinions given the fact that the borders between Cuban intellectuals and the West have become more porous, and that the state needs those borders open in order to receive some sort of real or symbolic revenue from intellectuals who have become, since the 1990s, free economic agents. The state cannot afford to lose its intellectuals, nor the support they have given its policies, but it can still set the right "political" line for them to follow.[11]

The existence and nonexistence of the book (or its validation, but not its circulation) also pertain to developments in the 1990s in the relationship among authors, their books, and their reading publics. Many authors living in Cuba have been published abroad, and they have brought new intellectual prestige to the island at a moment of symbolic and economic collapse. Many of their books have been commented on in Cuban magazines, before appearing in Cuban bookstores. Leonardo Padura's *Máscaras* (Masks) (1995) won a prize in Spain before Cuban readers had access to the tangled tale that mixes revolution, graft, and homosexuality. The two novels by Pedro Juan Gutiérrez, *Trilogía sucia de La Habana* (*Dirty Havana Trilogy*) (1998) and *El Rey de La Habana* (The king of Havana) (1999), exposing the hardships of the Special Period, were a success in Spain before they were published in Cuba, though the author lives in Havana and has been frequently interviewed in the Cuban press.[12] Antonio José Ponte lives in Cuba but has been published mostly abroad. Although Cuban readers within the tight network of Cuban literary circles certainly know his poetry, his first full-length novel, *Contrabando de sombras* (Contraband of shadows) (2002), was published in Spain, but not in Cuba.

These displacements create different readers, in spite of the continued appeals to the collective and cohesive nature of Cuban cultural discourse. This is important when looked at with an eye on the past, in terms of the importance the book and the lettered city had to the construction of revolutionary Cuba.[13] But they also signal a new relationship between the lettered city and political power that goes beyond the question of censorship. From the transparent symbolic value the book has in Daura Olema's *Maestra voluntaria,* the book in the 1990s *openly*—this transparency is one of its contradictions—stands as a metaphor for knowledge possessed and not readily available, as well as for a hierarchy of knowledge where what is most valuable is hidden from sight. This was of particular importance as the book in the 1990s became haunted and pursued by the dollar sign, and a new "kind" of Cuban literature appeared: the aptly named (by Esther Whitfield) "Special Period genre."[14] These books are not merely commentaries on the social hardships suffered by most Cubans during this period; they also signal a new relationship in terms of money and symbolic value. Many of them appear in foreign markets, while at the same time posing as the "authentic" "inside" experience of Cubans.[15] That many of these books were not read in Cuba—certainly not by the broader reading public—is part of the interesting effects this situation creates in terms of readership. How can the press, or the Ministry of Culture, or the National Union of Cuban Writers and Artists (UNEAC) create a Cuban book without Cuban readers? Exiled Cuban writers have grappled with this problem and insisted on its political foundations. What happened in Cuba in the 1990s was a question not simply of censorship, but of economics. The book sold abroad was part of a marketing franchise, a trademark. Not that politics is not part of this equation; but control reveals literature as the area of cultural production that still commands the biggest range of symbolic power. The novels of the Special Period highlight this fact precisely by migrating from one publishing context to the other, and this underscores how careful the government needs to be when it is dealing with the excess of symbolic accumulation that pertains to them. As Katherine Verdery has remarked in terms of the Eastern European context after the collapse of the Soviet Union, literature sits "atop an immense reserve of prior symbolic accumulations, arguably the largest of any area of culture."[16] This was true for the Soviet Union, for Eastern Europe, and for Cuba as well.

THE SPECTACULAR PAST OF THE LETTER

Recent generations of Cuban writers try to forget a memory that was constructed for them the moment the revolution saw itself as providing for the future. The children of the heroic struggle have been accused of taking for granted the achievements of the past, and of uncritically assuming positions that do not take into account the difficult situation the country has faced since the revolution. The divide is generational, and it can be seen as the product of failed expectations and lost illusions, but also in the belief that the present and the future will only offer more of the same. The aftermath of heroic history has produced impatience with the sheer fact that life in Cuba has been extremely hard since the early 1990s, and that the present conditions of the literary and cultural world are "weighed down" by the important role literacy has played in the Cuban revolutionary project.

Cuba was the first territory of the Americas to free itself from illiteracy, and the fact that there is a *date* to this state proclamation—December 22, 1961—engages its own temporal logistics within national history. More than four decades after that, the state can still remember and celebrate the utopian thrust of that moment. To this day, the symbolic value of that project has erased in the international circuit the later history of censorship and repression. Reading, back then, was directly related to ideology, and the aim of creating a nation of readers entailed having faith in human liberation. This liberation in turn demanded that the citizen master the tools to make sense not only of letters, but also of the world. The aim was to create what Magaly Muguercia has called "a democratic, egalitarian, dignified and communal body."[17] It was, of course, a communal body that lived in Cuba and believed in the revolution's promises, and did not openly disagree with its major policy decisions.

The visibility of the revolution was sustained by images, but it also depended on texts. The act of reading as the basis for liberation and national unity was exemplified in Roberto Fernández Retamar's *Calibán,* in which writing and reading entered into a state pact. Beyond the strictly national effects of this policy, the revolution fostered the creation of a continental reading public that consumed the latest Cuban novels and kept abreast of Havana's dazzling literary life.[18] It was a reading public that fashioned a pan-national form of identity. What held it together, and what it saw incarnated in the Cuban scene, was a successful struggle to demolish the borders of the lettered city itself, a will to usher in a new, revolutionary time when aesthetics and politics could be brought together.

The first decade of the revolution was lived with a sense of historical fervor that more recent generations can only try to identify with. Even participants who later became more hostile because of state repression, such as Reinaldo Arenas, could call the period the "glorious Sixties."[19] The revolutionary government founded Casa de las Américas, the film institute (ICAIC), and the writers' and artists' union (UNEAC). There were magazines such as *Casa de las Américas* and *Revolución y Cultura,* and the newspaper *Revolución,* directed by Carlos Franqui until 1963.[20] As *Lunes de Revolución,* the semi-independent supplement directed from 1959 to 1961 by Guillermo Cabrera Infante gave way to *El Caimán Barbudo,* the situation became more tense.[21] But still, the revolution could command wide admiration and respect throughout the world, and a near-unanimous show of solidarity, at least until the early 1970s.

During the 1960s, the relationship with Latin America was deepened by the Latin American Boom, a period of about ten years that produced brilliant iconoclastic and experimental works, such as Julio Cortázar's *Hopscotch* (1963), Mario Vargas Llosa's *Conversation in the Cathedral* (1963), Gabriel García Márquez's *One Hundred Years of Solitude* (1967), and José Donoso's *The Obscene Bird of Night* (1970). The Boom was a capitalist publishing machine that had Barcelona as one of its epicenters and cast its web throughout Latin America.[22] Cuba was one of the central nodes in this machine, and it gave the Boom a sense of grounding. The synergy of this book-publishing market with Cuba is unparalleled in developments after the 1970s. Gabriel García Márquez, Carlos Fuentes, Julio Cortázar, and José Donoso all had Cuba on their minds at one point or another.[23] Fuentes finished his first major novel, *The Death of Artemio Cruz* (1962), in Havana, and Cortázar was, throughout the 1960s and 1970s, a fellow traveler of the revolution—criticizing its policies at some points, though not at others.[24]

The network involved more than the prestige offered by individual writers. It also included journals, magazines, and prizes conferred by Casa de las Américas. The decentered grid also had its moments of institutional friction between Cuban official institutions and literary networks elsewhere in Latin America. The most important of these was surely the one between Emir Rodríguez Monegal's journal *Mundo Nuevo* and *Casa de las Américas,* with the latter exposing *Mundo Nuevo's* ties to the political power and capital of the United States.[25] But a look at the tenor of these two journals also reveals how political opinions were related to aesthetic positions. Not only was *Mundo Nuevo* a more "individual" (or "individualistic") project, but *Casa de las Américas* was linked to a whole network of institutional power via the revolutionary institution in which it was housed.

The emphasis on institutions, as opposed to the celebrity culture of individual writers, may or may not account for the fact that no Cuban author living on the island was closely associated with the Boom to the degree that the Boom itself marked the work of Fuentes or Cortázar. Major Cuban writers of the time, such as José Lezama Lima and Alejo Carpentier, did not have the same relation to capital the other writers had. Although they wrote, arguably, their best work and their most ambitious projects from the early 1960s on, they fit imperfectly with the broader economic contexts of Latin American narrative. García Márquez, Fuentes, and Donoso had publishing contracts and lawyers, publicists, editors, and roy- alties. Cuban writers, on the other hand, depended on the state. Because Cuba did not honor international copyright law, Lezama's work, or Car- pentier's (and later on, Reinaldo Arenas's), was reproduced in countless pirated editions that circulated throughout Latin America but paid no royalties to their authors.

The role that institutions played in Cuban writers' lives separated them from many of their Latin American colleagues. Other Latin American countries created state entities to support the arts, but Cuba created them to an inordinate degree, and it insisted that all writers (and artists, film- makers, "cultural workers") be registered as members of an institution. Other writers of the Boom were, properly speaking, professional writers and free agents, not institutional figures.[26]

This institutionalization may also account for the fact that the major writers at the time, Lezama and Carpentier, did not just write novels, but inscribed them within broader critical parameters that guided their inter- pretation. Both originated a discourse with philosophical underpinnings that searched for an essentially "Latin American" way of seeing the world and history.[27] Although Lezama's and Carpentier's baroque poetics pre- dated the revolution, within the socialist network their critical framework was placed outside of the capitalist machine. The baroque became an object of study and a mode of writing that emanated out of the lettered city called Havana and then radiated throughout Latin America, giving the continent a sense of coherence and order that was not unrelated to the organized way in which the revolution interpellated its intellectuals. The baroque engaged a "style" that was also an architectonics of the world.[28] It was criticized by other Cubans from different ideological positions—such as, most notoriously, Guillermo Cabrera Infante—for placing characters in sets full of props. But it was also praised for the same reasons—the immo- bility allowed for a revolutionary validation of the aesthetic difficulty of prose, of the signifier over the signified, as revolutionary. Still, Carpentier's and Lezama's relations to state power differed. Carpentier worked during his later years at the Cuban embassy in Paris, and was allowed to travel outside of the island as a representative of the government. Lezama was not allowed to leave Cuba during his lifetime, though the state maintains that he never wanted to travel. His most important novel, *Paradiso* (1966), had only one Cuban edition during more than twenty years, even as editions abroad multiplied.[29]

It is possible to read the Boom as a peculiar capitalist machine—one that existed alongside the Cuban revolution as a state machine. Although the state was chiefly concerned with the insular Cuban world, it also disseminated its symbolic values and legitimacies to the capitalist machine that it spawned. These machines related—even gravitated—to each other even as they distanced themselves from each other at different points. Cuba influenced the institutionalization of the Boom, just as the revolution institutionalized a country that possessed weak institutions throughout its history.[30]

Keeping in mind Lezama's difficulties with the revolution, it is useful to recall the sad narrative of Reinaldo Arenas's attempts to publish outside of Cuba during the very same period when the Boom was producing its most memorable works of art. State policies produced petty infighting as authors jockeyed for position in order to receive validation from the state that was their sole publisher. This validation in turn allowed writers to travel abroad, receive important posts, and be taken into account within the broad network of prizes and support that the state provided. In *Before Night Falls,* but more important in *The Color of Summer,* Arenas vents his ire on individual writers, and a careful reading of these texts reveals how difficult it was to distinguish writers from their institutional frameworks. Indeed, in *The Color of Summer,* institutionalization (the "Institution of Cuban Culture" broadly defined) is evident in the initial, theatrical chapter. It is an allegory in which José Martí and almost every conceivable personality of Cuban letters appear in a broad satire and carnivalesque romp, a grand spectacle that takes place on rafts in the Florida Straits. It has a cast of thousands in its own Cecil B. DeMille delirium, including most of Cuba's poets and writers, living and dead. That they have all been condemned to the perpetual resurrections intended by the state in its allegorical drama shows to what extent culture and ideology had been meshed at this time. But it is also clear that the world of Cuban culture that the state manipulates is not contingent on the island (the allegory takes place between Key West and Havana), and is not limited to a contemporary period. Past and present, North and South have been mixed here. And the allegorical play is a desperate mode of purgation, as well as a call for renewal that can only take place in another, parallel universe out of which this one originates.

FRAGMENTATION AND RESISTANCE

The Palacio del Segundo Cabo, where the Cuban Book Institute is housed, is an exemplary site. The unity proposed in terms of Cuban culture in the 1960s and the 1970s could only produce, after the debacle, a more fragmented lettered city, one that validated the utopian thrust of the past, as long as it was allowed to pursue different and differing poetics within the same cultural space. Fragmentation is one of the ways novels and books implicitly or explicitly question purported unitary narratives, collective discourses, and the notion of cohesive popular will. Many books written during the Special Period in the 1990s are fragmentary in nature: Pedro Juan Gutiérrez's *Dirty Havana Trilogy* is a collection of tales assembled in order to achieve some kind of unity, but the novel still retains a kind of polyphonic arrangement. Zoé Valdés's *La nada cotidiana* (translated into English as *Yocandra in the Paradise of Nada*) has a story line that is interrupted while it shifts from present to past and back again toward a present that gives no clue as to what the future will be. In Leonardo Padura's *Máscaras* (Masks) the unfinished business of the past is interjected into a present where the main character is also the author of an unfinished tale—a frustrated writer. And in Pedro de Jesús's *Cuentos frígidos* (*Frigid Tales*) we are meant to understand fragmentation within the fragmented tales of a short-story collection that plays with the reader's attempt to piece the stories together into one cohesive narrative. Even literary criticism echoes this mode of writing. Margarita Mateo Palmer, in *Ella escribía poscrítica* (She used to write post-criticism) presents a loose arrangement of critical essays that are constructed and deconstructed into an image of the critic struggling in difficult times.[31]

This fragmentation can be understood by relating it to appeals for unity that took place throughout the Special Period, when "resistance" as a mode of action was insisted upon in all official discourse. It was the perfect term, part of a 1960s vocabulary that embedded itself into new realities, including the relationship of Cuban culture to the "migratory" community of Cubans now living outside the island, as noted in remarks by Minister of Culture Abel Prieto.[32]

The reasons for the focus on resistance are clear, and they are economic as well as political. For a state that had prided itself on facilitating access to culture, the small number of books published in the early 1990s amounted to a total collapse of the book-publishing industry and of the cultural apparatus Cuba had known in the recent past. Because of this economic constriction, the state faced ideological obstacles in imposing new policies. A famous letter, known in Cuba as the "Carta de los Diez," was signed by ten intellectuals in 1991 and published in the *Miami Herald,* demanding democratization and humanitarian aid in order to prevent the "collapse of Cuba as a civilized state."[33] Some of those who signed this letter were important members of the UNEAC, including María Elena Cruz Varela.[34] That resistance produced desperation can be seen in many poems and writings of the Special Period. There is a general sense of doom, best expressed in the works of younger poets. There was good reason for this, because they came of age at a time of social scarcity. Antonio José Ponte contemplated a landscape that had now been irremediably changed. Obliquely and elegantly talking about the present situation, he writes: "One municipality is blacked out for another to exist. / My life is already made up of borrowed matter. / I complete with light the life of an unknown one. / I say in the darkness: another lives the life that I am lacking."[35] Like modern-day Robinson Crusoes, Cubans wanted to write in spite of the closing down of printing presses, the demise of publication prospects because of the unavailability of ink, or the absence of magazines because of the lack of paper. Because all the means of production were controlled by the state, and the state could not finance these endeavors, it stopped publishing books. If there is no material, can there be cultural products? And if there are no cultural products, in what way can culture manifest itself? This was the crux of the dilemma faced by the cultural authorities at this time.

In a prose poem titled "Monólogo de Augusto" (Monologue of Augustus), Pedro Marqués de Armas voiced how the poet and the city related to each other in the Special Period: "The city burns and I am at its center" (Arde la ciudad y estoy al centro).[36] The line validated the voice at the center of a burning city: there was no sense of urgency, and the poet did not intend to save the city, nor even to reconstruct it. Marqués de Armas just ponders the possibility that the city might fall: "This city can open itself up into a thousand heads" (Esta ciudad puede abrirse en mil cabezas). The sense of freedom expressed in these lines verges on the absolute: the city is free to burn, while the poet allows himself the liberty (is this an act of treason?) of merely watching as the city destroys itself. There is no question,

or even questioning, of the sense of agency (why is the city burning?)—
only the quiet desperation that surrounds the voice as it speaks.

The poetry of the Special Period reveals the dense context of the time,
but its literary origins can be pushed back to 1989. The 1980s had been (in
the cyclical way in which cultural policy takes place in Cuba) a particularly "open" period, during which censorship had become more relaxed;
the visual arts moved to the fore, with the 1980s perhaps best seen from
the context of art and performance rather than literature, which still was
more subject to vigilance and control. A literary tradition existed in 1989
that could be firmly placed *within* revolutionary Cuba, while those who
had fled the island during the Mariel crisis, if not earlier, had produced a
considerable amount of work, including novels, magazines, and journals.
The generation that came of age in 1989, born after the revolution, was
starting to win prizes in various writers' associations and had begun to
publish poems in magazines.

Because of the shortage of paper for longer narrative works, poetry
better than other genres registered the cultural and economic conditions
of the times. Poetry had its own communal form of organization, and it
nurtured its own readership by virtue of its democratizing form: it promoted readings, parties, and meetings where poems could be recited or
passed from hand to hand. A deliberate obliqueness of language became
a form of resistance to the never-ending slogans issued by the state. With
its appeals to emotion as well as to a critical assessment of the economic
situation, the explosion of poetry during the early years of the Special
Period was a phenomenon that once again underscored the central role of
poetry in Cuban culture. Poets responded to the parameters imposed by
the state with their own forms of collective organization, and they were
able to carve out for themselves an independent space.

It is impossible to minimize the real as well as the symbolic value of these
new forms of literary organization. Cuban poets circulated their work in
anthologies that they crafted for themselves. The first and most important of these, *Retrato de Grupo* (Group portrait), appeared in 1989, and it
assembled writers who had been born after 1959.[37] Many of those who
appear in this collection already knew each other, knew *of* each other, or
were linked to each other. Among them are names that became important
during the 1990s: Rolando Sánchez Mejías, Damaris Calderón Pérez, Juan
Carlos Flores, and Carlos Augusto Alfonso. Sánchez Mejías became one of

the editors of *Diásporas,* along with Pedro Marqués de Armas. Damaris Calderón Pérez, who has been living in Chile since 1995, has published two other books of poetry: *Duro de roer* (Hard to gnaw) (1999) and *Sílabas/Ecce Homo* (1999). Juan Carlos Flores, another poet in this collection, went on to write *Los pájaros escritos* (Written birds), which won the prestigious David poetry prize in 1990, but was not published until 1994, in the collection Pinos nuevos. Omar Pérez is another important member of this group, and he published a book of poetry titled *Algo de lo sagrado* (Something of the sacred) in 1995. Carlos Augusto Alfonso won the Premio Abril in poetry with *Fast Delivery* (1996), a collection that recalls the history of Cuba since the fated assault on the presidential palace on March 13, 1957.

The poems of the early 1990s give readers the impression that something is about to happen, that reality can be found walking on a tightrope. A text by Damaris Calderón Pérez (Havana, 1967) recalls with irony how the population was mobilized for heroic sacrifice: "This is the only lie in which we shall always believe."[38] To believe in the lie, a lie described with such conviction and in such absolute terms, throws the poem back into the past from which it came, from, a fact underscored by the dramatic ending of the short poem: "It is a sad story / playing at perfection."[39]

In the cyberjournal *La Habana Elegante* (the title pays homage to the modernist poet Julián del Casal, but is also an ironic comment on the disastrous condition of the city), Francisco Morán recalled the lifestyle of the early 1990s in Havana, and the role played by the meetings at Reina María Rodríguez's *azotea,* her rooftop apartment: "We lived in individual catacombs that the 'azotea' connected with the bigger catacomb: the city." *La Habana Elegante* still has a poetry section titled "La azotea de Reina," a direct reference to these meetings, for the space became a meeting place for poets who read and commented on one another's work. In this context, hunger was not merely a metaphor of desire, but also referred to a real lack of food. Sigfredo Ariel (Santa Clara, 1962) presents a scene that suggests Van Gogh: "These are the plantains that my sister / has sent from Oriente, and a bit of coffee / because she imagines / that at the dinner hour penury falls / like lightning.[40]

Desire is related to the metaphorical (and real) desire to flee, to leave, to escape circumstances both physically and mentally. Emilio García Montiel (Havana, 1962) writes: "I longed for a journey, a long and clean journey so as not to rot."[41] Alessandra Molina's "Laminas," from *Anfiteatro entre los pinos* (Amphitheater amid the pines) describes a sense of flight accompanied by exhaustion: "Surely imagined for flight / we were already birds of tired forms."[42] Norge Espinosa voices a desire to flee in "Dejar la isla" (Leaving the island), but departure haunts the speaker with its own circular dynamic: "Everyone who leaves, returns," he says, adding "Everyone who returns: burns."[43] The city was not burning, however, but rather crumbling. Buildings that had suffered governmental indifference were simply collapsing, and this furthered the impression that the social project that had promised a better life for all Cubans was imploding.

In the early 1990s, Cuban culture was memorialized with symposia in Havana on the centenary of Julián del Casal in 1993, and the fiftieth anniversary of Lezama Lima's journal *Orígenes* in 1993 (which followed *Retrato de Grupo* in 1989, in which many of the same poets participated). These two events underscored how Cuba had one of the great poetic traditions of the continent, and how poetry had always been at the center of public life.[44]

In fact, one of the most important acts of historical revisionism took place precisely during the centenary of Casal in 1993. If Martí had become related to state power and with the revolution, younger writers turned to the more aesthetic poetry of Julián del Casal as a way of countering the utilitarian notions of literature deployed by the revolution. For this generation, Casal embodied the tensions of nineteenth-century Havana, and he was one of the most misread figures in Cuban letters. The poet that Martí had praised in heartful and eloquent terms was turned by literary history into the effete intellectual, the castrated Casal, who was often read from the point of view of the man of action, the heroic Martí. This was seen as the ruling dialectics of the republic, and the revolution demanded this contrast. But young writers in 1993 went back to Casal in order to reclaim him. In the work of Víctor Fowler Calzada, Francisco Morán, and Antonio José Ponte, as well as in the work of Cuban critics outside the island such as Óscar Montero, Casal turned into a sharp social observer with a keen understanding and a well-argued position of creative resistance against that society. Revising Casal turned him into a historically queer (*raro*) figure, and this queerness is part of a legacy that has resisted, to this day, the normative visions of the state and society. As Víctor Fowler Calzada observes in "Casal disputado y una nota al pie" (Disputed Casal and a footnote) included in *Rupturas y homenajes* (Ruptures and homages) (1998), "Casal is still a mystery."[45]

Some of the poetry of the Special Period could only read the nation through the lens of a negative epistemology. In *La isla en su tinta* (The island in its ink), published after Francisco Morán left Cuba in the mid-1990s, the section titled "Palma negra" (Black palm) gives an account of this pessimistic view of past and present history. Since *Mariel* magazine in the early 1980s, writers were insisting that throughout Cuba's history, literature was mostly written either in exile or against the state and power. *Mariel,* created by Reinaldo Arenas, Reinaldo García Ramos, and Roberto Valero in New York, published iconoclastic reviews on the tradition, and this work was continued in the 1990s inside Cuba.[46]

A reader who has access to work produced during the early 1990s has to actively engage not only with what the text says, but also with its presentation.[47] The editions themselves are a semiotic indication of the hardships of the Special Period—small, sometimes *plaquettes,* or the "artisanal" books produced by Ediciones Vigía, a publishing project in the city of Matanzas that at first used cardboard paper to publish a very limited number of writers.

History and reconciliation were important themes in the work of these poets, as was reference to the past, recent or otherwise. In contrast with other periods in Cuban life, there is no common, cohesive project, except for a validation of self that leads to a slippery subject. There is irony in the works of these melancholic subjects. They confess only obliquely at times, they call attention to the self and display their hunger for other places and other spaces. In terms of reconciliation with diasporic Cuban culture, the work continues the productive line already present in one of the first encounters between Cuban poets living in Cuba and abroad—encounters which were tolerated by a government that seemed to have relaxed its controls during the early years of the decade. The first one was called the "Encuentro de Estocolmo" in 1994, and it produced the "Stockholm Declaration" on May 27, 1994, signed by Lourdes Gil, Reina María Rodríguez, Pablo Armando Fernández, and Heberto Padilla.[48]

The writer who emerged as the key figure at this time is Antonio José Ponte, who along with Víctor Fowler Calzada wrote the preface to *Retrato de grupo.*[49] Ponte's wry vision of the world was already noticeable in *Un seguidor de Montaigne mira a La Habana* (A follower of Montaigne looks at Havana) (1995) and in *Asiento en las ruinas* (A place amid the ruins) (1997). His story "Corazón de Skitalietz" (Heart of Skitalietz) (1998) narrates the encounter between a historian who has lost his past and an astrologer who cannot make out the future.[50] In his lyrical and poetic tales, Ponte has produced a literature unlike anything else that has been published in Cuba recently. He is a fine reader of the Cuban tradition, which in his hands undergoes a strategic retelling. Already in 1993, during the Special Period, Ediciones Vigía in Matanzas had published two hundred copies of his essay *La lengua de Virgilio* (Virgilio's tongue).[51] Ponte has managed to skew some platitudes and obfuscations of the Cuban state, and has achieved a degree of freedom in terms of his publishing venues. Most of his recent work has been published thanks to the efforts of an exiled Cuban painter named Ramón Alejandro who is responsible for Deleatur Editions in France. There, Ponte has written *Cuentos de todas partes del imperio,* translated as *Tales from the Cuban Empire* (2002), and *Las comidas profundas* (1997), which is certainly destined to be the definitive account of life during the Special Period (parts of which have been translated by Mark Schafer as *Wanting to Eat*), a long essay that is also a meditation, but at the same time a literary account of a man sitting at a kitchen table and writing a book about food and longing at a time when there is very little food of any kind to be had in Cuba.

Las comidas profundas is a small book that moves in time and space, though it is centered in Havana. The author explores the surface of things (he looks at the mantel that covers his writing table but never explores what the table is made of) and carefully avoids asking as to the reasons for a physical hunger that in many ways is assuaged by engaging in comparisons with other moments of scarcity, particularly those in the context of war. The reference here is to the refusal to eat as well as to the inability to eat: King Charles V is portrayed with a pineapple that he contemplates but does not eat; a countess in Madrid keeps her pantry full of tubers that come from the tropics. The Lezamian feast, which appears in Lezama's *Paradiso* and which is also referenced in Senel Paz's *El lobo, el bosque, y el hombre nuevo* ("The wolf, the forest, and the new man") is here understood as a metaphysical hunger for incorporating food. "Cubans eat their land," Ponte explains, quoting from Lezama, and the text underscores the sense of insularity and lack of options up to its final page, dated November 1996. If it does not (irresponsibly) substitute culture for hunger, it does broaden the meaning of hunger to include something more than the mere physical act of "wanting to eat." In seven short sections, the prose moves from one space to the other, including not only references to disparate periods and times, but also to the popular culture of the period. It includes a fascinating account culled from popular memory about cleaning rags sold as steak, while it also manages to render, in one short paragraph, the links between Lezama's supposedly atemporal writings on the question of incorporating metropolitan discourses and the political and ideological vocabulary used in 1970s Cuba. *Las comidas profundas* is striking in that it makes no attempt to disguise a socioeconomic and political situation by metaphorical means, yet it also steers clear of an overt critique of the ways the situation has taken the form of an undeclared war in which real voices find themselves with no options.

· AUTHENTICITIES OF THE BOOK

The dearth of novels published during the Special Period was directly related to the lack of publishing options at a time of economic need. It was more economical for narrators to publish short stories, which could be anthologized in one volume. It was also more expedient to publish anthologies than complete works.[52] Narrative explored themes that were previously judged to be "too sensitive" in the Cuban context. There was a lifting of restrictions beginning the early 1990s—what Esther Whitfield calls an "unpredictable—and always retractable—tolerance."[53] At the same time, the presence of a market has made itself felt at all levels of the Cuban cultural apparatus, particularly in terms of what gets published both inside and outside of Cuba.

Previously taboo subjects were first explored by using the homosexual as a literary character that could give an account of the past as well as the present. Homosexuality had already featured prominently in the work of Reinaldo Arenas, as well as other members of the Mariel generation, published outside of Cuba after 1980. As a belated response to this generation, homosexuality was featured in literature, first by Roberto Urías in "¿Por quién llora Leslie Caron?" (Who is Leslie Caron crying for?) (1988) and by Leonardo Padura in "El cazador" (The hunter) (1988). This subject was more resonant after Senel Paz's "El lobo, el bosque y el hombre nuevo" (1991), which in turn was the basis for *Strawberry and Chocolate* (1994), the film adaptation by Tomás Gutierréz Alea and Juan Carlos Tabío. The male homosexual in these stories is a symbolic prop that allows writers access to themes of marginality.[54] In Urías's tale he is disaffected, does not believe in family or state, and takes his cultural pointers from foreign movie stars living fantasy lives. In Paz's story—and, later on, in Padura's *Máscaras* (Masks)—he is a more literate homosexual, an inhabitant of the Havana cultural demimonde who is deeply committed to the reconstruction of the city in ruins, while also holding the key to repressive events that do not necessarily figure in the official histories of the past. Lesbians were invisible in these first accounts, owing mostly to the fact that the male homosexual was rendered more visible as a source of social malaise by the gendered politics of the revolution. When a lesbian narrator appeared, in Ena Lucía Portela's stories in the late 1990s, she played with a clearly defined auto-biographical narrative that was also a scathing critique of male Cuban literary circles. Portela was thus able to pick up on the social defiance present in Roberto Urías's tale, which was also narrated in the first person. The appearance of the male homosexual helped to open up cultural expression to whatever had been taboo in the previous period, and it allowed writers to start exploring aspects of social reality previously considered unrepresentable, such as prostitution, hunger, drug addiction, and petty crime.[55]

In many ways, the figure of the homosexual bears responsibility for the explosion of novels sold as a Cuban "Boom" to the Spanish book market. This was accompanied by other kinds of Cuban "products," most notably music. The Spanish literary audience was promised a more "open" political discourse—similar to what Spaniards, reading the situation from their own point of view as post-Franco subjects, understood as a *destape* (opening up). But most of the Cuban literary works published abroad afforded no escape and no solution to Cuba's problems. They pivoted around the desire for change, but in many ways they were also densely allusive. One of the best anthologies, *Nuevos narradores cubanos* (New Cuban narrators), edited by Mihai Grunfeld, has in its cover a black-and-white image of a boy on a broken fence. But the stories in the collection do not really deliver on the promised unshackling and freedom. They do offer excellent writing, a rare skill that underscores the literary, and that only occasionally delivers the raw sex promised by other referents available to Spanish readers. The book offers a snapshot of a cultural space in which authors openly experiment with form and content, and this experimentation offers different views of Cuban society, though not very conflictive ones. The stories do suggest the absence of a project like the one that had guided the revolution from the start. Some are nostalgic for a general sense of direction, as in Ponte's "Un arte de hacer ruinas," and others engage the reader with detached irony, as in Ena Lucía Portela's "El viejo, el asesino y yo."

PAST ENIGMAS, SEX, AND DIRTY REALISM

Three writers best illustrate changes in Cuban narrative during the 1990s: Leonardo Padura, Zoé Valdés, and Pedro Juan Gutiérrez, and they deserve to be treated separately. In terms of their relationship to state policy, their situations differ: Valdés left Cuba and lives in Paris, while Gutiérrez and Padura still reside in Cuba.

Leonardo Padura Fuentes was the first writer in Cuba to focus on corruption, both present and past, by recasting the detective genre in line with new social and political realities. He began publishing novels centered on the detective Mario Conde in 1989 with *Pasado perfecto* (Past perfect), followed by three more works, each set in a different season: *Vientos de cuaresma* (Winds of Lent) (1994), *Máscaras* (1995), and *Paisaje de otoño* (Fall landscape) (1998). The cycle is composed of four novels that correspond to a different season of the year. But they also deal with different repressive moments in the revolution. In *Máscaras,* the most famous and well known of these narratives, Mario Conde tries to solve the murder of the transvestite son of a high-ranking party member. The transvestite appears strangled one morning in a Havana park, and Conde has to explore Havana's homosexual world in order to solve this crime, and, because the boy is the son of a high-ranking party bureaucrat, he needs to address corruption at the highest levels. Previously banned literary figures are memorialized, because the murder victim was dressed not simply as a woman, but as a character in Virgilio Piñera's highly resonant tropical Cuban version of Electra, *Electra Garrigó.* The victim left behind a number of clues that ultimately point to the social and political scandal that forms the book's conclusion.

Into efforts to solve the murder Padura inserts fragments of a history that is not linear but cut up, a pastiche of different times and places. The action of the novel is interrupted—or fragmented—by the diaries of a man who travels to Paris during the 1960s (an homage to the exiled Cuban writer Severo Sarduy, who developed a theory of transvestism), as well as accounts of a cynical homosexual who was purged from his work in the theater during the 1970s. In parallel narrative lines, Conde's friends have suffered during the 1990s for various reasons: the economic hardships of the Special Period, the lack of government support for veterans of the Angola campaigns, and the fear within the detective bureau itself because of the massive purges that have taken place in the government apparatus.

Padura, who was himself a journalist, has taken on aspects of life untouched by journalists and social commentators in Cuba.[56] One of the interesting features of these novels—which never allow readers to forget that they are, in many ways, potboilers—is that they are reconstructions of the underworld of revolutionary history, that the detective, by virtue of his association with the underworld, can shed light on the "other" Cuba conspicuously absent from the glaring lights of the media gaze. In Padura's dark novel *Máscaras,* the Cuban revolutionary process has produced a sequence of disenchantments covered up by institutions, and which are presented to the reader as mutilations and interventions within a literary text. His tale allows for a linear narrative while at the same time it breaks it up. A key element is the fact that it is impossible to understand the present Cuban situation in a linear fashion, that the different temporalities that coexist in one space need to be taken into account.

Though Padura has been able to talk about political issues that no other writers had been able to touch, the more recent Cuban boom in writing was initiated by Zoé Valdés, who moved to Paris in 1994 and has portrayed the difficult social and economic conditions of Cuba in her novels *La nada cotidiana* (*Yocandra in the Paradise of Nada*) (1996) and *Te di la vida entera* (*I Gave You All I Had*) (1995), causing a stir in Europe for their unabashedly sexual content and their scathing critique of life within the revolution. Although many in Cuba and elsewhere cast a skeptical eye at Valdés's work and focus on her savvy manipulation of the literary market, these critiques are often ill-disguised attempts to downplay her significance and reveal a bias that counterposes market success and literary quality. The fact that Valdés published her novels in rapid succession and that she used her gender position to deconstruct a literary circuit that had not produced one major female novelist in two generations are the common threads in critiques of her work. Yet, Valdés has placed herself within her own literary genealogy (Cabrera Infante, Virgilio Piñera) and within her own context (Havana in the 1990s), and if she has not perfected the formula used by Isabel Allende, or even Laura Esquivel, it is because politics, broadly understood, play a role in her work, which, like that of many of her compatriots, is full of references to the specific internal Cuban milieu. By leaving the island and becoming a dissident who openly exposes the government as a dictatorship, she lives outside of insular (or even trans-territorial) controls. She has gained a following for her work, and has been a key figure in disrupting the links between the European (principally Spanish) left and the Cuban government. She has also been at the fore-front of protests against repressive Cuban policies that have placed many journalists and writers in jail.

Yocandra in the Paradise of Nada is an indictment of the times narrated by Patria, a woman born in the early days of the revolution, who later on changes her name to Yocandra—a name that combines two Greek char-acters, Yocasta and Cassandra, which underscores the character's position between a past she does not want to see and a future that is still unknown, but that is bound to produce more suffering. She is torn between two lovers—one she calls the Traitor, the other the Nihilist—who, respectively, represent two sides of the Cuban cultural world, literature and film. Posi-tioned as she is in a dialectical impasse between past and present, the nar-rator contemplates her present circumstances in terms that recall Virgilio Piñera's long poem *La isla en peso*. Disenchantment with revolutionary promises goes together with an unveiling of the revolution's errors. The promise for national redemption that Patria incarnated at the beginning has turned into a Greek family tragedy. Patria's father was emotionally destroyed during the Ten Million Ton Harvest, and her mother has lost all contact with time. Yocandra's first lover is an "official" writer sent to Paris, but his paranoia does not allow him to fulfill his revolutionary promise; the Nihilist believes in nothing; her best friends have left the island—the Gusana managed to leave Cuba for Spain as a prostitute, and the Lince has landed in Miami—and all of these characters feel an oppressive sense of nostalgia, as they contemplate lives that have been ruined by a destructive social process. The novel begins and ends with Yocandra contemplating the webs of misfortune that have produced a suicidal condition. It is in part a tragic tale, but one told with a parodic bent. It mixes humor with despair, and is completely frank in terms of the main character's sexuality. It joins sexuality to politics by letting go of the moral pieties sponsored by

the state. If it is in many ways a nihilistic narrative, it also expresses a redemptive faith in the ability of Cubans to surmount seemingly intractable
odds in order to start anew.

Valdés's novel can be seen as the starting point for a new Cuban literature that engages dirty realism. If the creation of the Cuban Boom by
Spanish publishing houses owes a lot to the work of Valdés, it has been
continued especially in the work of Pedro Juan Gutiérrez. Social squalor,
sex, petty crime, political corruption—all of these appear in Gutiérrez's
Dirty Havana Trilogy (1998) and *El rey de La Habana* (The king of Havana)
(1999). These works focus on the underside of the revolutionary project, a
world that bears no relation to the "official" representation of the country
as nobly trying to overcome the difficulties of the Special Period. They
offer a lot of sex, filth, and deadpan realism amid the ruins of Havana. If
they do not engage in the romantic melancholia that tourists sometimes
seek in Cuba, they also do not allow their characters to mourn the loss
of utopia. Curiously Gutiérrez's novels served to cement the mystique of
Cuba as a site of collapsed dreams. If it might seem unreal for a reader to
want to visit Cuba after reading one of his novels, they nevertheless do
appeal to a very masculine sense of sexual—as opposed to political—em-
powerment in their treatment of women and homosexuals. Gutiérrez
hardly serves up a cool tropical drink for his would-be tourists; instead,
the seduction of his tales lies in a combination of aesthetic realism and
freedom from constraint.

The best account of what this relationship with the market has produced may be found in a memorable piece by Ena Lucía Portela in the collection *Cuba: voces para cerrar un siglo* (Cuba: voices to close off a century),
edited by René Vázquez Díaz for the Olof Palme Center in Stockholm
in 1994. In "Literatura versus lechugitas, breve esbozo de una tendencia,"
Portela opposes literature to the demands of the market (*lechugitas* are like
"greenbacks"—pieces of lettuce, hard currency). She portrays the conflicts
of the Cuban writers in terms of a market that demands the local color
of the "Cuban reality," and she defines that "local color" as a folkloric
aesthetics of hardship. She explains that, as a female writer who at age
twenty-four had won the Cirilo Villaverde national prize for her novel *El
pájaro: pincel y tinta china* (The bird: brush and Chinese ink), she was
immediately approached by editors who wanted her to engage the Special
Period from a feminist point of view. She defines this literature of the

Special Period in succinct terms, though states that it is impossible for her to participate in this dynamic. Of course, she needs money, even likes money, and has nothing against it. But she cannot bring herself to participate in the "Cuban Boom." She concedes that one or two of these novels may be good, but she still believes in the notion of "literature" as something that lives in a kind of isolation from market forces. At the end of her essay, however, almost as if winking at her reader, she allows herself to strike an exotic note, yet on her terms. She closes the essay with a paragraph that could find its place in the literature that sells overseas. It is a paean to community life, to life in the space of the "barrio," that yields an image of society. In speaking about that Cuban "reality"—one that is specifically Cuban and that is sought out by foreign publishers—she riffs on what it actually contains:

> With special period, blackouts, misery, building collapses, soy meat, henequen sutures, boniato bread, dirty broken streets, mud, flies on top and worms underneath, *balseros,* prostitutes [*jineteras*], witchcraft, punks [*rockeros*], marijuana, anxiety pills, homosexuals (bisexuals, trisexuals, and others), pilgrims, Angola wars, etc.[57]

She goes on like this for a page, describing in minute detail what that "reality" is, except for the fact that the "reality" becomes the list of things, the "baroque" profuse, overwhelming, poetic fragment, or collection of fragments, that Portela seductively offers her readers.

THE LETTERED CITY REVISITED

It is strange to watch how the present cultural moment unfolds within a revolutionary project that allowed so many images to seep into the collective consciousness of Latin America and the West. The literary world in Cuba is still composed of writers' unions and cultural associations like the UNEAC, but at this point it is impossible not to register the disenchantment that many writers feel with so many aspects of the project. If the publishing situation has recovered, largely thanks to the aid of foreign capital and some very creative management from those who lead the institutions themselves—as well as a more open Ministry of Culture under Abel Prieto—at the same time the fragmentation has produced a self-referential literary context as writers trade accusations openly or by means of coded messages in their texts. This new play with language and context, more-over, is not sustained by the kind of theoretical framework that supported Severo Sarduy's or José Lezama Lima's work, but rather by stories culled from the oral histories of those who live in the Havana lettered city. Resistance as state policy has produced a thoroughly self-referential text, one where the narrator hints at clues to what the text means, while playing with the reader's awareness of those codes.

According to Margarita Mateo Palmer, one of the sharpest Cuban scholars living in Havana, intertextuality, sexuality, and disenchantment (the collapse of a project that was seen as a mirage) are the defining features of Cuban literature from the 1990s. She argues that many novels outside of the framework of the "Spanish Boom" let their readers know exactly what they are doing, as if, above all, they validated unveiling as method. For her, intertextuality is the key for understanding writers such as Pedro de Jesús, Alberto Garrandés, Jorge Ángel Pérez, and Ena Lucía Portela, and she notes to what extent they borrow from both present and past Cuban literature: Pedro de Jesús incorporates the work of Lino Novás Calvo and Onelio Jorge Cardoso; Garrandés borrows from Ezequiel Vieta; Pérez refers back to Ronaldo Menéndez or the work of contemporaries such as Pedro de Jesús and Ena Lucía Portela; Portela constantly inserts references of her own previously published or written work, in a process that she rightly classifies as "autophagous." For Mateo Palmer, these texts do not "feed" off of reality, they deal above all in cultural signs and codified aesthetics. In this way, the text turns the dependent relationship between reality and literature upside down: it frees itself from other texts and gains a degree of autonomy that it did not previously have.

Intertextuality gives the text this much-desired autonomy as a reaction to the political imperatives of revolutionary literature. At the same time, individual figures occupy the space left by the relative demise of the institutional network. Socialism privileged the collective over the individual, the social process over the personal project. But already by the late 1990s, the individual is at the center of aesthetics, and marginality becomes a valid literary theme. The early focus on the homosexual as marginal being has been supplemented by other marginalities. In Raúl Aguiar's *La estrella bocarriba* (The star upside down) (2001), punks (*rockeros*) invent their own language, and the novel abounds in powerful and shocking descriptions.[58]

Whereas from 1959 to 1980 literature was influenced by the political processes taking place in Cuba, in the 1990s socioeconomic conditions took center stage.

In the early 1990s, the educational system produced more intellectuals than the system could absorb. The government could only manage the situation by encouraging the collaboration of some intellectuals while allowing others, for a time, to live on separate spheres thanks to the cultural authority they possessed. In this way, the state favored some intellectuals at the expense of others. As a result, contests for larger allocations of cultural power were soon brought to the surface, as different factions of the cultural elite competed with each other. Political status, in this case, was distinguished from cultural authority. Some intellectuals can have political status (they can occupy formal bureaucratic posts, for example), while others have cultural authority. In cases where cultural authority involved disputes over past mistakes, the state slowly tried to mend its ways by co-opting intellectuals into placing their cultural authority at the service of political status. This was the case when Antón Arrufat was given the National Prize for Literature in 2000. Cultural authority and political status can allow the writer to consolidate his or her cultural standing and gain increased access to resources. Hence, many figures in the cultural world are deeply suspicious when the state confers political validation (a prize or a medal) on their work. Although cultural authority is somehow tainted by contact with the party bureaucracy (it is very hard to "sell" oneself as a "dissident" writer on the capitalist book market after having won a Cuban literary prize), at the same time writers want to capture cultural authority while steering clear of the political influence it confers.

Much of the intertextual debate in recent Cuban literature concerns the hidden plotlines of this situation as it is manipulated by the state. If the implicit promise of the Spanish book market lay precisely in the fact that Cuba was opening itself up to the world, the still overwhelming presence of the Cuban cultural bureaucracy as a partial intermediary between writers, publishers, and readers has resulted in writers turning inward or, as they find the situation increasingly intolerable, deciding at great personal cost to leave the country and sever, partially or completely, ties to the Cuban establishment. In the last chapter of his memoirs, *Informe contra mí mismo* (Report against myself), Eliseo Alberto lists the diasporic network of friends and acquaintances of the Cuban cultural world who left the island during the 1990s. The catalog is impressive not only for the number of people involved, but for the clear sense of loss involved in the lives that have been disrupted. This loss is one of the themes in the work of Reina María Rodríguez, as her translator has pointed out.[59] This situation allows the state to consolidate more power, as it broadens and amplifies its reach over different segments of society that it had more or less "freed" at the beginning of the Special Period.

The case of Abilio Estévez is interesting in terms of how struggles in the literary realm can affect cultural production as well as writers' lives. Ever since his novel *Tuyo es el reino* (Thine is the kingdom) was published to great acclaim by the Tusquets publishing house in Barcelona in 1997, certain members of the Cuban literary establishment tried to minimize its value. One Cuban author, known only as Ernesto Ernesto, alleged that some fragments of the novel had been lifted from his own unpublished work, and he requested that UNEAC intervene on his behalf. There were no formal mechanisms to sue for plagiarism and the case at first seemed one of an unpublished and little-known figure attacking a widely published and successful writer. Estévez submitted the complete manuscript of his novel, and the paperwork at his disposal, and the UNEAC commissioned a group of experts to investigate. They ruled in Estévez's favor, even if Estévez himself could not be described as a writer with both political and literary power. He had published an early book of poems titled *Manual de tentaciones* (Temptation manual) but had been ostracized for a period of time because of his friendship with Virgilio Piñera, and because of his homosexuality. For a long period of time, his was not the kind of literature that Cuban cultural authorities had wanted to promote. But the fact that he had gained fame abroad did not render him "untouchable," especially in view of the racial overtones of the case (the accusing writer was black).

Estévez's case is particularly instructive: foreign success does not guarantee political power. On the contrary, it may be the basis for increased resentment given the lack of resources for which writers must compete. After the case was settled in his favor (recall this was not a legal case, but rather a dispute between members of the writers' union), Estévez left Havana and settled in Barcelona. He has not become an openly dissident writer and has avoided the kinds of political statements made by other writers when they leave the island. However, he has confessed to being disillusioned with Cuba and with Havana, and has remarked that Havana has become a city that he cannot live in and that he cannot recognize as his own anymore.[60] These are powerful comments from a writer who has always professed love for the city. But for Estévez, Havana has become inscrutable, a hermetically sealed text where writers are on the constant lookout for each other—a court of mandarins where social climbing is accompanied by ferocious backstabbing, a kind of dress rehearsal for impending doom. Reinaldo Arenas had made the point before, in *The Color of Summer*, that no amount of theatrical gestures could explain the level of aggression that forced writers to spy on each other. Estévez's voluntary exile, as well as the bitter tone of his remarks about the city where he had lived all of his life, show that the anger felt by Arenas has now turned into melancholia. The disenchantment is not only Estévez's. It is symptomatic of a process that uses visibility paradoxically to mask terrible processes taking place elsewhere. These processes repeat themselves over time, turning out ever more illegible texts that readers approach like spies, trying to nail down the elusive reason for their being.

The Beat of the State

RHYTHM SECTION

The boom in Cuban music during the 1990s took up considerable shelf space in U.S. stores. There was a wide variety of projects, both ambitious and modest, selling for a lot of money or copied cheaply in Miami from old archives. In the wake of the success of the elderly musicians of the Buena Vista Social Club, there were so many collections by the end of the decade that it was hard for aficionados to make sense of it. It gave the impression that Cuban music had devoured the International collection, so it was moved to the Latin sections at many stores. It was hard, during the Cuban "Boom" of the late 1990s, to pick the good from the bad, though the compact discs were generally of superior quality. They were targeted to more educated consumers, and many spared no effort in creating a stylized product. The presence of the music itself in record stores could not erase the absence of dance-hall venues where that music could be heard, nor the fact that distribution trumped promotion—that the only place one could generally hear and dance to contemporary Cuban music was the record store or a private party. The music was not heard on the radio— except in specialized radio shows—and it moved to a different beat than the one sweeping Latino communities in the United States, with its penchant for pop or rock *en español,* or Tejano music, or merengue, rap, or newer beats such as reggaeton. For an island that produced such great music, the absence of the sound in a live context is a dramatic contrast to the rest of what the stores offered.

There are many reasons for this absence of Cuban music on the circuit. The economic embargo is the main one, but also the particularities of the Cuban music and recording system before and during the 1990s, as well as the broader migratory currents of Dominicans and Puerto Ricans in the Northeast who listen to a different beat, and Mexicans and Central Americans who also prefer a different sound. In Miami, the explosion of South American rock promoted by transnational recording companies and fostering stars such as Shakira, los Rabanes, Ricky Martin, and Marc Anthony created a context different from the one in Cuba, where audiences favor either big bands or troubadours who more closely resemble folk singers.[1] Paradoxically, the best place to hear Cuban music from the island may be Miami, where audience support for it has translated into dance clubs that foster its development, in spite of the city's ban on musicians from the island performing there, and despite the ruckus in 2001 when the Latin Grammys were forced to move their annual ceremonies to Los Angeles.

Complications arising from the embargo also account for the venues where Cuban musicians can play in the United States. In Spain in 1998, Cuban musicians toured in dance halls, where the contact between audience and orchestra provided the context for a great show in which bands and audience members took cues from each other. In the United States, even before the George W. Bush administration tightened restrictions, getting booked in big dance clubs did not provide the financial returns necessary to transport a large group of musicians around the country. The halls they played in were concert halls, where, in spite of musicians' efforts, people were not allowed to dance. As Juan de Marcos (the main impresario behind the Buena Vista phenomenon) explained to Eugene Robinson, "[t]o succeed on the road in the States you have to play music that works in the concert hall. The old stuff, it works. We proved it."[2] To hear Cuban music in the context where much of it has any meaning, a trip to Cuba is obligatory. Robinson begins his account of the music scene in Cuba at La Tropical, one of the best of a dwindling number of venues where Cubans without dollars can listen to their favorite bands. His description of it is pure magic: a sublime instance of collective frenzy organized in such a way that it seems "an exercise in massively parallel computation, many minds each solving its own bit of an otherwise unsolvable problem . . . It was brilliantly human and clever and aware, both spontaneous and purposeful, and it was one of the most stirring and beautiful sights I have ever seen."[3]

As the dancers spin around each other and embrace, try out complicated moves for the other to follow without missing a beat, and still manage to occupy a relatively constricted space, the meaning of Cuban popular music becomes clear. The music is predicated on the dancing, but also leads the dancers around while the band provides the beat, and the audience calls the beat out to the band. Dance music becomes a metaphor of the island: for scholars such as Robinson, one has to be there to experience it, and it allows for an understanding of the call-and-response pattern of Cuban popular attitudes to authority. It also serves as a venue for Cubans to let off steam in a context based on the counterpoint of expression and repression. What Robinson finds is a contradiction in terms that can only be resolved by the sheer physical trance that the dancers and the musicians experience—the island is an amalgam of postmodern beats within a historical setting. This is where the context of resistance colludes with global corporations invested in propping up the resistance to their own insertive transnational penetration, and where the vanguard of expression collides with a vanguard that wants to preserve tradition. The liberating force is music, but the beat of the music is never allowed to stray from the beat of the state. Music and the state seem to dance around each other, and with each other: music involves musicians and dancers, and these demand venues, and the venues produce a collective expression that may or may not fall into line with what government policies seek to promote.[4]

Music was always the background to Cuban intellectual discourse. It turned poems, slogans, exhortations, and even historical narratives into song. If images referred to the call of history, then music was the beat of popular response, the mambo line that moved the masses at the parade or the march. One of the most striking examples of this can be seen in an account by Antonio Benítez Rojo, who memorably explained why nuclear fallout was not to be in 1962. Recalling the moment when the whole world feared annihilation because of Russian missiles on Cuban soil, he saw two black women from his balcony walking on the street below, moving their bodies lackadaisically with their own sense of rhythm and beat. At the risk of sounding racist or sexist, Benítez Rojo makes a striking observation: it was at that point that he came to the conclusion that the end of the world was impossible in this context, because the Caribbean was not an apocalyptic space. This scene is presented at the beginning of *The Repeating Island,* where Cuba and the Caribbean engage in their own particular flow, moving with the rhythm of the waters that have brought culture back and forth from the Americas to Europe, and from Africa to a meta-archipelago—the constant theme of Benítez Rojo's work.[5]

Since the revolution, music in Cuba has been linked to state policies. This linkage was always predicated on the popular, but it was also a question of the way in which the popular was represented, and what kind of citizen was being represented by song. Thus, music became part of a *political* discourse, and subject to shifts in cultural policy explained by intellectuals who "channeled" popular will. There was an attempt to create a new context for music, and in the early 1970s this produced the Nueva Trova (loosely translated as "New Song"), a musical movement that countered the negative images fostered by the recording industry and capitalism and that benefited from state sponsorship, including television programs and radio airplay, which paradoxically marginalized popular music, understood as dancing music.[6] Nueva Trova singers became immensely popular throughout Latin America, and have been a big factor—to this day—in explaining the bonds of solidarity felt with the revolution in the region and internationally.

Alejo Carpentier and Natalio Galán wrote famously about music in Cuba, but neither focused on economics, on music's relation to the state, or on government in music (Carpentier's book, of course, dates from 1946).[7] Both books discuss the origin, diffusion, and popularity of music in a context in which the state was not the major participant in music or the recording industry. Although musicians may adapt, manipulate, seduce, or be consumed by the market, it is the continuous dynamic set in place between intellectuals and music that collaborates in making this situation difficult. Associating music with intellectual discourse is the main thing distinguishing the Cuban musical industry from that of its Caribbean neighbors. Even in the 1970s, when salsa throughout the Caribbean became a musical genre that spawned its own intellectual discourse, it did not influence what people heard or danced to in the streets. Within the capitalist recording industry in the Caribbean region, validation from below generally accounted for interventions within the public sphere. The same certainly did not apply to Cuba during the 1970s, when music was tied to political messages or cultural uplift. Only in the 1990s, and after gradual and always retracted openings, did the Cuban musical scene resemble the one produced in its broader geographic context. But to this day these dynamics are subject to state intervention in ways that need to be mapped out in historical terms.

THE END OF THE CABARET

Music was always part of the revolutionary educational program. Already in his June 1961 "Palabras a los intelectuales" Fidel Castro included music as part of the state's educational mission. He announced plans to establish a school (which would become the Instituto Superior del Arte) in one of the most elegant Havana neighborhoods to teach music, dance, and visual arts to students from all over the country.[8] Because the state understood music as part of a broader academic and pedagogical project, what used to be called entertainment was now understood as culture. This also implied linking music to the social context in which it was produced.[9]

Cubans did not listen to different music immediately after the revolution, though later the music industry changed: political processes of the 1960s and 1970s isolated Cubans from the rest of the Caribbean region.[10] Thus, while Cubans to this day still talk about music within the context of nationality, the idea of music as a *national* entity may not totally explain recent processes taking place in the Caribbean. At the beginning of the twenty-first century, Dominican merengues are sung by Puerto Rican singers, salsa is played by Mexican *orquestas,* cumbia may be refashioned in Miami or Los Angeles, while rap moves Latino and African American youth in New York or Cali. Indeed, the fact that the state can still talk about "Cuban" music may seem like a regressive gesture or, paradoxically, an echo of how it markets its products—in this case, to the transnational music industry, which in the 1990s marketed "Cuban music" as an authentic Caribbean musical expression—undiluted, that is, by capitalist influences.

The narrative of how the state, recording industries, and music impresarios created a "Boom" for Cuban music in the 1990s may or may not be related to what Cubans actually "heard" and danced to during those years. But the separation between popular taste and the music market can be traced back to the early years of the revolution. In the early 1960s, many of the country's important musicians and singers left Cuba to explore better options elsewhere (Olga Guillot, Celia Cruz, La Lupe, Olga Chorens, Tony Chiroldes, and others) because the economic and political changes brought about by socialism rendered irrelevant the context in which they existed. Record distributors and producers set up shop in New York, where there was already a growing circuit of Latino (principally Puerto Rican) musicians. There, they benefited from closer access to means of production and a wide network of recording studios.[11]

With socialism, the capitalist consumer in Cuba disappeared. Because musical education and promotion were financed by the state, the nominal musical audience was the nation—understood always in territorial terms— or those outside of the island who sympathized with or supported the state project. After the 1970s, Cuban musical production always had solidarity with the state as its ultimate goal. There being no private entity as such, musicians recorded with EGREM, the state agency, founded in 1963. EGREM was chiefly concerned with music as a cultural venue, and thus it did not take into account popularity or profit in its recording decisions.[12] In addition, EGREM was supposed to set certain parameters in terms of what music revolutionary citizens (not consumers) should listen to.[13] It was only in 1986, when the state formed the Cuban Institute of Music, and then, in 1990, Artex, an independent entity financed by the state to represent Cuban musicians abroad, that a system that more or less replicated market mechanisms was established on the island.[14]

Contrary to popular misconceptions, these changes were more gradual than drastic. Conflicts over literature, film, and other artistic expression took precedence over conflicts relating to music—although it should be noted that one of the first films banned in Cuba was precisely a *musical* documentary. This was the notorious *P.M.* (1961) by Sabá Cabrera Infante (brother of novelist Guillermo Cabrera Infante), a documentary that represented Cuban dancers and musicians in Havana nightlife and that openly celebrated not only Cuban music but also the kind of lowlife sociality where it flourished.[15] *P.M.* served to underscore how music was intimately linked to the social scene where it thrived. Although the revolutionary authorities banned the film, the musical cabaret circuit continued more or less until the early 1970s, when a revolutionary offensive closed down the last vestiges of nightlife.

The closing of the nightclubs represented more than the end of an era. A way of life associated with it was rendered irrelevant, as poet Sigfredo

Ariel has pointed out.[16] Although some of the artists popular in the cabaret circuit remained in Cuba, their repertoire was rejected completely, as one Cuban observer remarked of Omara Portuondo's appearance in Wim Wenders's *Buena Vista Social Club*.[17] The whole milieu, for example, associated with *filin*—a Cuban musical genre that flourished in the late 1950s and early 1960s—was displaced by more proper revolutionary models, and this genre of song was not validated again until the singer Pablo Milanés, in the 1970s, devoted a whole album to the genre as an homage to the past.

When the state in the late 1960s eliminated cabaret and entertainment artists' ways of earning a living, a new crop of singers appeared. The singers of Nueva Trova, principally Pablo Milanés, Silvio Rodríguez, Noel Nicola, and Sara González, were meant to channel Cuban youths' appetite for American singers such as Bob Dylan and Joan Baez, and even the Beatles (they were banned in Cuba and long hair was frowned upon by a puritanical revolutionary regime).[18] These artists benefited from the fact that, no longer dependent on the dictates of the market, and at the same time fully financed and sponsored by the state, music dissemination in Cuba was now under the rubric of the "cultural" and educational experience.[19]

That music was now *culture* and not *commerce* was reflected in material terms in the way it was produced and exported during the 1960s and 1970s. Back then, buying a Cuban record outside of Cuba meant buying the record at a specialized store (a bookstore, perhaps—not necessarily an ordinary record store—and above all a "leftist" or "alternative" bookstore) and keeping track of artists one had never heard of but who carried the Cuban imprimatur as a cultural alternative. Records were invariably produced by EGREM, the sole state recording venue, and they generally carried a note on the cover that announced, "Este disco es cultura" (This record is culture). Records were, indeed, culture, and many of the Nueva Trova singers set out to experiment and refashion cultural texts of Cuban nationality. At this time, the more open experimentations of the Grupo Experimental Sonora del ICAIC put a jazz inflexion on Cuban music in 1972, Pablo Milanés and Amaury Pérez musicalized many of José Martí's poems, and singers such as Virulo presented themselves as troubadours commenting on Cuban history.

From the EGREM studios the record was sold throughout Latin America by licensing the rights to a number of alternative (generally progressive, or left-wing) distributors, who then printed cover art, and in many cases reproduced liner notes. For example, the Grupo Experimental Sonora del ICAIC created one product expressly geared toward distribution in Puerto Rico, in order to support the Puerto Rican independence movement. The music was recorded in Cuba, but it could be sold in Puerto Rico in the 1970s because of the new U.S. policy on transmission of cultural products.

Cuban records in the 1970s stressed a particular mix of the aesthetic and the political contained in the notion of a *vanguardia*—a term that underwent various inflexions at least since the 1930s in Latin America, but which in the 1970s was firmly allied to the notion of a political avant-garde. The Nueva Trova was predicated initially on the tradition of the troubadour, but it also incorporated traditional Latin American instruments such as the quena, the vihuela, the Andean flute, the accordion, and the lute in order to broaden its appeal to a pan-Latin Americanism that was inspired by the revolution's status at the helm of a "new" continent. In recordings such as *Credenciales,* the first record by Grupo Moncada, one can find the following mix: an Andean folklore song, a song from the Isle of Pines in Cuba, a Venezuelan *son,* and a musical version of a Nicolás Guillén poem dedicated to Chile.[20] The record, distributed in Mexico by agreement with EGREM, includes in the inner liner notes a long, unsigned text that narrates the group's history in the context of Cuban political changes. The music is related explicitly to the parameters set forth by the First Congress of Education and Culture celebrated in Havana in 1971, which aimed to eliminate the "old culture" through a political and cultural decolonization process. And the liner notes explain that in 1972, a movement of *aficionados* (identified as a cross section of "workers" and "students") formed the Nueva Trova with a modernist political program: to stop singing the songs of old and sing about the new realities.

It is interesting that the songs of "old" mentioned by this album engaged thinly veiled references to the cabaret circuit where the slow songs of the Caribbean bolero reigned supreme. The artists insist that new listeners should forget, and cast aside "perfect women and women who were 'traitors,' impossible loves, bucolic picture-postcard landscapes, tropicalistic tourism, and other similar concoctions."[21] At another point, the text makes this more explicit, with a Marxist reading of the links between what the audience listens to, and the social and political culture in which the nation lives. Neocolonialism, according to this new reading of music history, produced "its easy music, its banal themes, its texts replete with corniness, its idols fabricated by record monopolies."[22] The members of the Grupo Moncada opted, as they said, to sing "of history and war, of the Fatherland and of heroes, of the daily struggle against the enemies of the people, and of the anonymous labor of any worker.[23]

But the question was not to validate popular music per se, for this music also reproduced the socioeconomic fabric in which it thrived. In other words, the masses were not always at the vanguard of artistic change, and the artists grappled with the fact that these traditional songs, validated as creations of the people and the masses, also contained objectionable elements. The Grupo Moncada in particular—as well as many other artists at the time—pointed out how machismo and male power were reproduced in popular lyrics. Because "new" songs of love should take the place of the "old," the Grupo Moncada includes a song that deals with women "now" as the *compañera* of the male, who shares with him the agonies and frustrations of revolutionary struggle. The song about the new *compañera* aimed to correct the misrepresentations of the past—even if the new representation could also be criticized in terms of the gender roles it depicted.

The Nueva Trova that buried the world of the cabaret was invested in a discourse of *construction,* very different from the discourse of *resistance* that would be the norm in the 1990s. The discourse was predicated on the elaboration of a "new" form of song out of the disparate elements of Latin American reality, which could also entail a new way of representing Latin America to "ourselves."[24] In the Grupo Moncada record, which is paradigmatic of many of these projects, the fundamental aim is to bridge the divide between past and present, between "folklore" and "contemporary music." But these changes also took place along the axes of production and reception, because they aimed to break with the traditional venues where music was played, as well as with the audience that received the message. The political was part of the group's educational mission, but it also informed the aesthetic function of this new intellectual musical aesthetics in the lettered city. All the songs, the group says, have been played "in university schools, factories, high schools in the countryside, preuniversity preparatory schools, workshops, campesino communities, student and worker festivals."[25] This represents clearly the breakdown of old intellectual spaces where music could be heard. The old venues and the women who sang in them were replaced by the new cultural sites that the Grupo Moncada performed in.

The song that gives the album its title—"Credenciales," written, according to the liner notes, by a poet named Héctor de Arturo and published in his book *Pido la palabra* (I ask for the word)—alludes openly to the political scandal surrounding Heberto Padilla's *Fuera del juego* (Out of the game) in 1971. When the poet, in a sentimental, slow tune, apologizes in the name of those who stand "outside of the game" precisely at the moment in which the people are "playing" to change death for life, the jab at Padilla could not be more explicit: his polemical book of poems, *Fuera del juego*, marked a turning point in the state's repression of intellectuals in 1971.[26] Arturo's poem seeks forgiveness for the duty that brings him to sing of new realities. He distances himself from those who bring styles from Paris to "our reality," and this culminates with his asking those other poets to receive "bullets" (a metaphor for words) signed by guns ("balas firmadas con fusiles").

The Nueva Trova movement was complicit with a notion of time and history: it challenged youth to partake of the utopian impulses of the time, and it sought to redefine how the past could be incorporated into the present. As it appears in the Grupo Moncada liner notes, the movement resurrects the energies of folklore, which is deemed not a "museum" genre but a living thing. In this way, the Nueva Trova was not invested in recapturing the past, but rather in making it valid in the present, because oppression and neocolonialism do not turn folklore into a "dead" relic. The Nueva Trova, then, saw itself as dreaming of a future; it is forward-looking, belonging to a time that originates in the Cuban Revolution and that goes on toward a future that is also a present—what could be called "messianic" time. This is further underscored in the notes, where the group talks about Cuban history in terms of the popular solidarity created by the narrative of war: "War has been our way of life" (La guerra ha sido nuestra manera de vivir), and this was to be reflected in an ambitious undertaking promised for the future: a fourteen-part song that narrates the battle of the Moncada in 1953, where a revolutionary force met fierce resistance from the Batista army. Whether this epic project was written and recorded or not, what is important is the way in which it illustrates the sense of cultural service to the collective endeavor.[27]

The isolation and distance from other forms of Caribbean music in the 1970s are remarkable, especially when one compares Cuban music to the luxurious voluptuousness of New York salsa popular during that time. Until the advent of the fast-paced beat known as *timba* in the 1990s, no lyrical form in Cuban popular music took into account marginal social realities the way Héctor Lavoe and Willie Colón did, for example, in "Juanito Alimaña" from their record *Vigilante* (1983). This is not necessarily because the social realities that the song talked about (thievery, picardía, and urban threat) did not exist in Cuba, but because of other, interrelated factors: in Cuba, the state exercised control over the lyrics, the lack of a commercial culture turned the music away from the notion of scandal and defiance that was a trademark of New York salsa, and there was a lack of contact with the Caribbean dancing public in New York. Salsa portrayed, in fact, many of the moral nightmares of the revolution, at least in terms of its lyrics: an underworld that struggled for representation, a combative attitude against the system, and a context of drugs, social dislocation, and despair. In musical terms, salsa was too fast-paced, too brassy for many Cuban musicians. For intellectuals, it was simply heard as bastardized Cuban music.[28] Other issues relating to the very means of production were, of course, important in this regard: the fact that Cuban musicians were employed by the state also meant that they received a fixed salary, regardless of where or how often they played.[29] As these changes were being reflected in music pedagogy, music halls and dancing halls seem to have disappeared.[30]

It was only toward the end of the 1970s that Cuban musicians collaborated with foreigners, but these contacts always took place on a quasi-official level, and were tinged by the negative reading of salsa developed by the cultural authorities. The exchanges happened mostly between Cuban and American jazz musicians, not *salseros*. Jazz artists such as Dizzy Gillespie and Stan Getz went to Cuba in 1977 and jammed with members of the Cuban band Irakere, who also toured the United States at that time. In 1979, CBS records organized a series of concerts in Havana's Karl Marx theater that included artists such as Billy Joel, Kris Kristofferson, Weather Report, and Stephen Stills, and while Havana and rest of the Caribbean were tuned in to Ruben Blades and Willie Colón's more socially conscious salsa, Oscar D'León played in Havana and Varadero.[31] However, this exchange was short-lived: the Mariel exodus of 1980 changed the equation, and Ronald Reagan's extremely hostile policies toward Cuba lasted throughout most of the 1980s. One of the first markers of this change was Paquito D'Rivera's very public defection in 1980 in order to pursue a solo career that was in many ways denied by the musical establishment in Cuba, and in order to collaborate more openly with other jazz currents than the ones he had access to.[32]

THE *CROQUETA* CURTAINS

Croquetas are fritters cooked in Cuba and throughout the Caribbean, and the term "*croqueta* curtains" comes from Enrique Fernández's liner notes for the compilation *Diablo al Infierno,* describing the optimism felt in the early 1990s among music critics in the United States.[33]

Any attempt at a "history" of music during the Special Period is bound to dehistoricize what is perceived very differently by different publics. There is no way to determine which cultural products move in and out of Cuba, and how musical circuits negotiate relative political isolation while at the same time picking up different beats and musical inflections from visitors, from radio, or from increasing contacts and travel abroad. Faced with immense economic and political obstacles in the early 1990s, the state understood that cultural discourse had to go hand in hand with a new pride in nationality. This revival of nationalism occurred while the state was opening up to entrepreneurs who mined the island's untapped musical legacy.

At the beginning of the decade, selective reissues of old recordings kept the cultural focus at the forefront. In a quasi-ethnographic vein, record entrepreneurs sought to rescue important performances of the past and bring them to the market in order to show the richness of the Cuban musical tradition, as in recordings made by Cubans in Paris during the 1930s, or the excellent compilation *Cuban Counterpoint: History of the Son Montuno,* assembled by Morton Marks.[34] These compilations generally had well-informed liner notes and even at times took issue with the way Cubans understood the dynamics of the music.[35] These first recordings were the work of individual entrepreneurs, who acted as intermediaries and negotiators between the Cuban recording studio and the government bureaucracy, on the one hand, and the "global economy," on the other. They were "concrete actors" who "linked socialist institutions with the transnational corporations that dominated the worldwide dissemination of mass culture."[36] The entrepreneurs possessed an extraordinary sense of agency in opening up Cuban music to the transnational circuit, and many of the available recordings reflect their taste and their particular interests. As a result, the Cuban bureaucracy encountered transnational markets first via concrete actors, not faceless institutions.[37] In many cases, they were just "musicians and music lovers in search of new frontiers . . . the contemporary equivalent of old colonial traders, self-made men, exponents of the individualistic values of capitalism."[38] One of the important elements in this picture is the fact that rescuing Cuban musical tradition, or even exporting it to the wider circuits of the world market, was not an exercise in traditional forms of nostalgia. There was no link with the diaspora per se, but a commitment to Cuban music, as well as the desire to earn money in the process.[39]

Deborah Pacini Hernández's distinction between the term "world music" and the term "world beat" allows us to understand how "Cuba" was packaged and exported. World music was used by music scholars to refer to all that was not necessarily Western (linked, then, to "root music"), whereas "world beat" refers to more modern products that took into account the cross-fertilization of styles between the First and Third Worlds.[40] The "world beat" circuit is more tied to African roots than the more generalized "world music" circuit. Promoted in the late 1980s and early 1990s by means of the "world beat" category, Cuba benefited because of the emphasis the revolution gave its ties to Africa during the 1980s.[41] It was not a new product or a new beat, and in turn it fulfilled the desire for authenticity that was essential to the world music public. Inside Cuba, these sounds were registered as "old" and "dated," and were not massively popular. But they put Cuba on the map for the transnational world music public.[42]

By the time Cuba Classics 3, *Diablo al Infierno,* came out in 1992, with liner notes provided by the *Village Voice*'s Enrique Fernández and Ned Sublette, the country flavor had yielded to the Havana urban sound. Some of the optimism paradoxically produced by this difficult period in Cuban history, after Soviet subsidies had ended, permeates Fernández's liner notes:

Gloria Estefan has played Havana. So have Latin stars Willy Chirino, Hansel (with and without Raul), Carlos Oliva and the entire suave Miami sound. Pablo Milanés has played Miami, as have Silvio Rodríguez, Los Van Van and Orquesta Revé. Vinyl, tape and CD's cross the sugar and croqueta curtains. They are light contraband, to be sure, not even illegal, just sospechoso (suspicious), like stolen kisses between cousins. Miami and Havana listen to each other's recorded music, sometimes, no doubt, to hear messages banned or shunned on either side. But mostly to hear Cuban music. To love it.

Diablo al Infierno even took authenticity and played with it, as in a recording of Los Blues singing a version of "Rompe Saraguey" that sounded like a 1950s bluesy jam. It was electrical guitars, an open concert (authenticity and the rawness of the recording were insisted upon) lasting six minutes on the compact disc. The fact that its compilers knew Cuba is evident. They registered, for example, the ominous tone of Carlos Varela's song "Guillermo Tell" (William Tell), and the live recording included in this CD is one of its emotional highlights. Varela's song turns William Tell's trope upside down. If the father in the legend put the apple on the son's head in order to try out his marksmanship, now it is the son's turn to experiment with his father, by putting the apple on *his* head. A wrong shot, of course, would mean death, but that is precisely the poignant scenario Varela sang about, at a time in which Cuban youth were tired of being experimented on, supposedly for their benefit. "Guillermo Tell" summed up what the new generation coming of age during the Special Period felt about the political and economic changes taking place, and it was an instant classic.[43] It is clear that Sublette was taking the pulse of changes happening in Cuban youth, and this sensibility, along with that of the heavy metal song by Zeus that titled the collection, pushed the limits of official tolerance at the time. *Diablo al Infierno* also gave a broader vision of Havana music, and thus it included such popular bands as Irakere, Los Van Van, NG La Banda, Dan Den, and Pablo Milanés (the Luaka Bop label also brought out a collection by Silvio Rodríguez). The liner notes insist on this mix with tongue-in-cheek irreverence: "It is also, perhaps, a selection that few Cubans would have made. Singer songwriter Pablo Milanés on the same record with Cuban ska band Los Blues? What this collection says is, if you thought you knew what Cuba was, think again."

These compilations were seductive and they were packaged to seduce. In terms of transnational capitalist venues, however, their audience was relatively small. Byrne and Luaka Bop even tried to establish links between the old and new music by recording a compilation of Silvio Rodríguez's songs. But nothing would quite succeed like Ry Cooder's *Buena Vista Social Club,* and the film by Wim Wenders, which can be used as a marker

that closes off this period of Cuban music—and it does so with a paradoxical gesture: revealing how the past returns to the present in order to
capture what Román de la Campa has brilliantly termed "the sublime
charm of cultural nostalgia."[44] It was certainly not urban, but it wasn't
country either. And Cooder's project was very different from the one that
David Byrne sought to sell with his Luaka Bop label. While Byrne was
working on the "urban" "pop" "alternative" feel of Havana, Cooder aimed
to go back to the roots and add to those roots some inflexions of his own.
The market does not always respond in ways that can be predicted by even
the savviest pop entrepreneur.

THE BUENA VISTA DEBATE

Buena Vista Social Club was a worldwide phenomenon when it was re-
leased in 1997 by World Circuit Records. It sold more than a million and
a half copies in three months; it won the Grammy award for best Tropical
Latin recording that same year, and each of the album participants negotiated excellent contracts, aided in no small part by the success of the
1999 film version directed by Wim Wenders. The musical product was put
together by the intellectual and musical intelligence of Juan de Marcos
González, who had rounded up the Buena Vista musicians and brought
them to his studio to record. Ry Cooder had come to Cuba to attend a
meeting with musicians from Mali who could not show up, and Nick Gold,
who already had contacts in Cuba—one of them being Juan de Marcos
González—put them in contact with each other.[45] Recorded in Cuba, it
featured Compay Segundo, Omara Portuondo, Ibrahim Ferrer, Eliades
Ochoa, Rubén González, Barbarito Torres, and Orlando "Cachaíto" López.
In addition, Ry Cooder played the slide guitar, and his son Joaquim per-
cussion. The album mixed in a number of different styles, mostly from the
1920s to 1940s, and it appealed to a world circuit audience by not merely
exploring one aspect of Cuban music, but many. The film, which is insep-
arable by now as a visual register for the music, moved from the concert
hall to the daily lives of the musicians, photographed at different points in
Havana, and interacting with people on the street. Bracketing that dual-
ity, two concerts divide the film into two parts: first, in Amsterdam, and
then in New York's Carnegie Hall. On a third, dialectical level, there was
the magical encounter between these musicians and New York as a world

capital, underscoring anachronism and cultural dislocation. All the dialectical exchanges are structured. Wenders juxtaposes downtrodden and
almost crumbling Havana buildings to the fast-paced New York nightlife, featuring musicians who seem to belong to a different time. What is
absent here is verbal: politics and history. *Buena Vista Social Club* is all
about vision and hearing. The musicians not only avoid all references to
the political situation, but the film manages to deflect the political histories embedded in these musicians' careers.

For Rufo Caballero, who emerged in the late 1990s as an important
voice in Cuban cultural criticism, this lack of context is appalling. His
"La excusa: Semiosis, ideología y montaje en Buena Vista Social Club" is
a long tirade against Wenders, comparing him negatively to Rainer Fass-
binder and Werner Herzog among German directors. His critique moves
between scorn toward what Wenders had done in representing certain
stereotypes marketed to the world as the "reality" of Havana, to his use
of montage for political purposes, especially in the final scenes, which he
analyzes with structural precision as manipulative in the broadest sense of
the word. Caballero's language is at times elitist, as he dismisses the film's
"vulgarity" and "superficiality" in terms of its handling of history.[46] He
claims that Wenders is not a "real artist" (*artista verdadero*) because he only
scratches the surface of the phenomena he explores. Caballero also resurrects the fact that Omara Portuondo, though never a well-remunerated
singer, did once sing revolutionary songs, such as "Junto a mi fusil mi son,"
which compared the Cuban musical *son* to a weapon (*fusil*) and for which
she became a symbol of political power during a period that, Caballero
adds, is now thankfully in the past.[47] The combination that Caballero
embodies—the highly literate critic of Wenders's semiology and the rough
political language of accountability—is important because of the strong
passions this cultural product aroused.

The film was first shown in Cuba on March 26, 1999—it coincided
with the Baltimore-Cuban baseball game—and then again to the general
public during the 1999 Havana film festival.[48] The international opening
salvo to the debate about the *Buena Vista Social Club* record and movie was
given a year later by Michael Chanan, who in March 2000 published an
essay simultaneously in *New Left Review* and in *La Gaceta de Cuba* titled
"Play it again o llámenlo nostalgia."[49] Translated by Ambrosio Fornet, it
compares the *Buena Vista* film by Wim Wenders to a Dutch documentary,

filmed by Sonia Herman Dolz, about the Cuban *trova*. Chanan discusses the relative merits of each (he prefers Dolz's) and questions why Wenders's film has been the more popular one. It was clear that, like *Strawberry and Chocolate*, *Buena Vista Social Club* was made for literary debate, because in spite of its emphasis on music, there was something intellectual—and thus literary—about it.

The most important, and the most interesting, debate was sponsored by the journal *Temas* (July-December 2000). It was moderated by Ambrosio Fornet and included Julio García Espinosa, Vicente González Castro, María Teresa Linares, Helio Orovio, Frank Padrón, Germán Piniella, Luis Ríos, and Alan West.[50] They represented film, music, official ideology in varying degrees, and one Cuban living abroad. As with many of the debates sponsored by *Temas,* it revealed different opinions about the present and the past state of the issue, and took into account globalization and Cuban music abroad. It voiced mistrust with regard to Cooder's and Wenders's motives, though Cooder comes out better than Wenders, because his previous collaborations are seen as impeccable examples of interesting encounters between East and West. Wenders's aestheticizing gaze is judged unfair, unbalanced: the corresponding shots to those of dilapidated Havana neighborhoods should have been taken in the Bronx, not on Fifth Avenue. For María Teresa Linares, the film was aggressive.[51] For Germán Piniella, it was upsetting because at no point did the film explain the specific facts of social history that account for that poverty. Many of these academics wanted a more "ideological," or at least ideologically precise, representation.[52]

The debate is interesting for what it reveals about the history of music within the revolution—a subject the film purposely does not represent. It is a history of governmental mistakes, of harsh decisions that may have been rectified but that still produce a bitter aftertaste. Helio Orovio, the foremost Cuban musicologist living on the island, discusses this most extensively. He does think that these musicians were subsisting in the precarious and difficult conditions that the film represents, and he cites a number of records made by the EGREM as being better than *Buena Vista Social Club*. But he agrees that there has been a problem in terms of the relationship between musicians and the state:

> The fact that the organization of music in our country was a mess [*un disparate*] is something else; that musicians had a fixed salary, that they were

programmed by a person sitting in a bureau, in an enterprise—that is all true and they were enormous blunders [*disparates*]. The fixed salaries [*la plantilla fija*] for example, resulted in musicians breaking their own bass so that they would not have to go out and play in Bejucal, because, after all, they earned the same amount at the end of the month; and in Bejucal people at the dance were waiting for the orchestra that never showed up because "the bass broke." These are all mistakes [*disparates*], as is preventing students in the Art Schools from playing Cuban music . . . These are blunders [*disparates*] for which we have to assume responsibility, and make a historical criticism, but they have nothing to do with the fact that all of that is now being manipulated, to the extent that people throughout the whole world are now interested in Cuba because of the Buena Vista Social Club.[53]

What Orovio calls "manipulation" is interesting in this context, for it is the way in which the *state* is organized that produced the situation that Cooder and Wenders in turn "manipulated." As Orovio points out, the problem was always a state problem. The state treated the musician as a "cultural worker" when the musician cannot or should not be, and never should have been, considered as such.[54]

It is interesting to note the extent to which this discussion refers back to the scene that was presented in the Grupo Moncada record. On the one hand, it argues for more liberty, and it condemns as "excesses" the kind of "cultural worker" mentality that produced music in the 1970s; on the other hand, it calls for more government intervention in terms of the symbolic meaning and images attached to music. In other words, instead of using Wenders's movie as overriding argument for "freeing" up musicians, the debate takes on an eerie quality by insisting on validating the intrusion of the state into the cultural arena. Julio García Espinosa argues that the state should engage in a massive educational project, and Vicente González Castro states:

I think we should aim to get Cuban Television, or the Ministry of Culture, or the Institute of Music, I don't know who, to finance or in some way subsidize the creation of popular materials on our music; far removed from the demands of these institutions that produce these materials in order to sell, and end up developing a label, just the way they produce toothpaste, or the texture of a shoe; in other words, they are fabricating something that is salable, commercializable, and that is immediately going to be converted into money.[55]

This discussion turned into one about how the state should finance and control its own image—the image of Cuba. Faced with the growing popularity of a seemingly "independent" phenomenon that freed musicians from the rationalizing impulses of the state, these intellectuals argue for a new form of state participation in culture, one that ensures the creation and reproduction of "authentic" music and "quality" artistic expression.

Buena Vista Social Club thus points to two related phenomena that are relevant to any discussion of cultural policy in a state that, during the 1990s, once again deployed an ideology of resistance as one of its principal ideological propositions. First, internal and external events affect Cuba in ways that are different from the way they did during the more "cohesive" 1960s and 1970s. The relationship between the state's internal control and the image it wants to convey internally and externally now must pass through cultural intermediaries that are not necessarily under its control. The second phenomenon pertains to internal and external validation of new musical communities. What the foreign media values as authenticity increasingly affects what gets recorded, played, and performed in Cuba. If the state is to be the ultimate guarantor of *cubanía,* it needs to process these cultural modes in one way or another. This is why debates on music were part of a broader series of debates on literature, visual arts, and film. With music (Cuba was marketed abroad as "La isla de la música"), a nationalist construction was spawned by some predictable essentialist categories. And while *Buena Vista Social Club* was taking the world by storm, other phenomena were taking place in Cuba, and these showed to what extent music, as the most "authentic" Cuban artistic expression, faced new challenges.

HOW CUBAN IS IT?

Intellectuals who participated in the discussion about *Buena Vista Social Club* do not debate much about what is understood by "Cuban" music at this point in time; they all take its existence for granted. For them, there is, as Carpentier famously put it, "music in Cuba," but there is also Cuban music that has resisted for years the nefarious effects of the transnational dilution of culture, as well as the more "terrible" effects of the Miami sound.

The only voice to dispute this assessment is in the second debate on music sponsored by *Temas,* "La música popular como espejo social" (Popular music as social mirror) in 2002, and that is Roberto Zurbano's sharp comments on popular music.[56] Zurbano cautiously notes that the rhythm of this intellectual conversation may or may not be in sync with the beat of what is happening, with how Cuban music goes abroad and then gets restructured. He points not only to Gloria Estefan's *Mi tierra* as representing a radical break in her career, but also to the fact that Celia Cruz sang Cuban work by Cándido Fabré and Pedro Luis Ferrer. These mixes produce new things: Cuban singers do not do solely Cuban work, and the immense success of a transplanted Cuban group such as Orishas in France shows how transnational diffusions break down myths that Cuban intellectuals have about music, and shines a new light on notions such as efficacy or cultural value. Zurbano concludes by observing how complex the present moment is—one that sees a coexistence, within the same cultural field, of disparate and opposing social expressions.[57]

This line of thought was not pursued much within Cuban intellectual discourse on music, though cultural relations with the diaspora have been more pronounced with writers. What debates on Buena Vista and on the contemporary musical scene addressed was the question of the "image" that Cuba wants to portray abroad. The reasons for this concern were self-evident: during the late 1990s, "Cuba" became almost a kind of franchise within the capitalist music scene. There was a glut of recordings that used Cuba as a point of reference in order to provide background for other, more experimental mixes. Although Zurbano did not address this concern, the tenor of his words suggests that he understood and accepted this new cultural field.

That music would be so intricately intertwined with "image" was one of the more conservative concerns of intellectual discourse, and it was a direct result of the implicit equation of music with nationality, and nationality with the state. What kind of image was being exported? This question haunted state intellectuals. A random example is the compact disc *Urban Cuban,* which combined Cuban music and French Afro pop. *Urban Cuban* was mixed in Paris, and it traced a direct line between the

Parisian *banlieues* and raw Centro Habana or Alamar marginality—a mix of Pedro Juan Gutiérrez's "dirty realism" and graffiti-like postmodern cool. Politics here takes a back seat to the hyperdesigned construction of the music itself: the "Yayabo" piece (a Cuban standard) is presented as a fast-paced, funked-out number with horns and a steady beat; the "Light and Fire" track revs up techno and synthetic elements. At the same time, the group P18, creators of this mix, is capable of being as authentic as can be, including a song on this CD to the Afro-Caribbean deity Yemayá.[58] *Urban Cuban's* techno-syncretism is not necessarily looking for authentic experience, but for what an authentic experience *should be*. It does not mark the opposites of past and present as *Buena Vista Social Club* did, but is more concerned with spatial categories. This can be seen at a very "raw" level in the long recording period, from April 1996 to October 1998, and in the fact that it was done at the ICAIC in Havana and a number of other places around the globe, with the final product mastered in London.[59] It is not even "deracinated" music, but rather uses juxtaposition: the Eiffel Tower with the dancing *mulata*. It was not necessarily operating at any level of reality, but rather heightened all sensation to a level of unreality with Cuba as its center. This is a very different world from the one contemplated by the intellectual discussions that were taking place in Havana. And it was manufacturing a notion of "hipness" that is nowhere to be seen in the Wim Wenders or Ry Cooder productions, which are quite "literary" and culturally nostalgic, or sentimental, in comparison. *Urban Cuban* partly captures the imagination of what Cuba is. But Cuba merely provides a referential image for something else, always elusive. It is a French fantasy that uses Cuba as the originating quotation and reference, as when the introduction to "Somos el futuro" samples Che Guevara. Cuba is here a mental abstraction, as decontextualized as it would be to wear a Che T-shirt in an upscale New York restaurant. Because of this, *Urban Cuban* falls outside of the sociopolitical discussions taking place in Havana. The real discussion about "image," and the question of state control over it during the Special Period, concerned the *timba* explosion and the rap phenomenon.

Timba appeared in full force during the late 1980s and especially in the early 1990s, and was a popular response to a stagnating Cuban musical scene.[60] Like salsa in the 1970s, it depended on big bands with a big brassy sound and irreverent lyrics born in marginal milieus. It was a male phenomenon, a music so loud, so rough, so macho, that the mere fact of attempting it with women singers was enough to attract attention.[61] Un-like salsa, the dancing style did not depend on one partner leading the other but on both dancers pressing their bodies provocatively one in front of each other (what Helio Orovio calls the *tembleque*), simulating frenzied intercourse.[62] It was a brassier sound than the one used by bands on the island, and it quickly became the music of choice in two venues: the newly created tourist spots where *jineteras* (Cuban prostitutes) could be seen dancing with foreigners, and on Cuban neighborhood streets, where *timba* lyrics described the social hardships of the Special Period.

Bands would still play at popular spaces such as La Tropical, but *timba* was ever present in tourist locales, such as El Palacio de la Salsa in the Hotel Riviera, where Cuban men or women and their foreign escorts could be seen dancing a kind of simulated foreplay. *Timba* lyrics were full of innuendo and double entendres; they validated individuality and status symbols such as money, cars, or personal wealth. The music was closer to transnational Caribbean salsa in its brassier sound, and the bands wore outfits similar to those seen in contemporary Dominican or Puerto Rican bands. García Espinosa alludes to this in the debate on *Buena Vista Social Club* from *Temas:*

> More and more, musicians, in the world, adorn themselves with costumes, makeup, lights, and rhinestones. They do a spectacle, and one doesn't know whether one likes the spectacle or the music they are offering. Our musi-cians are the antispectacle, and this is the way they are presented in these documentaries: without makeup, without lights, rhinestones, without any phosphorescence: music, without any kind of backup. That, in a world that is losing more and more a sense of authenticity, is an important value. I think that in the world as a whole there is a very strong desire for authen-ticity, in the face of so many cheap spectacular products [*baratija espectacu-lar*] that permeate the music scene.[63]

But what García Espinosa is validating here is the opposite of what *timba* is, for *timba* did not make a claim for authenticity but rather for exhibi-tionism. *Timba* became so popular and so massive that at one point the authorities had to clamp down on popular performances. The story of what happened to the immensely popular band La Charanga Habanera comes in different versions. Robinson points out the fact that the "furious, danceable music and lyrics . . . spoke of real life . . . [and were] often risqué enough to provoke government disapproval." But his account of the changes in the band stem from the fact that David Calzado, its popular leader, one day fired the band—though the musicians claimed that it was they who fired Calzado—and two competing institutions were formed: Calzado's Charanga Habanera and the rival Charanga Forever.[64] But at no point does he mention the most important event in this story—when, as Roberto Zurbano explained in the *Temas* debate, the band was given a sanction in 1997 for a concert that took place at the Festival Mundial de la Juventud y los Estudiantes (World Festival of Youth and Students).[65] According to people in Havana, they landed on a huge stadium in a helicopter, dressed in what the authorities considered "outlandish" costumes, and proceeded to move their bodies in a rhythmic and provocative dance. La Charanga was banned from performing in public for more than six months, and their act had to be reconceptualized.

The ban on La Charanga was part of a broader clampdown. The *timba* scene had gotten out of control, and the social disparities it created had produced an ostentatious—indeed, flashy—lifestyle that the government immediately recognized as projecting the "wrong" image of Cuba to foreigners. The Palacio de la Salsa was closed down temporarily by the Ministry of Tourism; it reopened with the kind of cabaret-style venue that seemed a throwback to the big hotel musical revues that tourists used to frequent in Havana, Miami Beach, or Las Vegas in the 1950s. Banning La Charanga was a sign of harder times for the whole *timba* scene, but it also pointed out the limits of the permissible for the Cuban state. In this case, the problem was not a question of lyrics being too political, or of the dance being too provocative, but the validation of material wealth.

This was curious insofar as there was nothing "political" per se in *timba*—no overt antigovernment messages in the music like those found, for example, in Carlos Varela's "Guillermo Tell." But in a context where music is equated with "culture" broadly understood, and where culture itself is the mark of *cubanía,* there was no cultural value to be added onto the genre, in spite of a complex musical beat that refashioned both traditional Cuban music and the New York salsa of the 1970s. This appears to be the context for the *Temas* debate on popular music as social mirror, coded behind the term "efficacy"—the extent to which the music in itself is projecting certain kinds of values. For Zurbano, efficacy and cultural value are contingent on the kinds of crossings music can achieve as a form that is always cultural; for Margarita Mateo, efficacy has to concern the means of distribution and diffusion for the music. How many Cubans can afford a compact disc is part of the question, as well as how much one has to pay to hear it, and where.[66] *Timba* depends on a social space, partly because there are so few means of diffusion, and the same is true of rap. What the state ultimately did was close off the spaces in which *timba* was diffused. *Timba* was creating an interesting kind of public—one that defined Cubans as citizens within a particular economic configuration, while erasing some boundaries between the music Cubans heard and the music heard abroad as being "distinctly" Cuban. Foreigners' validation of traditional Cuban *son* was not popular in the Cuban street, but *timba* surely was.

Popularity "en la calle" (on the street) in Cuba does not necessarily translate into broader musical venues or a wider diffusion of the music. This is especially true when music courts communities joined by a similar view of sociality, as can be seen in the case of the budding rap movement in Cuba. The authorities' initial discomfort with rap was certainly political, but it also involved the fact that in the United States rap was associated not only with the culture of inner-city resistance, but also with the validation of easy money, easy women, flashy outfits, and drugs. In the case of rap, the emphasis on material flashiness was bound to be more lethal than it was in *timba,* for although *timba* thrived in a kind protocapitalist setting, rap was associated with a hip-hop community understood in racial terms, and racial constructs had always been problematic for the revolution.[67] Hip-hop creates a fluid zone, it exploits the tensions between an open space that is multiethnic, multiracial, and diverse, while at the same time it can present itself as an exclusionary phenomenon that insists on, for example, the fact that neighborhood identity sometimes may be more important than ethnic or national forms of interpellation.[68] Originating in the fusion and exchange between African American and Puerto Rican communities in New York from the early 1970s on, hip-hop is rooted in the urban culture of the underclass, where, on the one hand, there is consistent and ever-present miscegenation, and, on the other hand, fluid ethnic and social boundaries are always associated with the economic conditions that produce them. Because of the urban nature of hip-hop, it stretches the boundaries of what nationality and culture are.[69] In Cuba, in a context of besieged nationality centered on a culture of resistance, hip-hop was first of all seen as an invasion, an element foreign to the nationalist Cuban sentiment; for hip-hop does not subsume tensions between race and ethnicity, but grants them open play, and it also plays with the notion of an underground that has an organized vernacular from which it can claim authenticity.[70] If validating the existence of this underground was problematic in the 1990s, the fact that it could be openly represented in music was an extremely delicate proposition.

Hip-hop came to Cuba via radio airwaves from Miami. The music started filtering in from U.S. radio stations during the late 1970s and early 1980s in Alamar—an immense housing project of around a hundred thousand people built in the late 1970s to the east of Havana, and separated from the city proper, resulting in better radio and television reception from the north. Alamar was once the pride of revolutionary housing construction, but with the absence of Soviet subsidies it fell into disrepair. Transportation to and from the city was difficult, and the crammed residents of the huge satellite city—many, if not most, Afro-Cubans—found themselves in a dire situation. In the 1990s, young people in Alamar started to rig their antennas to catch Miami radio stations.

Initially, Cuban authorities looked on hip-hop with mistrust. Radio stations did not play it; it was deemed black music and not popular with the audience. Around 1998, Ariel Fernéndez, who had been working at a Havana radio station, started a campaign to get rap validated within state institutions. Fernández, who now works at the Asociación Hermanos Saiz in charge of hip-hop, wrote a manifesto declaring hip-hop an "important cultural phenomenon" and published it in the *El Caimán Barbudo*. In 1999, Abel Prieto, Cuba's minister of culture, declared hip-hop "an authentic expression of Cuban culture" and immediately it began to receive an official imprimatur.[71] Annelise Wunderlich noted that Fidel rapped with the group Doble Filo at a baseball game. Eugene Robinson sees it as wholly state-supported, though he admits that it is a new phenomenon and that it further broadens the limits of expression. He sees it as a way of permitting the impermissible so that the situation does not get out of control, and he detects a tug-of-war within Cuban hip-hop between the political and the material: an "embrace of Western materialism on the one hand and increasing stridency against state authority on the other." There is an air of dangerousness to rap, he notes, though there is no "direct challenge to the state, no questioning of the fundamental tenets of socialism." What rap talks about the most is police harassment and racism.

Fernández was instrumental in making this happen, for it was he who convinced the cultural authorities that hip-hop was not against the revolution. This validation had to occur first of all by remotivating some of rap's more problematic features, and making sure that rap did not cross any lines and turn into "dissent." Criticism of the social circumstances of the Special Period was tolerated, but mass protest was not. As Robinson puts it, "[t]here was a fine line between slamming the police who acted on behalf of the state and slamming the state itself."[72] This is where Pablo Herrera, Cuba's most important hip-hop impresario, enters the picture. Herrera, who at that point was teaching English and Russian translation at the University of Havana, tried to instill in rappers a more socially responsible outlook—to do away with the materialism that they were imitating from the north and to deal constructively with the problems facing Cuban society. Herrera turned not only into rap's promoter, but also its ideologue—in Robinson's phrase, "the Cuban Dr. Dre."[73]

Hip-hop had to position itself in a different space from that of salsa or *timba*—uniformly derided as "too frivolous," too commercial, and too easy by the Cuban hip-hop community. As Robinson makes clear, it also enjoyed the blessing of African American revolutionaries from the United States who fled American justice and have resided in Cuba for more than a decade, such as Nehanda Abiodun, who encouraged the participation in Alamar of such U.S. rap groups as the Black August Collective and the Malcolm X Grassroots Movement—groups that avoid the materialist bent of much of U.S. rap and focus on social problems. In this way, rap turned into what Abidoun calls a "movement."[74] For Annelise Wunderlich it is the belated equivalent of the American Black Panther or revolutionary movements. It blends together African diaspora fights as well as support for Mumia Abu Jamal (whose son has spoken at rallies in Cuba).[75]

Still, the line was not going to hold for long. At the 2002 annual Alamar rap festival, the young rapper Humberto Cabrera took the stage and rapped the lines "Police, police, you are not my friend; for Cuban youth you are the worst punishment," while two young men behind him hoisted a banner that read "Denuncia Social." There, in front of the world media that had come to cover the event, Humberto crossed the line. The authorities did not shut the event down, but it was clear that he was issuing a "blanket indictment," a kind of formal complaint against the system itself.[76] Subsequently, the authorities clamped down: they closed off some venues for hip-hop while "smothering it with bureaucracy and structure and oversight."[77]

This co-optation of hip-hop is a temporary retrenchment that will only be useful in the short term, as a different set of social actors take their place. Hip-hop articulated the question of race in Cuba in terms very different from the discourse on race that the revolution had always produced. But the discussion of race and music also has to take into account nationalism and nationalist traditions. Pablo Herrera has explained that "what makes Cuban hip-hop Cuban is simply that it's being made by Cubans. They're talking about our society from the perspective of people who were born and raised in Cuba during the socialist revolution. It's authentic music in that it's our own."[78] Yet some *raperos* express their distance from Cuban music as an institution—even as a *state* institution. They not only highlight economic difficulties in terms of production and distribution, but also proclaim their distance from the category of *Cuban* music itself. *Raperos* produce music by sampling other people's work, by manipulating equipment, by playing around with sound and beat. In the economy of means and in their use of technology, they stand apart from the presentation of the virtuoso *timba* musician.

Positioning themselves at an angle, in sharp dialectical terms, *raperos* raise questions of *cubanía* and transnational communities of color in ways that are not evident in *timba*'s fusion of *sones* and *charangas*. That the movement came from below, that it points out and leads directly to the "New Cuban Revolution," is part of what makes it so threatening. But the fact that its history can be plotted out with such precision—rigged antennae in Alamar catching radio stations from abroad—as transculturated in the strictest sense of the word, as "invasive" and not necessarily "organic" in its origins, is also part of the question. And the links with U.S. communities of color and their critique of capitalism protects *raperos* from a massive faux pas that would destroy Cuba's long history of contacts with the African American left.

Race and economics are the two categories at play during the 1990s, as they are evidenced in the relationship between hip-hop and *timba*. The revolution can understand race as a discourse and establish a dialogue in ways that are not that precise when it comes to economics—which I have here associated with *timba.* The commercial webs surrounding *timba,* the wealth it was creating, and the image it was giving the island abroad were harder to contain than the more discursive and verbal (i.e., linguistic) realities of rap.

Image is a key revolutionary preoccupation. What the Nueva Trova did was fight against the image, and obliterate it to produce a discursive presentation. The language of words is easier to deal with than the semiotics of the image. Sabá Cabrera's *P.M.* was banned outright, while poets and writers were slowly accommodated or, finally, banished. The lyrics of *timba,* despite their sexism and naughtiness, were not really the issue, because social reality was presented in terms that a heterosexist and misogynist culture could essentialize or brush off. Women's bodies were not the issue— money and capital were. With hip-hop, the rhymes of the young fighter against repression created a combination between images and words that cannot be banished outright. Thus, during the 1990s, the cultural authorities responsible for the production and dissemination of Cuban music, both on the island and abroad, showed a remarkable awareness of the way in which national and transnational publics may collude or collide in terms of apprehending Cuba as a symbol. Having dealt with the economic webs that link Cuban music to a broader transnational market, they guaranteed that, internally, these links would not upset their aims to maintain the population as a cohesive whole. If the capitalist market balkanizes according to consumer taste, the Cuban state will make a note of the fact that there is variety within Cuba, but at no point can this difference threaten the collective project of a unified population, which is an image that should prove indelible in the future.

Still Searching for
Ana Mendieta

I never met Cuban artist Ana Mendieta (1948–85) in any of the places where our paths might have crossed, and our only connection is the fact that we were born on the same island. Our lives did not intersect, even if in the late 1970s and early 1980s we moved among similar political circles. Her first return to Cuba was in January 1980, and mine was in July of the same year. I have replayed my own mental Super-8 film, and found nothing until I realized we are linked not by content, but by arbitrary relations placed at one site like a crossword. She established contiguous relationships with things; events happened in particular spaces, and part of her work was fully controlled yet completely open. So, this is really not an essay about Mendieta and myself, but rather an essay on Mendieta and our relationship to Cuba.

Mendieta was a visual artist, a sculptor, and a performer. She created land-body art, assumed all of its physical challenges, and embarked on a journey that allowed her to deal with the past, with identity, and with heritage. She traced connections between disparate things, placed herself in different sites by means of different media (Super-8 film, performances with earth, blood, and wood) and dealt with critical issues (feminism, identity, politics, antimuseum efforts) in work whose themes were displacement, ubiquity, movement, absence, space, and time. She invited those receptive to her work to witness events she created using natural elements, and these events were deceptively simple: lumps of sand and flowers washed by the ocean, a figure consuming itself as it was lit by fire, or twigs and branches as they floated downstream on a river. Mendieta created crossings and paradoxes—of film and body, of organic reproduction and decay—that then became transcendent by virtue of mechanical repetition, because film was the only trace of their existence.

The nature of the engagement Mendieta produced through her art was affective at all levels; we script ourselves into the art, and read our own lives through it. There is nothing to be gained by resisting this process of identification because it was one she demanded. Mendieta always claimed her place of birth and the traumatic events that as a child forced her to leave it as central to her art. She derived her strength, however, from playing with, and moving out of, the expected narrative of exile. She turned that narrative upside down by insisting on the way in which she was always *more,* not *less*: her working agenda seems to have been addition, not subtraction, layering one image over the other, not paring it down. She returned to the Cuban space that so many of her compatriots in exile during the 1970s thought it a crime to visit, and she created works in a cave (hidden works

Ana Mendieta, *Untitled* (from Silueta series), 1976. Red flowers on *silueta* on sand, Mexico. Courtesy of the Estate of Ana Mendieta and Galerie Lelong, New York.

she called the *Rupestrian Sculptures*) as an homage to Caribbean native populations decimated by imperialism. It was the vague recollection that I
had that these pieces existed that motivated my search for them, and for
the trace that Mendieta as a Cuban-American artist left in me. I did not
set out to find the real meaning of her work, or to retrace her journey. It
was not the search for my roots that brought me there; it was the search
for a particular time and space. I was not clear about what I was looking
for—perhaps a way to *forget* Cuba, not necessarily reclaim it, or perhaps I
was looking for a way to forget the particular circumstances of having been
born there, and then leaving. I know what Mendieta meant for me, but I
really didn't know what I was trying to see by means of her work—except
that it had to do with Cuba, and Cuba can only be forgotten by being there.

Engagement with Cuba had been a subject of interest for me for years,
but it reached a new level when I visited the island in 2000—a different
time from the present Mendieta lived in 1980. I went on that trip fully
aware that the present was not a carbon copy of the past. Life in Cuba had
changed in ways that affected both art and economics. Some of the artists
Mendieta had met in the early 1980s had already left the island; others
stayed, or negotiated different ways of living within the revolution. Her
generation now had a time and a space in history, and they have been
the subject of homage and retrospectives. The arts institutions that she
dealt with and that allowed her permission to work have now transformed
themselves into NGOs, although they still are governmental associations.
They market Cuban art and artists abroad, serving as agents, publicists,
and disseminators.

I enlisted two poets for an expedition to Jaruco, to search for any traces
of the *Rupestrian Sculptures* she had carved in 1981. The poets were Carlos
Aguilera and Pedro Marqués de Armas, who published an independent
journal in Cuba called *Diásporas,* a very "Mendietan" name. *Diásporas* was
not really a journal, though, but a bunch of papers photocopied without
any support from the state and distributed by the two remaining members
of a collective that had left the island during the past five years. I did not
contact any of the appropriate authorities in Havana, did not ask about
the sculptures, got permission from no one, and received no guidance or
orientation for this trip. Mendieta was an important artist—she was remembered on the island, and Carlos and Pedro had heard about her work.
This was initially just an outing, a day in the country, a kind of picnic.

Just as Mendieta's work demanded all sorts of transgressions, from the beginning the act of searching for her sculptures involved various kinds of crossings, legalities and illegalities. We took a beaten-up Chevy from the Plaza del Vapor and, because these cars are reserved for use by Cubans living on the island, technically I was not allowed to ride in one. We were silent on the way out of Havana, until at one point it was clear that the driver would not and could not turn back. Unlike drivers Mendieta must have hired back then, this one worked on his own, not for a government agency. Ownership of the vehicle was hard to determine—it might have been his, or he might have borrowed it from a neighbor and split the profits—and it was quite possible that he was not allowed to take it beyond the city limits. At various points along the road, vendors were selling their own fruit; the state seemed everywhere to be in the process of being dismantled by its citizens. During the trip a strange sort of history began to weave itself into this tale, almost like a hidden history of the revolution that was slowly being uncovered.

It always seemed to me that the sense of being Cuban those of us had who were raised outside of the island of our birth (what is termed *cubanía*) could only be grasped by means of paradox, or chiasmus: it was a sense of pride and place that was also marked by interruption and traumatic absence. Mendieta's was a *cubanía* of interruption that had its own coherence: a sentence left in mid-phrase, a chapter left uncompleted, a book half read, a tale broken up into fragments. It was also a *cubanía* of reproduction, one that flourished outside of the island, in the most dissimilar places and circumstances. What I saw in Havana was hard to understand in terms of how the recent past had created this present, and it was a strange combination of interruption and continuity. In spite of the sense of organicity and historical continuity the revolution insisted upon, I did not feel that there was necessarily an organic relationship to a history that had taken place as recently as 1980, when no private enterprise was yet allowed on the island and the Soviet Union was still a world power. In fact, I had the distinct feeling that there had been a break between then and now, or perhaps that the time in which Mendieta and I had visited Cuba was a bounded moment, a closed-in space that would return no more, and that now Cuba once again was related to its Caribbean neighbors. It was that *other* time in 1980 that was an interruption, and not the present. Although in 2000 we were in what the government called the "Special

Period in Times of Peace," the Special Period seemed to be the other one, not this one.

Mendieta's story gets repeated in every essay on her work; hers was a conscious aesthetic and political decision to inscribe within the work of art the life story of the artist who produced it. When Mendieta was taken out of Cuba in 1961, the country felt new, and so did exile. She was born in 1948, her maternal grandmother was the daughter of a general who fought in the wars of independence, and Carlos Mendieta, her granduncle, was president of Cuba in the 1930s. Before her mother and father left the island—the mother in 1966, the father in 1978—Mendieta's parents sent Ana and her sister Raquel, ages twelve and fifteen, to the United States in 1961 as part of Operation Pedro Pan, a program run by the Catholic church and the U.S. government.[1] The girls arrived in Miami on September 11, 1961, and were separated from their parents for five years until 1966, when her mother was finally granted a visa to leave. Her father left the island in December 1978, and came to the United States in April 1979.[2] During the years when Ana and her sister were separated from their parents, they spent time at a camp in Miami and then were sent to an orphanage in Dubuque, Iowa. They were shuttled from one foster home to another, where they encountered a different racial climate from the one they had been accustomed to at home. Although they were "white" Cubans, they were seen as "brown" or even "black" and suffered racial taunts. Mendieta turned these traumatic childhood experiences into a concept that would become crucial for her work: detachment or separation:

> All detachment or separation provokes a wound. A rupture, whether it is with ourselves or what surrounds us or with the past or present produces a feeling of aloneness. In my case where I was separated from my parents and my country at the age of 12, this feeling of aloneness identified itself as a form of orphanhood. And it manifested itself as consciousness of sin. The penalties and shame of separation caused me necessary sacrifices and solitude as a way of purifying myself. You live it, like proof and promise of communion.[3]

For thirteen years, from 1972 to 1985, in Iowa and then in New York, Mendieta produced an extraordinary body of work, from Super-8 films and videos to performances, site-specific installations, sculptures, drawings, and prints.[4] Her images were totemic in their *search* for a kind of raw power. "Imperialism," she explained, "is no longer a problem of expansion so much but of reproduction."[5] Her art was predicated on form understood as a living thing, within a process of transformation. This emphasis on change is what draws spectators to her work: they feel drawn not because they want to complete the work, but because they are in it as witnesses to an act that occurred at one specific time, and that can always be reenacted. At some level, the jump from event to film creates the work of art as something that has crossed borders. There was an essence to the artistic piece—it existed or had existed at a given point in time—but what was important was the change produced *on* it, as if it had a life cycle of its own. From event, to film, and then to photography, the object defined itself differently depending on the means used to reproduce it. The camera crossed the border between site and representation. It created ubiquity—the sense that the work could be at any place at any time—and it allowed for the visual to be a trace, one that could allow the viewer to relive the moment in which it originated. As in Michelangelo Antonioni's *Blowup*, photography allows us to multiply the site of representation, but also to take an event from one place to another. The photographer in *Blowup* amplifies the images he takes of a murder to such a degree that the event itself takes place in the space of reproduction: the apartment where the images are being displayed.

In retrospect, it is hard not to succumb to the temptation to see this work as a commentary on the exilic situation. I should emphasize that my intention is not to "Cubanize" Mendieta's work, but to understand the context in which it was formed, and allow the work itself to illuminate the situation that produced it. It seems that for Mendieta the only response to exile was the desire for reproduction, and I can see traces of this same operation when the memory of a site in Havana becomes a picture of it in Miami. We could be living, all of us, amid the photographic traces of the things that disappear—or, perversely, we could say that the building we see in the Havana photograph taken in 1959 is still there, though our memory of it is what is fading with time. The paradox in Mendieta's work is that, for example, she did not photograph her house in Varadero and allow it to be changed by the art of time, but she created an impermanent work of art that achieved the same consistency that the house in Varadero once had.

In terms of her own *cubanía* as well as in her art, Mendieta assumed that taxonomies existed a priori and then cut them loose. She reminds me of poets who intuitively know that chance operations imply searching for a form and structure that are not necessarily created by the self. She reined in the elements in order to allow them to disperse once again. The object was not contained but could inhabit different times and different spaces by means of film and photography. This could be seen as a parody of what was understood as a work of art, with all its transcendent and immutable implications, and it was also a celebration of the impermanence of art. That the object disappears and that we have access only to its reproduction is just one part of the equation. What it loses by means of its disappearance is gained by a corresponding notion of ubiquity: the work could be in many places at the same time. To speak of this along an axis of "parody" and "tragedy" may not do justice to the works themselves; better terms might be "emotional" and "distant." We feel a loss in terms of the evanescent object being filmed, but Mendieta wants us not only to mourn its loss, but also to celebrate its transformation.

This distance created by means of the emotional attachment to the object—an attachment that was guarded and controlled so that it would not produce a sentimental reaction—can be seen in Mendieta's way of shocking, startling, and bewildering her audience. In *Glass on Body* (Iowa, 1972) she put on panty hose and deliberately contorted her body, or pressed her body—breasts, buttocks, stomach, pubis—against a plate of glass.[6] The work demonstrated to what extent contortion is its own construction, a result of seeing things in a different way. She could heighten the audience's perceptions by using all available means, impacting the viewers with viscera and blood, as in her filming the reactions of passersby to a pool of blood on the street in 1973, or, in the most shocking such event, when people in 1973 came into her house and found her covered in blood. This was done in response to a series of rapes on the Iowa campus, and it was in this piece that she most forcefully turned her body into the subject and the object of the work. From the very first, her works revealed a fascination with the viewer that was also a fascination with herself, with her own reactions to the work. She traced the blood outlines of a decapitated chicken, she did blood work on her body. She wanted to blur the contours, play with the edges, start out from a localized space and then move about. This was not necessarily an organic blending that proceeds from one place to the next, but a process that leads to a transformation.

Transformation was also the theme of an early work called *Facial Hair Transplant,* done in Iowa in 1972. It is one of the most important of her early works. She and another student, Morty Sklar, engaged in a ritual exercise: Morty shaved while Ana attached *his* hair to *her* face. The pictures follow the procedure from the beginning, and at the end Mendieta had herself photographed with the hair pasted onto her face. Her description of the piece was simple, and she mentions as background Marcel Duchamp's drawing a mustache on the Mona Lisa:

> What I did was to transfer his beard to my face . . . By transfer I mean to take an object from one place and to put it in another. I like the idea of transferring hair from one person to another because I think it gives me that person's strength.[7]

The transfer is a transfer of energy, and she understands this transfer (never a robbing of energy, in a zero-sum game, but rather an exchange) as part of a ritual whereby she will become something else: "After looking at myself in a mirror," she explained, "the beard became real. It did not look like a disguise. It became part of myself and not at all unnatural to my appearance."[8] The hair is naturalized, it can grow on one surface but be pasted onto the next and become more than a simple disguise for the subject who wears it; Mendieta does not seem to be concerned with how

Ana Mendieta, *Untitled (Facial Hair Transplants),* March–April 1972, University of Iowa. From a suite of seven color photographs documenting Mendieta's facial exchange (beard) with a fellow student. Courtesy of the Estate of Ana Mendieta and Galerie Lelong, New York.

the spectator reacts, or whether he or she deems the object a disguise. The process entails an act of self-observation and self-recognition; the artist is in front of a mirror, and the mirror itself is an important component of the piece. Mendieta is not trying to hide who she is by pasting on the beard, nor is she trying to use the beard to reveal something about herself. The beard "becomes" natural; it acts upon the self just as the artist's gaze acts on her own face. The object changes because of the act of looking at it. The observer—in this case, the artist who observes herself—changes what is being looked at. The gaze itself works just as the object (the beard) works: they both bring about change.

I can imagine the piece originating in an offhand comment, even as a joke. What is significant for me is the act of Mendieta's becoming a *bar-buda*, with all the connotations that being a "bearded" one had for Cubans at the time. Her rebel's way of understanding the revolution also entailed inhabiting that character, becoming the feminine revolutionary by means of an object pasted onto her face. That the object (the beard) had a genealogy—it comes from Marty Sklar—establishes a clear filial line. The observer sees where the hair comes from, and is allowed to perceive other beginnings to the act of becoming. I don't think Mendieta is exploring gender—her own self, for example, as a drag king—but something else. The romance of the bearded revolutionaries produced the early images of the revolution, the photographic register of the golden years of photogenic construction that traveled throughout the world. Mendieta's *barbudo* is not portrayed at a moment of panache, talking to Jean-Paul Sartre or Malcolm X, or in a quiet, melancholic moment imperfectly assuming the weight of the world. Here, black and white is substituted for color and the sideways picture is frozen in a statutory pose. She cuts a classical figure, the end of the *barbudo* as historical star, the death knell of its symbolic significance in the present.

Not diluting the beard, but precisely *pasting* it on, played with the idea of culture as pastiche, reality as a simulation, and transculturation as an active mode of engagement. There is an economy to the inorganic tufts of hair that has nothing to do with filial relationships; it is not necessarily carried in the blood but rather pasted on with the same sense of mediated agency (it is Mendieta herself who demands that her friend cut those pieces of hair) that compels and demands at the same time a given position. The beard is not an assumption of a male persona, but rather, precisely, a mode

Mendieta as a *barbuda,* or bearded revolutionary. From *Untitled (Facial Hair Transplants),* March–April 1972, University of Iowa. Courtesy of the Estate of Ana Mendieta and Galerie Lelong, New York.

of questioning essentialism in art. What happens at a specific moment in time is less important than all the possible permutations that temporality can bring to bear upon the object. The object in itself transmigrates. It does not come in stealthily in order to reveal itself later; its transmission is done openly, cut up from one body to the other. To cut and to paste, and to exhibit the operation as the hair moves from one body to the other, from one hand to the other's body, exhibits its own interruption as spectacle. It is as if the act had to include the moment in which the hair itself is suspended in air.

SILUETAS (SILHOUETTES)

When Mendieta returned to Cuba in 1980, in the first of seven trips, she wanted to bridge a gap—in her life, in her art, in the nation's politics.[9] She placed her body between two geographies and aimed to join them into one temporality. She managed to work with this idea as part of a national construct, for she surely understood that Cuba is made up of elements pasted onto a national surface that is constantly changing. Mendieta was a visual artist working with technology and earth, but she was also surrounded by paper, and her work colludes and collides with the paperwork of citizenship, nationality, politics, and government. She had to deal with permissions and with authorizations in Cuba, and sought guidance from artists in order to figure out how to secure them from the Cuban Ministry of Culture. She had to surmount resistance and then official indifference to her work. She was suspect not because of her political affiliations but because she was an exile. As such, she had to apply and reapply for permission to enter the country of her birth. Mendieta may have felt Cuban, but the Cuban state classified her as something else.

Even in 2000, when Pedro, Carlos, and I went to look for the caves in Jaruco, the Cuban state raised the question of ownership. Who owns the piece of land where the sculptures are placed? What government entity is in charge of its slow unfolding into disappearance? It would seem that in Cuba, Mendieta just went and did her stuff—but such was the deceptive simplicity of her work. In order to be realized, her work also needed government paperwork granting permits. A provincial government official in Jaruco disputed the assertion that an institute in Havana owned the site, saying it was under the control of the provincial government even if it was in a national park. But the official, who had lived in Jaruco all her life, had no idea that there were sculptures there, that an art object existed within a national park, and that this art object was visited by people from abroad. No schoolchildren came to look for Mendieta on a holiday trip, and no homage to the work of exile was possible in a context in which fragile carvings on rock were stealthily viewed by visitors from abroad accompanied by Havana authorities. Other caves have been set up as visitor sites, but not these. Mendieta's work might not have attracted a constant stream of visitors, but what was interesting was that in spite of her insistence on her connection with earth, there was no connection here in terms of the work's surrounding administrative context.

Clearly this was a solitary work that had remained in its solitude for decades, with few *jaruquenses* knowing of its existence; it was also clearly an intervention from abroad, a deracinated piece that disappeared, only to leave the trace of its absence. In terms of capital and tourism—even literate tourism—it is not clear what the question of the cultural object in the land is all about. This paperwork is part of the problem, and it surrounds the work, especially in terms of crossing the border into Cuba, which was a difficult and contentious border to cross in the early 1980s.

The Cuban context for *Rupestrian Sculptures* is broadly political. Between November and December 1978, 140 Cubans participated in two discussion sessions that from then on were called the diálogo.[10] They were meant to soften the tense relationship between Cuban exiles and the government.[11] It was not really a political movement, as some in Miami have thought, but rather a kind of synergy put into motion by factors inside and outside the island. Many of its younger members had been students radicalized in the 1960s and 1970s in the United States. The *diálogo* was open, but many of those who participated demanded a right of return and some formed travel groups, modeled on other work-study groups popular at the time. Cuban-born residents, or citizens of the United States, traveled as the Antonio Maceo Brigade, in honor of the Cuban nineteenth-century independence fighter. Its members held a variety of political views, but it seems that Mendieta did not want her art to be associated with politics. The Brigade was part of a broader network of associations that included the Círculo José María Heredia, the Center for Cuban Studies, the Círculo de Cultura Cubana, and *Areíto* magazine.

These events were extremely important for those of us who lived abroad.

For the first time in twenty years, it seemed an opening up was possible, that the Cuban–U.S. impasse was going to come to an end. This accommodation was tentative, from the government's side, but it did signal a change. Although in 1976 the Cuban Ministry of Culture tried to put an end to inconsistencies in dealing with artists, Cuba as a whole was still a repressive place throughout the 1970s. Cubans on the island now refer to this period as "el quinquenio gris" (the five gray years), when the government's repressive apparatus was felt keenly. They tend to limit it to 1971–76, but censorship was fierce throughout the decade. That there was, in the latter part of the decade, a cautious openness toward an accommodation with the United States and with some segments of the exile population suggests that the government was searching for ways to open up.

For those of us who took advantage of that moment in time, the revolutionary state recognized citizenship by virtue of birthright, not by naturalization. Although many of us were naturalized citizens of the United States, Cuba did not recognize that citizenship in any person who had been born on the island. Because it was an exceptional country, the Cuban state turned us into an exceptional category. In order to travel to Cuba in the late 1970s, Cuban-born U.S. citizens were given a Cuban passport, issued as a *new* document, meant to replace the previous one, given to the citizen at the moment of departure. With this new passport, which the state kept after the visitor left the island, Cubans were allowed to travel in and out of the island. The paperwork that produced this classification (or the classification that produced this paperwork) created a euphemistic category called the Cuban Community Abroad (in shortened form, *la comunidad*). This name, this category, allowed us to travel to the island for the first time in twenty years. Visits were allowed for a fixed amount of time (two weeks) and for a specific price. But "visiting" had economic repercussions. Visitors from capitalism needed capitalism—they needed products—so the state set up stores where "visitors" could buy consumer goods, at exorbitant prices, for Cubans living on the island (called "relatives").

I mention all this because it considerably complicates Mendieta's work as an artist, her position within Cuba, the work she did in Cuba, and what critics see in that work. Critics have seen her work within the sentimental parameters that Mendieta herself employed: Mendieta was "home," she created these works as an homage to "Cuba." And certainly, within the system of classification that defined citizenship back then, Mendieta was literally "at home," just as many other Cubans (including myself) "returned" to Cuba and went "home" in 1980. But the question of "being home" is also mediated by the particularities of this art, by the particularities of this subject, and by the particularities of this state. None of us really went "home" to Cuba in 1980; too many events had already happened in the preceeding twenty years, and home was in many ways a constructed fiction, an imaginary landscape, an alternate past in the present that lived on in memories repeated almost mechanically.

The first of Mendieta's seven recorded trips was in January 1980.[12] It was organized by the Círculo de Cultura Cubana, and participants were taken around the island on a fact-finding mission to visit hospitals, factories, schools, and other revolutionary institutions. These may have been political and ideological tours, but it was hard at that time to negotiate other kinds of trips. One traveler later recalled that Mendieta convinced the tour driver to take a small detour to Cárdenas so she could visit family, and she was later granted permission to stay in Havana one more week.[13] This says something about the way Mendieta was treated by the government. On other trips, the authorities insisted that every part of the schedule be adhered to, for these encounters were also important ideological statements, given the complex relationships between Cubans. The revolution saw these visits as opportunities to educate Cubans and other foreigners, while many Cubans saw them as deeply personal journeys. The personal and political agendas frequently collided, as many returnees wanted to revisit their past, while the revolution was constantly showing them the present. Sources close to Mendieta have explained that during her seventh and last trip she was interrogated and searched by the authorities, because she was taking out of the country china belonging to her grandmother. The state did not consider it personal property, and Mendieta had to leave it behind.

On her second trip, in January 1981, Mendieta began to make inroads into the art scene in Havana. Between her first and second visits, the Mariel exodus took place (in June 1980), though this event apparently did not diminish her desires to reconnect with the island. On her second trip, Mendieta met Cuban art critic Gerardo Mosquera, as well as those who were her generational cohorts: José Bedia, Ricardo Rodríguez Brey, and Flavio Garciandía. She also established a closer rapport with her cousin,

Raquel "Kaky" Mendieta, who was instrumental in steering Ana toward revolutionary history, as well as Cuba's indigenous past. It was during this second visit that she met Beatriz Aulet and José Veigas, who worked at the Ministry of Culture and arranged for her work in Jaruco to be given an official imprimatur. The Ministry of Culture did not finance the project, but it did issue the required permits. She proceeded to visit the Escaleras de Jaruco, a national park about ninety miles from Havana with rocky terraces and caves made of a soft, porous rock that could be carved with relative ease.

Mendieta was introduced to the caves in Jaruco by Ricardo Rodríguez Brey, who taught at the Casa de la Cultura there. She undoubtedly chose Jaruco because of her contacts and because the caves resonated with hidden connections. There may be some significance to the fact that, as Luis Camnitzer points out in *New Art in Cuba,* the Almendares River, which flows through Havana and out to sea, starts in Jaruco, but it is more likely that the caves appealed to Mendieta because of their alternative history in contrast to the grander events of Cuban history: they had been used by indigenous people, and they had served as a refuge for pirates, for escaped slaves, and for the nineteenth-century independence fighters known as Mambises, in their war against Spain.

There were ten larger-than-life figures in the *Rupestrian Sculptures,* carved on two locations in Jaruco.[14] Mendieta created a film with them appearing in sequence, but only exhibited the large-format pictures of the individual figures. She named each of the pieces with Taino names and to make her meaning clear she attached to those Taino names English explanatory titles. These were Itiba Cuhababa (Old Mother Blood), Guabancex (Goddess of the Wind), Atabey (Mother of the Waters), Maroya and Guanaroca (The First Woman), Guacar (Our Menstruation). She wanted to suggest, at some level, primitive cave art, and intended to create for the viewer the effect of having just stumbled onto an ancient site. She worked with the natural contours of the rock, but she also used paint and chisel to bring out defining details. The sculptures were not imposed on the site, but rather seemed to have been brought out from it. The lines carved onto the rock are shapes more than figures per se. One of them (Itiba Cuhababa) seems like the imprint of bones upon the rock, as if the sculpture in itself were the remnant of that which created its sequence of nine parallel bones, resembling a rib cage.

Jaruco did not simply allow Mendieta to rediscover origins, but to inscribe in a Borgesian manner her origins onto the future—*her* own creation of *her* own precursors inscribed within the temporal space of the present. It was an intellectual pursuit that she understood as a personal quest.[15] Her fascination with the Indian was the product of a Cuban-American's intellectual work—chiefly, of Yale professor José Juan Arrom's investigations into the subject.[16] Arrom, even before Mendieta, had straddled the

The carvings at Jaruco are the most ambitious artistic work done by a Cuban exile in the island after the revolution. Documentation of *Guanaroca (Primera Mujer)*, *Cuerva del Águila, Parque Jaruco, La Habana*, 1981. Courtesy of the Estate of Ana Mendieta and Galerie Lelong, New York.

political divide between the two countries with his investigations into the Cuban pre-Columbian heritage. Mendieta wanted to create a book to document Arrom's work, and she wanted him to write an introductory essay. She understood this heritage as part of her origins: "I have thrown myself into the very elements that produced me," she explained.[17]

The search for Taino roots was also part of the cultural imaginary of the Caribbean at the time, which was rediscovering its roots in disappeared Taino cultures. It was validated in the Nueva Trova, a popular Cuban musical form that migrated to the wider Caribbean area during the late 1960s and the 1970s with an anti-imperialist message. The pieces in Jaruco incorporate feminism, anticolonialism, earth art, and the autobiography of exile. This makes the sculptures very specific but it also allows them to cross over into distinct territories negotiated by the images themselves.

Searching for those sculptures in 2000 proved to be an exercise in putting together pieces of a different puzzle. And it produced a new understanding

Documentation of *Itiba Cahubaba*/Old Mother Blood (Esculturas Rupestres/ Rupestrian Sculptures), 1981. Courtesy of the Estate of Ana Mendieta and Galerie Lelong, New York.

of time in a context in which it was the work of art that had disappeared. Insisting on the Tainos as a point of origin was a way of reconnecting with something that is totally dead and leaves barely a trace. Mendieta saw herself as the heir to that culture: "as a Cuban-American and cultural inheritor of the Tainan Culture." This statement's power derives from the authority given to cultures that leave traces, and to the fact that there are subjects who also engage in the work of connecting and reconnecting cultures, by means of underground contacts. These contacts bore fruit in the work of young artists in Cuba who followed Mendieta's example throughout the 1980s, after her untimely death.[18] Even as she was working on the *Rupestrian Sculptures,* a generational shift in art was occurring on the island, marked by the exhibit Volumen 1 in 1981, and the opening of the Centro Wifredo Lam in 1983. She knew many of those artists, yet she could not exhibit with them because she lived outside the island. She presented work in 1981, and she contributed a photograph in 1982 to a Casa de las Américas exhibit on Cuban photography, becoming the first Cuban exile to be invited to exhibit work along with that of Cuban nationals. She also had a solo exhibition of her work in 1983, titled Geo-Imago, at the Museo Nacional de Bellas Artes. In 1984, she sent a small drawing executed on a leaf to an exhibition at the Havana Biennal. The leaf, in the collection of the Centro Wifredo Lam, is one of the few surviving pieces of her work in Cuba.

The contentious dynamics between the government and new artistic groups continued throughout the 1980s. The last Arte Calle show, in October 1988, was closed down by the government. The same happened that year to exhibitions of Tomás Esson, Carlos Cárdenas, and Glexis Novoa, titled A brazo partido II. Exhibitions at the Proyecto Castillo de la Real Fuerza in 1989 were closed down by the government, and the vice minister of culture, Marcia Leiseca, was removed from office.[19]

These very public events stand in marked contrast to the stealth events that surrounded Mendieta's stay in Cuba. The slow dismantling of her pieces on-site seems to uncannily anticipate the slow demise of the revolution itself. The revolution was a work of art also, and when one looks for traces of its past one finds unfoldings and permutations. The process by which Mendieta rescued and revisited events from the past in order to bring them to the present implied a notion of time that was also part of the historical landscape of the revolution.

CAVES

It was a utopian gesture, back in 1980, to think that all traumas could be resolved if only we went back to the place of our birth and tried to achieve closure. It was not clear what exactly this gesture could accomplish—perhaps a rebirth, an erasure, or a detachment. It might also produce a fatalistic understanding, an acceptance, of the inexorability of time: you could go back to the place you left, or the place you were forced to leave, but ultimately you can never go back and reclaim a decision that was never yours to begin with. Epistemologically, you were something else, other than Cuban, even if Cuba was always the ontology that gave some meaning to existence. Erasing or consigning to a deliberate amnesia everything that had happened during the intervening years was an option, and there was a political investment in accepting history as it had been lived, with its twists of fate and its chance events. These were real debates about identity, and the choices they presented were difficult. In order to accept the way things were, one had to accept the revolution uncritically. Ultimately, I suppose that at the end of those trips to Cuba there was a process of what many might call a process of healing. But to look at the *Rupestrian Sculptures* as the end of that process may or may not be a satisfying gesture. Yes, the old wounds were healed, but the acceptance of the wound entailed its own kind of phenomenological closure. To claim a Cuban identity that could be in solidarity with, but also in disagreement with, the revolutionary process entailed a mediated distance that was hard to negotiate in personal terms, when so many events demanded a firm and resolute position. To this day, it is extremely hard for those of us living outside of the island when artists or writers in Cuba defy the expectations of solidarity inherent in governmental policy and end up being ostracized. The bonds of solidarity we feel with the artist are pitted against the bonds of solidarity we feel with the political project. At other times, solidarity with the project is belied by a governmental decision to critique its own mistakes. Those of us who went to Cuba in 1980 felt allegiance with policies that later on, in the 1990s, the government itself realized were in error. We also heard countless denunciations of those who were, back then, leaving the island through the port of Mariel, though many years later the government itself took a more conciliatory position toward them. At what point does one collude or collide with the other, within the "us versus them" context in which this political discourse exists?

Mendieta must have found this a difficult terrain to negotiate, given the different accounts of how she reacted during her various trips with the different audiences she related to in Cuba. The desire to create the work of art trumps all political categories; to accomplish her work surely meant negotiating the terrains of loyalty to the project as well as faith in art. Her positionalities are partly the measure of this, as Mendieta moved in different circles. She did not talk politics with her friends in Miami who had left the island, but she could stake out adamantly pro-revolutionary positions with foreigners whom she perceived could not understand Cuban particularities. Within the leftist feminist context in which she thrived in New York, she faced demands of solidarity with Cuba expected from North Americans who approach the island's history with a mixture of fascination, imperial guilt, and redemptive politics. The difficult situation in which we found ourselves was reflected in our own kinds of mediation. Not wanting to seem fragile or wishy-washy, we modulate according to the speaker who is asking us for our opinions, until we find a comfortable space from which to venture our agreement or disagreement, dejection or critique. We can be very critical among friends living in Cuba, who are themselves critical of absurd government policies and arbitrary decisions, and we can triangulate ourselves in front of U.S. citizens according to race or politics, while holding on to principles of justice when dealing with absurdly reactionary impulses, and, at the same time, keeping a respectful silence faced with the pain and loss of exile.

It was clear in 1980 that we did not own completely whatever it was that brought us to the island, for we were part of a bigger puzzle where social justice, power, and politics were being played out. Mendieta was interviewed on Cuban television, and the trips, as well as those of her generational cohorts, were publicized in the press. Wanting to reconnect and engage with Cuba was paramount, and if that entailed allowing ourselves to be photographed and filmed, this was a space we could always rationalize; it did not mean a lack of commitment to resolving the problems at hand, but was a way of negotiating the personal and the political. It was interesting in this context to learn of the problematic nature of Mendieta's last encounters in Cuba—not because one needs to place her in any position other than the one she laboriously staked out for herself, but because it gives a measure of a silenced disenchantment that would have produced not open dissidence, but further nuance. Olga Viso has noted that Mendieta's last solo exhibition in Havana, Geo-Imago in 1983, was poorly attended and did not receive much publicity. She was allowed into the country then, though a month before the exhibit she could not secure a Cuban visa to attend her grandmother's funeral in Cárdenas. She was frustrated by the fact that venues for her art seemed to be more difficult, and the authorities did not seem welcoming. These negative feelings reached a critical point when Mendieta was stopped and searched by Cuban customs officials, who discovered some of her grandmother's personal effects, particularly a tea service. The officials told her that these effects now belonged to the Cuban state. As Viso puts it, "[t]raumatized by the experience and, by all accounts, unable to secure her grandmother's possessions, Mendieta left the island, vowing never to return."[20] I can relate to this stance, for the bonds of affection produce such gestures. Returning, and vowing never to return, are two sides of the same coin.

Reclaiming that past within this present was part of what took me to those caves in Jaruco with Pedro Marqués de Armas and Carlos Aguilera. The past I found was more than I bargained for, because the history that I had learned, and possibly the history Mendieta had read about, was not the one encountered once outside the established circuits of authority. We took side roads and went in and out of caves. We asked *guajiros* sitting out on the porch before and after lunch about the sculptures of a certain Cuban artist who lived abroad. Carlos Aguilera was very careful to explain this correctly: he put the accent on the Cuban, and he emphasized that she lived abroad—a territory that was not necessarily the United States but that had resonance as belonging to a world out there that was external (*el exterior* was the common bureaucratic formula he appropriately used) to the world of Jaruco and the world of the revolution.

It was one thing to visit Cuba on the political tourist route, and another to allow oneself the time to connect with other aspects of Cuban reality. As haphazard as it all was, I am sure that Mendieta too learned that some of the Jaruco caves held many recent memories of clandestine homosexual weddings, and that they had been used as places where rockers and pot-smoking disaffected youth would meet. As we searched for the caves where Mendieta created her works, the hidden story of the very visible revolution was slowly untangled for us; we understood that it was not a question of believing in everything that was visible, but of uncovering that which visibility somehow managed to hide. The patient driver of that old

beat-up Chevy took us up a mountain to an abandoned restaurant im-
plausibly called El Mesón del Árabe where there seemed to have been no
customers for twenty years and Spanish tiles were meant to reproduce a
Moroccan ambiance created by a Syrian owner in the late 1970s. These
were the remnants of the internationalist project that intervened in almost
every facet of Cuban life throughout revolutionary history—not the intervention of global capital that one can see now, but the webs of revolutionary solidarity. We were sent to a park, to which our amiable, patient driver
then took us, and Aguilera shouted out again to a woman who was patiently
sleeping her afternoon siesta under a mango tree if she knew where we
could find these sculptures that a Cuban artist who had lived abroad had
carved on a rock. Surprisingly, at that very moment when we were about
to go back to Havana, that woman sitting under the mango tree said yes,
she knew where we could find them.

She elaborated on her story, recalling that some Germans had come to
look for them two weeks earlier but couldn't find them. She called an amateur speleologist and Carlos and Pedro waited while the young man and I
went in and out of caves. I saw bats and bat dung and bees and centipedes
and huge tropical leaves and rocks, but no trace of any cave where Ana
Mendieta might have carved her sculptures for posterity—and certainly
not for us, three Cubans from two countries, perhaps one nation, paying
for a Cuban driver of a beat-up American Chevy in dollars to be taken to
a place where, perhaps, a Cuban artist who lived abroad and incarnated
the sad history that produced the present had carved out sculptures of
Taino goddesses that were claimed by a foundation in Havana as possible
sources of cultural revenue and hard cash.

There was no use rationalizing or even inquiring further into this tangled web that irradiated meaning in the process of its unfolding, rather than
in the fixed act that might produce the object. The act of not finding these
sculptures in no way meant defeat. It made no sense to me at the time
to call a foundation in Havana for directions in finding some sculptures
in Jaruco. It made more sense to figure out the dislocations and the ruptures of an intervention that was already marked by the elements that controlled it, and by the ones that were to refuse to be marked by it.

On another trip, I again asked about the sculptures. And one afternoon,
as I was looking into the, at the time, semi-clandestine collages of an artist
who had been an "official" artist who created posters and advertisements

for the revolution, but who was also homosexual, I was put in contact with someone from the Ludwig Foundation in Havana who told me, once and for all, and without a doubt, that Mendieta's sculptures had disappeared forever, that the earth had reclaimed them just as she wanted. The object no longer existed, except as the memory of the object, and time had worked as an element of the sculpture itself, as Mendieta had always wanted.

Any attempt at understanding Mendieta involves that process of looking for her, the unfolding of a narrative that allows us to be in different times and places and that forces us to join one signifier to another, relating them in unseemly ways. Stand on a bridge over the Iowa River in winter. Allow yourself the sort of deep understanding of things that Mendieta would have wanted you to have. Remain still as if you were performing in one of her works, and let whatever there is on the outside diffuse the clear boundaries you have set for yourself. Look at a group of ducks swimming on the river; notice how a particular tree branch cracks and falls; remain still and follow with your eyes a dead leaf floating on the water. Mendieta engaged that scene, framed it without really turning it into the object "nature." She let it remain what it is, what it was: a loose organization of things that could always achieve a loose sense of unity at a given moment.

I stood inside a cave, with the amateur speleologist at my side. I was not in Iowa, or in Miami, I was not reading this account anywhere, nor imagining how I would read it in the future, and I was not trying to make sense of what it is that I was looking for, nor what she meant for my own life or for the life of us Cubans who were raised abroad. I was in Jaruco, inside a cave, and I knew that I was not looking for sculptures but for something else: indentations on a rock, traces of black paint, a deliberately hazy framing of a natural outcropping, a surface that could trigger a memory of what had been. And even though the pieces were not there, I knew that this journey could only begin at that moment and that she was everywhere, having gained the privilege of ubiquity that is the privilege of all those who register their disappearance and allow us to learn what it means. There was only one place where I could be every time I searched for Mendieta's presence, and that was there, inside the cave, looking for something I had already found but could not explain—looking in.

The object was transitory but the photograph fixed it in time. From Ana Mendieta, *Silueta* series, 1976. Red flowers on *silueta* on sand, Mexico. Courtesy of the Estate of Ana Mendieta and Galerie Lelong, New York.

The Cuban Book of the Dead

Celia Cruz died on July 16, 2003, at her home in Fort Lee, New Jersey. The body was taken to Miami, the casket displayed on July 19 at a building called Freedom Tower, a Mediterranean Revival–style construction inspired by the Giralda Tower in Seville, Spain. She had insisted on being taken to Miami so that her body could be viewed there, so the body was moved from one city to the other according to specific instructions she had left for her wake and funeral. Funeral viewing was scheduled to take place from noon to 7 p.m. but the doors closed at 6:30 p.m. because of the throng of people trying to get in. The copper-colored coffin was draped with the Cuban flag, Celia wore a blond wig and a white silk gown, and her hands were folded over a white rosary. A crystal bowl with Cuban soil rested under the coffin.

Celia never distanced herself from *el exilio*, the term used by Cubans in Miami to define an extraterritorial condition that began following the revolutionary triumph of 1959. The choice of site was an homage to her past and it triggered for her fans one of the most traumatic moments in her life: for Cubans to this day, the building is known as El Refugio, because there the U.S. government provided services to recent Cuban immigrants leaving the island when Castro came to power. It seemed, even then, perfect for a future memorial: it was built in 1926 near downtown Miami as the newspaper offices of the *Miami News and Metropolis* and at one point it had a beacon light that shined out over Miami Bay. It was the Ellis Island for Cuban exiles, and the day Celia died the building displayed an immense Cuban flag, and a U.S. flag, because the Freedom Tower has its own story, layered onto Celia's body lying there. The flags were there that day because of the message she wanted to convey: freedom in capital letters, and a symbolic homage both to her compatriots and to her host country. Celia, already a star, had left Cuba at the beginning of the revolution, along with many others who later died in a less glorious exile. She did not stay in Miami but moved north, and after years of hard work within the budding New York Latino recording industry, managed by the 1970s to become a star of the salsa craze and then go on to be crowned the Queen of Salsa. She became an international superstar at a time when young Puerto Rican musicians were rediscovering old recordings, and she became the living proof that Cuban music also had beat outside the island. She had an honorary doctorate from Yale, and a National Medal for the Arts presented by President Clinton in 1994. In all those years of superstardom, and conscious of her own importance, Celia never went to Cuba and never ceased taunting the Cuban government in her concerts. If they did not want her, they were missing the party.

Her wake in Miami brought more than seventy-five thousand people onto the street, and her older sister, Dolores Rodríguez, then eighty-six, arrived from Havana after permission to travel was granted at the last minute. Her younger sister, Gladys Bécquer, who was sixty-seven and lived in New York, joined Celia's husband Pedro Knight in honoring her memory. The hearse was accompanied to Gesú Church by Andy García, Willie Chirino, Israel "Cachao" López, and Gloria and Emilio Estefan, among others. The memorial service tour began in Miami, but it continued in the next days in Manhattan and then the Bronx. Celia had a different outfit for each of these events, and enormous crowds gathered, shouted out her name and her trademark call, "¡Azúcar!" (sugar), which she screamed out with all sorts of different inflexions during her performances. People danced and mourned, in Miami and at the Frank E. Funeral home on the Upper East Side on Madison and Eighty-first Street, where the funeral director had not seen such crowds since Judy Garland's wake in 1969. Celia and her husband had celebrated their forty-first wedding anniversary two days before her death, and he said he dreams taking Celia's remains to Cuba, to be buried next to her mother's.

In the symbolic grammar of Cuban discourse, Miami is a necropolis to life that was always lived elsewhere. The day of Celia's wake, Freedom

Tower (El Refugio) became an abstract cemetery for a day, as the choice of site had the presumed circularity of the journey Celia wanted to share with those others who had followed her on similar narratives of exile. This could only happen, though, because the building had ceased to be a psychic tomb in order to turn into a memorial. Since the mid-1970s, when Cubans stopped coming to the United States, Freedom Tower has been sold many times. Nothing seemed to prosper at that site, as if the building brought Cubans memories too painful to bear, as if it were impossible for the building to provide closure for its particular narrative. Unlike the Hotel Theresa in Harlem were Fidel Castro received the foreign press on his visit to New York in 1960—designated an official city landmark in 1991—this was for many decades a painful site, not just because it signaled one collective event, but for the thousands of minor events that it contained.

In 1997, Jorge Mas Canosa—the entrepreneur who turned the Cuban American National Foundation into a powerful lobbying group—purchased the building for $4.1 million. He helped collect the money to refurbish it, and he had architects consult plans, sketches, and blueprints of the tower as it had once been. The idea was to turn it into a site of pilgrimage, a site in which history came alive—a memory palace. Reconstructing it even created the illusion of a Statue of Liberty, as if Cubans had glimpsed that Mediterranean Revival tower from a boat at sea.

But Cubans did not, of course, glimpse that tower from the sea. It was less poetic than that. Many of the donors responsible for this reconstruction arrived at the Miami airport, and with very little in their pockets. But the Miami airport was not a backdrop suitable for commemorating the most successful migration the United States had ever seen. So these men and women, not simply Mas Canosa, who in one generation doubled the fortunes they had left behind, put Freedom Tower together, like Freedom Park near it—*freedom* being a word with *implications,* with complex meanings in Miami after 1959. Freedom was something that had to be attained, that had to be gained. It involved a journey from poverty to influence, and it also meant the freedom to pursue that influence and use it for political purposes. Freedom became a trophy in this narrative, and it had to be displayed in one site. When they reopened the Freedom Tower in 2001, they placed the offices of the Cuban American National Foundation—the most successful political action group Latin Americans had ever created in the country—and a public museum on the first floor, detailing

Freedom Tower reclaimed by Cuban exiles was the site of Celia Cruz's wake.
Photograph by José Castelló.

the history of the Cuban-American community. It was a history told in its own particular way, a history that *el exilio* still felt had to be voiced.

Thus it was somehow fitting that Celia Cruz's body would be displayed at this site, and that an immense flag be draped around it. Even if there was nothing that materially connected the most visible symbol of exile (Celia) to the site of exile (El Refugio/Freedom Tower), a link had to be made. Lines connected those dots one to the other. One should not demand of a funeral that it be an exercise in historical accuracy. It had a power of its own, one that was expected and had been expected ever since Celia became the most visible and the most prominent anti-Fidelista Cuban singer in exile in the 1970s, and especially during the 1980s. Even if her death was expected—she had been ill for some time—the reality of death trumped the reality of history. For the Cuban community, rich and poor, no attempt at historical accuracy was going to get in the way of Celia's death. As far as real grief goes, this was personal and collective grief that did not display for the camera a unanimous ideological narrative. Not all of those who came were mourning exile and displacement, but many were. The different publics at the wake all felt the loss of her voice. For some, Celia's body illuminated a broader sense of grief, one that is more difficult to bring to closure. It was a strange, jubilant, and sad grief at a story that many could identify with, reflected in their own journeys from poverty to freedom. The body allowed the narrative of identification to be internalized as well as projected onto the queen of Cuban music, and it permitted many to think of their own circular journeys, almost complete even in the memory of loss and unfulfilled desire.

IN EXILE

A dead body in Cuban Miami will never make one think that the past has finally been put to rest. In Miami it is quite the opposite, for there every death serves as an emblem for a story that *el exilio* still thinks of as unfinished. Even if a particular dead body has lived a long and fulfilling life, the dead in Cuban Miami seem to be there always as the result of an accident, of a story that got truncated at a particular moment in time. One does not die geographically in Miami as in Ithaca, after returning from a long voyage; for many Cubans, to die in Miami means not having come full circle, not having returned.

Cuban Miami is not indifferent to the Cuban dead. However, the insistence on the territoriality of Cuban culture over time has furnished Miami with its own versions of a symbolic relationship between death and nation. As with funerary rituals in many parts of the world, the dead need to have some native soil; they need to be where they can rest. And for a country that has celebrated, deified, and rarefied Cuban soil as one of the most important elements within the memory of exile, to expect otherwise would not be feasible. The fertile Cuban soil produced sugar cane and tobacco. Cubans on and off the island are still rooted to soil in ways described by Antonio José Ponte in *Las comidas profundas* (*Wanting to Eat*). It was said at the beginning of *el exilio* that you could always transport tobacco seed and that it would bear fruit, but the tobacco produced was different, because it lacked Cuban soil in which to grow. It is not surprising that the absence of Cuban soil turns exiled Cubans into bodies buried "out of place." As Ponte recalls, Cubans eat their soil, as a way of underscoring the symbolic link between food and earth in Cuban life on the island and abroad. In an artistic performance, Tania Bruguera hung the carcass of a dead animal from her neck while eating earth in homage to the hungry Cuban natives at the beginning of the Spanish Conquest who were forced to eat it to prevent starvation.

From the point of view of *el exilio,* the lines between the real resting place where bodies are buried and the symbolic cemetery are blurred. Dying outside of Cuba has always meant dying in Miami. The city is the paradigm for death, in the way the exilic place becomes no place at all. I am referring to Miami as not only a concrete physical site, but as a representation for everything that is not Cuba. It is of no importance if the individual actually lived or died in Miami. Many did not die, and are not buried, in Miami. But the Cuban dead in *el exilio*—I use *el exilio* to designate both a site and an affective space—are a broad and dispersed network. The list includes Heberto Padilla, Enrique Labrador Ruiz, Carlos Prío Socarrás, Lydia Cabrera, Carlos Montenegro, the modernist poet Juana Borrero, who is buried in Key West, a good number of men from the Mariel generation, including Reinaldo Arenas, Roberto Valero, and many who belonged to the cast of the scathing documentary *Improper Conduct* that criticized the Cuban government for having once incarcerated its homosexual population and accused it of systemic homophobia. One of its directors, Nestor Almendros, is also buried in exile. It is of no importance where these people died. In the political imaginary of dead bodies, they belong to *this* side.

There are memorials to the dead in Miami: Freedom Tower itself, the Chapel of La Caridad (with the Virgin facing in the direction of Cuba), the Monument to the Heroes of the 2506 Brigade, and for many months makeshift homages in Calle Ocho to Elisabeth Brotons, mother of Elián González. As visitors from Cuba repeatedly confirm, physical reality— topography, architecture, the urban fabric itself—does not correspond to the mental reality that Cubans on the island had created for the place. It is more a sense of internal reality, of psychic structures and psychic tombs.

Miami is where it all comes to death, metaphorically, in one way or another. Joan Didion wisely apprehended Miami as the space where things always seemed to dissolve, and Miami blends the cave, the tomb, and the sea into one continuous site that means death. It is an imaginative death that demands the creation of an imaginary country as a response to a country that could never be properly buried.[1] It is also a death that can be referenced in the hidden histories of the Cuban diaspora, as when Eduardo Aparicio states, in his introduction to a photographic essay titled "Frag-ments from Cuban Narratives," "The personal history of each Cuban liv-ing in the U.S. is mostly unknown, unspoken, and often lies buried under a thick layer of inaccurate assumptions."[2] It is striking to note how the word *buried* appears in relation to Cubans. The photographic image ren-ders those bodies visible. As happened after the collapse of the Socialist bloc, when national communities engaged in repeated gestures of memo-rialization and symbolic burial, Cuban bodies have to be memorialized; they also demand to be turned into Cuban narratives.

MEMENTO MORI

In Havana, the dead are alive because they are dead. In Miami, the living belong to the realm of the dead. I mean this in very general terms, as when I say that there can be no pictures of departure but that all pictures show something as it disappears. Let us recall all those picture albums of the city, all the glossy Cuban testimonials produced in Miami. Those albums were the opposite of a souvenir; in Miami, in the 1960s or 1970s, they were fragments of a Cuba that could be reclaimed, and that was simply there, ninety miles away, waiting for what was perceived as a nightmare to end.

Postcard collections, picture books, records with happy or sad songs meant to keep Cuba alive, all these created an alternate reality that back then was studied and debated as a way to understand the present misfortune. Cuba was not a nostalgic entity at that point in time, but rather a country in a parallel universe: letters could still go back and forth, phone conversations were relatively easy to have, and a constant stream of exiles brought news of a lived reality. By the time all those things were once again possible in 1980, and more so in the 1990s, one segment of the population had already partly resigned itself to regarding Cuba as a memorial from the past, while the other, more recently arrived, was bent on living in two spaces at the same time.

Cubans have been economically and politically successful in their diasporic journey, but they have not been particularly creative when it comes to monumentalizing their diasporic deaths. This may be owing to the constant historical twists and turns of the Cuban situation, always on the verge of a final resolution. Many Cubans are still waiting to be returned, brought back, memorialized in Havana, or in the town they left behind, individually or collectively: the heroes of the 2506 brigade that assaulted the Bay of Pigs, the pilots downed when Cuban authorities fired upon them as members of the Brothers to the Rescue team, the *balseros* who have perished at sea, the organized network of *sociedades* in *el exilio*. All these will surely require their own monument when and if the narrative that produced it achieves its sense of closure. One can imagine, even if as a work of fiction, the return of all those dead bodies to an island turned into a necropolis.

There are reasons for this reluctance to memorialize death. The Cuban population outside of the island—mostly in Miami—still thinks of itself as *exilic* and not necessarily as *diasporic,* and thus is not prone to memorialize in grand terms. Exile is an interruption in time, a moment with a definite beginning and a definite end. Diaspora, on the other hand, has a different effect, a longer time span. It implies centralizing a space or collecting around a common center fragments that have shattered. Diaspora implies accommodation in a way that exile does not. Dead bodies within this exilic earth convey endless recomposition, not decay. When the dead are summoned in exile, they stand as emblems of something—not the finality of exilic time itself, but the passage of time, and also the end of time. Only some of the dead in Cuba may actually embody the revolution, but each and every Cuban death in Miami seems to be an emblem. The perceptive critic Gustavo Pérez Firmat understands this in *Next Year in Cuba:*

> Over the last three decades, demographers and sociologists have repeatedly counted the number of Cubans living in Miami. But has anybody ever counted the exiles who have died in Miami? Has anybody taken a census of the city's Cuban dead? Miami is a little Havana not only because of the Cubans who still live there but because, perhaps primarily because, of those who have died there.[3]

Pérez Firmat goes on to say that "the living can only move away; it's the dead who are a city's permanent residents, for once they stop living there, they never stop living there." It works like an inverted trope, it keeps the dead alive, chained to the meanings given to them by the living. To take a census of the Cuban dead in Miami would be an impossible future memorial in itself, but it speaks to a sense of aggrieved history that also encompasses all other exilic spaces, such as Hoboken, West New York, Los Angeles, Madrid, and Mexico City.

Former president of Cuba Carlos Prío Socarrás and dictator Gerardo Machado (as well as Anastasio Somoza, who was not Cuban) are buried at Woodlawn Park Cemetery in Miami, right on Calle Ocho, a number of blocks from what used to be the center of Little Havana. Woodlawn Park Cemetery is a place many would rather forget, and even before Little Havana itself became a memorial to the Cuban migration it was a place that provoked a particular kind of dread. It is not a place that mourners can stroll in, for it demands to be seen from a car; it is not the cemetery where baroque memorials to the dead overwhelm the living. There is very little ostentatious funerary architecture, it is all flat land and spread-out tombs, the "cool" space of a fragile memory, sprinklers wetting the well-kept lawn, while the sun shines mercilessly on pristine tombs, wiped clean of moss and dirt.

This antiseptic and hygienic death makes a kind of emotional sense, in a definitional sort of way. This is American (U.S) death, the place where the American Century entombed some of its dead. There is a Bacardí mausoleum, a small monument to the unknown Cuban freedom fighter, and a number of black marble markers with the Cuban flag sculpted in color. The cemetery does not have a public listing of the famous buried there, the official explanation being that it would create unfair distinctions among the dead, as if validating the fact that some dead are more important than others. But this is also a tacit acknowledgment that Woodlawn Park Cemetery is embedded in a political history of military takeovers, backroom dealings, espionage, and coups d'état, with U.S. airpower perhaps offered as backup for an assault on the Bay of Pigs. The history of resentment is still very much alive at Woodlawn. Fortunes that could never be amassed in order to bury the dead, hasty rituals, mausoleums mortgaged at the last possible minute. It is death that should have never happened in *that* space, nor in *that* time.

MEMORIALS IN FLIGHT

From the other side of the ninety-mile liquid gap, Havana *does* have its own dead, and the dead have come back to haunt the living in their own way after the collapse of the Soviet Union and the Socialist bloc. Since 1993, with the commemorations on the centenary of the death of Julián

Where the Cuban dead lie beyond the island: Woodlawn Cemetery in Miami. Photograph by José Castelló.

del Casal and the fiftieth anniversary of *Orígenes,* and with the symposium on José Lezama Lima, literary and artistic institutions in Havana have consecrated the literary dead with a baroque feast: Lezama Lima, Alejo Carpentier, Nicolás Guillén, and in particular Virgilio Piñera—these were the pillars of revised or unrevised memory, the shorthand language for a change that could only move as slowly as death itself consumes the body. Revisionism bred more symposia, and then books, Web sites, and finally a whole apparatus of cultural tourism where the literate city is preserved from a possible onslaught. In the midst of a ruined Havana in the 1990s, memory was all about the imperfectly buried, the persistence of *things.* John Lennon has his statue in the Vedado, and Ernest Hemingway is now memorialized sitting at La Floridita.

One could argue, correctly, that the revolution has always commingled with the space of the dead by rewriting the history of the republic in a way that projects the past as a cult to the sacrifice, even martyrdom, of the dead. Death was seen as a metaphor that had a "life" linking it to a long tradition of struggle. The cult of death and martyrdom has always appeared prominently in revolutionary slogans: "Patria o Muerte" (Fatherland or death) is the verbal shorthand for a revolutionary attitude toward life that is also on display at the Museo de la Revolución—bloodied shirts, ragged flags, bullets hitting their targets, and memorials to the many martyrs commemorated year after year in Havana. But in the 1990s, the celebratory ritual of the dead had a different feel to it in Havana; if previous solemnities rescued the past for the present, at this point revisionist history became the conscious recollection of a different mental structure. If returning the past to the living was the previous mode of remembrance, now the semantics of these events involved recalling the dead as having died once and for all. Memory reestablished continuities while the slow, creeping discourse seemed to use the dead to speak about the present, as in the final paragraph of Antón Arrufat's *Virgilio Piñera entre él y yo* (1994):

Reality destroyed part of that pleasure: I had to walk the same street a number of times looking for the house in vain. Finally, I recognized it. The gallery no longer existed. Not even the mosaics in which I had rested. The wood having been eaten up by termites, the owner ordered what was left of it demolished. With this, the house seemed diminished, reduced. It looked completely real. Or maybe with the dimension given to it by the present.

I crossed the street and I separated myself. The house was another, and my life another life. I felt then that strange experience that is exclusive to man: the knowledge that one has a past.[4]

Arrufat's play *The Seven against Thebes* was banned because it dealt with a fratricidal war back in 1961, and he was sent to a provincial library to process arriving books and jot down information on index cards, and was barred from reading any book. It was a cruel punishment for a man who saw the world around him crumble and who had the perseverance or fear of never having chosen the death-in-life of exile. Arrufat's National Prize for Literature in 2000 was a way of making amends for this, but the simple and melancholic elegance of this paragraph speaks more eloquently than any official proclamation. Because Arrufat's last words are so precisely temporal, the knowledge and the awareness of the past implies a moment of closure and a sense of distance. The house has probably been reconstructed in the haphazard way such buildings are reconfigured over time in an economy of scarcity. The act of returning to the house, and closing the book with this return, pays homage to all those years when Arrufat was not able to visit the site, protecting himself from memories that were surely too hard to bear. In this one instant, the destruction of the past and its avoidance over a long period of time are brought to the forefront. Avoidance does not turn into amnesia, but into a new, reconfigured present where memory is voiced. The book is already a sense of closure for a friendship mourned over so many decades.

Even if death had figured prominently in the collective memory of revolutionary history, it had particular resonance during the Special Period, when everything stopped. The spectral economy can best be illustrated in Colón Cemetery in Havana—the city of the dead. There were stories of exhumations in the 1990s, with Cubans stealing from the dead; the dead were piled on top of one another, a single tomb holding bodies from different families and different generations in order to accommodate the passing of time and the reduced space of the plot. On top or alongside the pantheons where wealthy families during the republic rendered homage to their dead, little mementos have been placed—flower cups, stamps, pictures, smaller plaques—indicating more recent burials.

In the early 1960s, Tomás Gutiérrez Alea played with a dead body in *Death of a Bureaucrat,* where the still new revolutionary system was "killed off" in the Havana cemetery because of the enormous complications that ensued from dead bodies. Gutiérrez Alea again sardonically deflated dreams of a better future in the 1990s by showing the bureaucratic nightmares involved in moving a dead body from one end of the island to the other in *Guantanamera* (1995), a polemical film that was publicly attacked by the *comandante* himself as a bitter indictment of the revolution at a time when the people needed more positive images of resistance in a hostile world.

Guantanamera was striking, among other reasons, because it represented the possibility of the dead body creating a civil society beyond the dictates of the state. It is interesting in this context that the dead woman was precisely a singer and that, like Celia Cruz a number of years later, the body's silence becomes an indictment on a state that seems to impede her being buried in the right place. *Guantanamera* not only used the dead body as a way to illuminate what the living went through, it also reserved its most unsentimental gaze for the actions of the state. As the characters struggle with the state's dysfunctional and "rationalized" system for burying a corpse, a new social order ensues, predicated on the transit of that one body from one end of the island to the other. There is no pity for the state, and no attempt to understand its policies as promoting the common good. The state is represented comically by intransigence and bad faith, motivated by petty, narcissistic concerns with its own exaggerated proposals, and completely out of touch with reality. In the film, civil society always attempts to patch up the disasters inflicted by the state. But *Guantanamera* also depicted a general fascination with the dead, with memorializing. The decade was marked by other deaths, and not merely the stuff of symbolic burials.

One of the most important acts of memorialization concerned a body long dead that came back to haunt the living in 1997. The story of how Che Guevara's remains were found and how a team of forensic doctors came to identify them was followed by Cubans for weeks. It was known that El Che's body was in Vallegrande, Bolivia, though this information had been contradicted many times, and what was done with Che's body after his death had been the subject of broad speculation. It was known that after debating whether to sever his head or cut off one of his fingers for identification, Che's hands were cut off at the time of death, and later were given to Fidel Castro[5] (and that they are stored in Havana at the

Palacio de la Revolución, where some important visitors have reported seeing them). Retired Bolivian military officers had indicated that they knew the location of Guevara's remains, and in July 1997, after searching for months, Argentine, Bolivian, and Cuban excavators found skeletons at a site in Vallegrande. They identified Guevara's body as the one with no hands. Guevara's remains were sent back to Cuba. They were buried not in Havana, though, for reasons that were mostly political, but in Santa Clara (site of his most important revolutionary battle) where the government created a monument to put the body to rest.

At that point, the iconographic image that had traveled for the past thirty years, and that had been reproduced in countless objects for material consumption, entered into a different kind of relationship with its viewers, remotivated as it was by the material and physical appearance of the dead body. Seven days of mourning were held at the end of the Fifth Party Congress, which took place from October 8 to 10, 1997, which was significant, because it publicly recognized the dire state of the nation. Cuban television and print devoted commentary, recollections, pictures, and interviews to the memory of the Fallen Hero. The official newspaper *Granma* devoted just one paragraph to Celia Cruz's death, but for Che Guevara's remains songs were played continuously on the radio, and the coffin was put on display at the monument to José Martí at the Plaza de la Revolución, where some 250,000 Cubans assembled in a line that snaked through the huge plaza to see it. There was a ninety-minute ceremony with Aleida March (El Che's widow) and their children, who live in Cuba. The event was followed by the burial in Santa Clara.

The traveling body was finally put to rest. The burial of El Che was not really a funeral, but rather an attempt to rectify his secret and ignominious burial in Bolivia, which signaled the collapse of the idea that the Cuban Revolution could be reproduced throughout the continent. The social order demanded continuity between its illusions, its failures, and its long history of social justice. If the collapse of socialism devalued the Cuban experiment, if it threatened to render it a failed project, burying El Che was a way to give material value to the experiment once again, establishing by way of kinship the fact that the revolution had a right to this cultural property, and that in a universe devoid of material symbols of the revolution, the mausoleum with El Che's body could accomplish the symbolic purpose of inscribing the revolution in eternity. The act was a way to meditate and provide commentary about the present, but it was also clearly addressed to the future. It reordered stability in the midst of change, without necessarily presenting any new options for the future. It was a past that was still laid open and that could still provoke a fluid aesthetic statement: a funerary art of memorialization.

The funeral in 1997 lacked the iconographic elements of previous events—from the news of El Che's disappearance in April 1965, to October 1965, when Fidel publicly read the letter in which El Che announced his departure from Cuba, up to October 9, 1967, when he was executed and his body publicly exhibited the next day, in the washroom annex to a hospital in the Bolivian town of La Higuera. If massive memorials to the death of El Guerrillero Heroico in Cuba in those days were photographed, the aesthetics in 1990 did not call for the same kind of photoreportage. The present event —this reappearance of El Che within the time and space of the revolution—did not produce *images*. The two events were thus a reflection of their times and had a dialectical relationship with each other, as if the first could only be conceived with the patina of time in a black-and-white image, while the second called for the strident immediacy of color. The image that was still capable of producing discourse was, instead, the picture taken by Freddy Alborta of El Che's dead body in the washroom. Jorge Castañeda commented, in his biography of Che Guevara, that the picture rendered homage to Latin American youth who fought the revolutionary civil wars of the 1960s. And as such it reappeared in a project undertaken by Leandro Katz and exhibited in Buenos Aires in 2003.

Leandro Katz's installation is called *El día que me quieras* (The day you will love me), an ironic comment on the incommensurability and finality of death, as well as the title of one of the most famous songs associated with the dead hero of tango, Carlos Gardel. As the spectator walks around the installation, there is a complete chronology of the guerrilla struggle that El Che fought in Bolivia, as well as details from the dirty internal war that Latin American governments fought against the best and the brightest of a generation. For Katz, Che is the first *desaparecido* (disappeared person), and he inaugurates one of the most difficult and still unresolved moments in Latin America's twentieth-century history. It is because of the lack of resolution in the broader narratives in which they are placed that the disappeared, the revolution, and Che can be fashioned by Katz into a common space. The artist did not create a monument to the dead, and has steered clear of fashioning their tomb. The rooms have an airy quality to them, which contrasts with the force of its subject matter. The installation encompasses the bare room where the observer sees the photograph, surrounded by the chronology of El Che's Bolivian expedition, culled from various sources and from the artist's own research. There are pictures of Che disguised as he entered Bolivia, which contrast with the picture of the *guerrillero's* body taken at La Higuera. Katz deconstructs the meaning of photography and disguise—there are, after all, pictures of Che's passport, where he appears in disguise in order to fool the Bolivian authorities—as well as the relation between photography and truth. He includes a film he made for the exhibit in which he questions El Che's final image, taken on October 10, 1967, in which he lies like a broken Christ, his eyes open, surrounded by his military executioners, and he interviews the photographer. Whether the body lives in the present or the past is also the subject of speculation, for Katz allows the film to be seen again and again as an intervention in time, and its repetition within the context of the exhibit drives home the point that this is an open death: it still carries meaning, and it will always carry the meaning that history gives it. Katz goes back to the artist at the moment when art is conceived and interviews the photographer. The observer is suspended between those two events: the picture and the interview with Alborta, interspersed with Katz's quasi-ethnographic shots of Indians in Bolivia. It is an exhibition of context upon context, as Katz rescues the filmstrip of that moment when the photographer encountered history, and asks to what extent the aesthetic effect of the photograph was the product of a deliberate or self-conscious effort.

Katz understands the power of images and he fragments the picture in order to at once contain and magnify its power. He notes all the classical resonances in the event: the body with the eyes open, the body exhibited in the washroom of a hospital, where corpses are cleansed. Katz turns the image into his own version of *Las Meninas,* an attempt to paint a picture in the picture. Alborta, who passed away in 2005, was the complicit witness to history, the man who hides, who is not in the picture. The filmstrip shows members of the military placing newspapers in front of El Che in order to establish the exact date, and they pinch the body to prove conclusively that this was a body and that it was truly dead.

There was something fragile and haunting about the Katz exhibition that was lacking in the reburial of El Che in Cuba. It might have to do with the multiplicity of images in relation to the monumentality of death. Even if Cubans understood the event as one suspended between past and present, the exhibition dissolves and moves. In Cuba, there is a Che monument eternally affixed to Cuban soil. And even before there was a monument, countless structures had already cemented his presence there as part of the lanscape itself, as nostalgic memory.

THE LIVING DEAD

The presence of the dead during the 1990s was more than an event, or even a series of events. The dead could not be contained in their tombs; they had to come out and once again give their message to the living, teach the living what the meaning of desire is. Mausoleums and public acts in which the dead are memorialized were not the only way death was present during the 1990s. The present had expanded, its borders were not as tangible as before, and the sense of mission that gave meaning to its temporality was lost. Tomás Gutierrez Alea's *Strawberry and Chocolate* (1994)

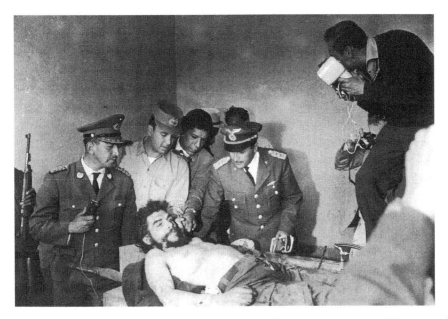

Leandro Katz's homage to Ernesto "Che" Guevara's final struggle, using Freddy Alborta's photograph of the dead hero.

already seemed to begin a new era, just as *Guantanamera* brought it to a close, as if he were responsible for embalming macabre changes in the revolution itself. But others also marked the changes, punctured by the ritual wakes that accompanied the burial of El Che in 1997, and in the death of some of the heroic figures of the revolution, among them Carlos Rafael Rodríguez, the dreaded Manuel Piñero, alias Barbarroja, and Tomás Gutiérrez Alea himself. The death of the old singer in *Guantanamera* came from a sudden heart attack, but the wake was prolonged.

In other recent works the cemetery is the mental space where the city lives, for example, in *Te di la vida entera* (*I Gave You All I Had*) (1996) by Zoé Valdés and *Contrabando de sombras* (Contraband of shadows) (2002)

An early homage to El Che on Cuban soil. Photograph courtesy of Zinnia Johnston.

by Antonio José Ponte. In Ponte's novel there is a sequence of metaphorical acts of displacement. The cemetery's borders separate the living from the dead, but that border is also a scar on the body of one of the protagonists, as well as a rip in the thread of a movie screen that the main character is watching while others around him masturbate in the closed confines of the movie theater. It is a significant piece of work where there is no interruption between the living and the dead, diffused in the novel and in the broader allegory of revolution itself for Ponte. It may be that he wants us to think of successive embalmings of Cuba, but he is also pointing out what lies *underneath:* he highlights the presence of the invisible in the luminosity of the false. The novel takes place in a Havana where history does not seem to *occur.* There may not be two cities (one for the living and one for the dead), but they all live in one city, after all.

There is, ultimately, only one cemetery, and it is at once physical and phantasmic. There are underground passages in this cemetery, just as there are tombs that communicate with different spaces and different times. Lydia Cabrera's work has been reissued in Cuba, and Heberto Padilla has been openly mourned in print; Severo Sarduy's novels, as well as those of Lino Novás Calvo, are echoed in the work of more recent Cuban narrators, such as Pedro de Jesús. The fact that the republic is being looked at with a scholarly eye is possible only because of a more open cultural context.

There are collective and public wakes, but there are also instances of solitary or collective mourning. Four poets in Havana during the Special Period in 1992—Francisco Morán, Víctor Fowler Calzada, Antonio José Ponte, and Jorge Luis Sánchez—wanted to commemorate the centenary of Julián del Casal's book *Nieve;* Casal was important for the generation living at this point in time. The poets went to the poet's crypt in the Colón Cemetery and filmed the event in a short documentary titled *Hojas al viento* (Leaves to the wind). To see the poets at that point, and to see them now, shows to what extent the Special Period involved hunger and distress. *Hojas al viento* documents a period in their lives. Sullen and extremely thin, they take turns talking about a modernist poet who lived at a different end of the century and whose work had been misunderstood during both the republic and the revolution as that of a refined, exquisite poet, out of touch with reality, a poet who had always been misread. But the poets had perseverance and the literary certainty that a statement needed to be made: that Casal's refinement and elegance could be motivated in a

different way, that it could be brought to life somehow, and that as a living thing it could illuminate obscure zones of Cuban life. Morán, Fowler,
Ponte, and Sánchez each give an improvised scholarly talk about the poet,
but this does not detract from its overall effect at a funerary moment in
Cuban history. It has all the characteristics of a happening: in the crypt,
they talked for a while about the poet's significance, in an act that had
greater resonance because of the story embedded within it.

The materiality of the body, the act of going to the tomb, is important
in and of itself. But this materiality has been brilliantly deconstructed in
ways that also bear on the memorializing of the dead time and the dead
poet. According to Morán, who was filmed in Julián del Casal's crypt, the
history of Casal's body is more complex. It is well known that Casal was
buried temporarily in the crypt of the Rosell-Saurí family. It is also known
that Eduardo Rosell, who later died in the war of independence, had requested to be buried next to Casal. But when Jorge Luis Sánchez, in one
of those morbid acts of love and affection that have been common in
Cuban literary history, decided in 1992 to open the crypt in order to identify Casal's body, Sánchez and the exhumers found only one body, not
two. To this day, the true resting place of Casal's body remains an unsolved
mystery—the missing body of the already too numerous dead, the absent
body in the overpopulated necropolis, where the aesthetic ruins never quite
seem to collapse.

BACK FROM THE DEAD AND READY TO PARTY

Dead bodies *do* travel and they do create meaning and reorder reality. The
funerary rites for Celia Cruz took place in New York and Miami, despite
many wanting her body to become affixed to one site, to one moment
in time. In nationalizing the dead (as happened with Che, who was born
in Argentina), by claiming the recomposition of that body, something else
was taking place: time and space were resignified, new identities were
created, authorities were investing themselves with the sacralized aura that
emanated from that body. This was because the past was invested with an
authority that the present needed to claim for itself. These were two different traveling bodies—Celia Cruz and the reclaimed body of Che. The
latter traveled more slowly; the former planned her funerary service while
she was alive. Che's body was brought to Cuba in all its materiality; with

Celia's body, a very specific and very particular *Cuban* body engaged in a symbolic dispersal. It is interesting to note how these lines multiply and intersect: the internationalist fighter who had left the Cuban state was reclaimed by that state, and buried in the site of his major battle. The very Cuban Celia, who always insisted on her *cubanía*, while also rejecting the Cuban government and identifying as Latina-American, became a transnational figure, buried not in the capital of Cuban exile but in the capital of the Caribbean one. In Celia's case, there was symbolic dispersal; with Che, it was containment. The transnational fighter paradoxically became linked to a state—even if a revolutionary one. In a politically expedient way it gave added meaning to Fidel Castro's visit to Argentina in 2003, while the Argentinean population was surmounting the worst economic crisis in its history.

With Celia, it was *el exilio* mourning one of its own, and when the appropriate time had elapsed for those in the capital of *el exilio* to pay homage to her life and song, the body was returned to New York for a service at Saint Patrick's Cathedral, where in 1987 she could not get a permit to consecrate her twenty-fifth wedding anniversary to Pedro Knight, because she was unable to get a baptismal certificate from Cuba. There were famous personalities in New York, and there were also famous personalities in Miami. It was the world of music and it was the world of politics: if, in Miami, there was Gloria Estefan and Cristina Saralegui, in New York at Saint Patrick's there was Gov. George Pataki, Sen. Hillary Clinton, Marc Anthony, and Paquito D'Rivera, as well as Melanie Griffith, Antonio Banderas, and Victor Manuelle.

The death was not unexpected. Several months before it happened, there was a tribute on television that had been planned for a year. It was a scripted party, where the new generation paid homage to the way she bridged generational divides, to the way she managed to keep herself relevant. And the song she chose to close off her life and career was none other than a version in Spanish of Gloria Gaynor's "I Will Survive," which Celia—it was rumored, against her doctor's wishes—joined Gloria in singing. The television special was a way of preparing us for her death, and deserves to be included as part of the baroque funerary rites death requested. It allowed us to see her in a different way, against the backdrop of eternal life. It did not make it any less sad or any less difficult to understand, though it was felt as an act of compassion toward her public, as if the dying Celia were responsible for making her death less sad, and comforted the living with the self-understanding of her own mortality. Her last hit was an appeal to live for the moment, and to understand that forgiveness is not forgetting, but rather the possibility of remembering without pain ("No es que recuerde, sino que no olvido / Eso es el perdón / Recordar sin dolor" [It's not that I don't remember, but that I don't forget / That is what forgiveness means / To remember without pain]). It was called, appropriately enough, "Ríe y llora" (Laugh and cry), and the refrain says that time will come for us all.

Even her posthumous album, *Regalo del alma* (Gift from/of the soul), where she appeared on the cover wearing a white platinum wig and white dress, had a note to her fans dated March 24, 2003. She thanked those who had been important in her life, including her family, her closest friends, and the staff at the Columbia Presbyterian Hospital. She noted the difficult times she had gone through, and offered the album as a gift from the soul. She dedicated it, poignantly, to her Cuban people, walking in earth's exile, and to all those Cubans inside the island who swim against the current so that her voice can be heard.[6]

The pictures taken in Miami and at the funeral service in New York allow us to see the different constituencies Celia Cruz appealed to: Cuban, Puerto Rican, Dominican, and Latino. In spite of her insistence on the coffin being covered by the Cuban flag, the body was not simply the sum of our attachments or our flags, but always something in excess of those attachments. There would be no contradiction between the *político* and the fan, between the Colombian immigrant and the Cuban *balsero*, between the Puerto Rican salsa aficionado and the Anglo record producer from Los Angeles. Each could claim the body as its own, and Celia wanted it that way—to render homage to her past and to the past of those who will remember her. As the body traveled from place to place, from New York to Miami, it reinforced those constituencies. It joined together in one space different communities that perhaps will never again share that space. It was predictable that many would question the rights of others, and that possession would be claimed by all. And, as always happened when Celia interjected her antirevolutionary politics into her persona, many of those who came to pay homage were undoubtedly turned off by the more outwardly political and partisan opinions expressed in the events. The Cuban flag, Freedom Tower, the statue of Our Lady of Charity, and the crystal bowl with Cuban soil were expressly chosen so that the past could be relived in the present; for many at the viewing in Freedom Tower, those objects represented *el exilio*. All these different signals, rites, and journeys can be seen as extraordinary demands made by the queen to her mourners—to accept her first and foremost as an exiled Cuban, to register her voice as transnational, and to follow her in all those journeys and with all those dresses, from New Jersey, to Miami, to the cemetery in the Bronx. Predictably, many felt that once again *el exilio* had hijacked a body and made it signify something other than what it was; also predictably that same *exilio* insisted on "you don't understand" as a response.

The internal mental landscape of *el exilio* seemed to find a reconfirmation of its pain in the body's physical journey and all the body's signs. At the same time, Celia's transnational public found comfort in the fact that she chose to be buried precisely not in Woodlawn Park Cemetery in Miami but in the Bronx's Woodlawn Cemetery in the (temporary, according to Pedro Knight) home away from exile—a gesture of solidarity, it was felt, in terms of class, to the poorer, working-class Latino communities of New York. Many took this—or wanted to see this—as a rebuff to those high-powered members of *el exilio* who wanted to claim her as their own. Death illuminates the points of contact that different publics had at one point but will never have again, because they were created in order to *possess* the meaning of that body. For an *exilio* that sees itself as isolated, besieged, and misunderstood, Celia's body offered a collective sense of identification in terms of the injustices suffered at living and dying in a foreign land. La Reina, Celia, stood for the historical script that predated all others, the one at the center of a narrative that had grown more complex over the years, and that had links to other narratives that may or may not be quite like it.

The service/event in New York on July 22 paid homage to Celia's roots in the transnational salsa communities that thrived in New York during the 1970s. It was also a made-for-TV spectacle: a white Cadillac convertible, a carriage topped by white flowers and lavender roses, and, at Saint Patrick's Cathedral, loudspeakers that broadcast the Mass to the public outside. Other famous musicians buried at Woodlawn in the Bronx include Miles Davis, Duke Ellington, and Celia's fellow artist, bandleader, and friend Tito Puente (1923–2000), with whom she recorded now-classic albums. New York was where she became an international star in the

1970s, alongside younger Puerto Rican *salseros,* and where she managed to transform herself from being a Cuban singer into a symbol for the Caribbean translocal and transnational communities. The funeral reminded those old enough to remember the glory days when Celia could be seen on album covers with the best and brightest musicians in the salsa pantheon, not only as a quote from ages gone by, but as a living presence who managed to combine present and past with the musicians that she chose to perform with, and who acquired a measure of legitimacy by means of her presence. On the album cover for *Celia, Johnny and Pete* she sits between the two other performers, decked out in their best evening wear, as if remarking that salsa was not only the music of the streets, but also the beat danced to in nightclubs and cabarets. This was not meant to plug into the barrio as the space for trickster figures who ran wild with the law, but into the celebratory beat of the night where all Latinos danced to remember or to forget.

In these services it was as if voice and body became unglued—with the voice recorded and thus living on through time. A late hit such as "La vida es un carnaval" was recorded already as a kind of intimation of mortality, and her last hit, the eminently danceable "Ríe y llora," was already a made-for-death song. She changed the Gloria Gaynor song "I Will Survive" into "Yo viviré"—as if there was the need to make the song more obvious by slightly mis-translating the title into Spanish, from "I Will Survive" to "I Will Live." Her voice invited all to dance in the face of adversity. It may not be entirely fair to separate the different points in this journey, but Miami celebrated her body and her presence, whereas New York gave us the imprint of her voice. There was a physical intervention with history and with finality in Miami—the mediated finality of death in exile—that made the event more "Cuban" and localized. Celia was generous to allow all to mourn, and to sing while mourning, and many who saw her for the last time in both cities were singing, and felt compelled to dance, while waiting to view her body.

How does one live among the dead without singing or dancing? Cubans have learned how to turn spaces into cemeteries, and they turn wakes into celebrations. It is an organic relationship and not exclusive to Cubans, but also true of other Caribbean populations. Yet recent Cuban history does add poignancy to this dynamic, in view of the psychic energy its population has expended on monumental projects, fratricidal warfare, clandestine

activity, and political intransigence since the revolution. In a strangely con-
flicted way, Cubans have been living alongside the space of the dead from
one country to the other and in the ninety miles that separate one from
the other. The relationship between Havana and Miami was memorably
expressed by Joan Didion: "Havana vanities come to dust in Miami."[7] But
the dust in Miami also haunts the vanities that Havana still deploys, while
Havana's crumbling buildings layer their historical dust at the entrance
to the skyscrapers that remind us of Miami's vanities. They have both
suffered from an excess of buried time: the celebrations of the victory of
Playa Girón (Bay of Pigs) in Havana have always been the flip side of the
stalwart, mourning remembrances of the Bay of Pigs in Miami. In the year

Celia Cruz album cover from her moment of glory as the Queen of Salsa, 1980.

2000 marches that demanded the return of Elián González to Cuba were echoed by candlelight vigils in Miami in his dead mother's honor. It could be that some bizarre twists of fate, or the cruel designs of a vengeful deity venerated under various names and guises, have been responsible for this situation. The relationship might even be apprehended as two sides of the same coin, a mental leap from sadness to the joke, from mourning to dancing, one as tragic as the other up to the limits of the absurd.

Reinaldo Arenas was fond of remarking that Miami was a kind of cemetery—the place where Cuba had finally achieved its perverse dream of becoming the culture of the living dead.

But he also said his native Holguín was a cemetery.

Acknowledgments

Thanks to Robert Vázquez-Pacheco, from whose Harlem apartment I first saw the Hotel Theresa and thought about what could have been and was not, in a kind of eternal present made possible by his generosity. Licia Fiol-Matta and Rafael Rosario have always been there, and I value them as interlocutors and interlopers more than I can ever express. Daniel Balderston shared days and nights in Cuba and in Buenos Aires and Santiago, and to him I owe so many things, among them a stroll through the Mitte district in Berlin where I went to the Bodeguita del Medio, or a foray into the hidden histories of Cubans in Iowa. I am indebted in happiness to Leticia Stella Serra and Nayda Collazo Lloréns in so many complicit ways.

Jossiana Arroyo, Patricia Gutiérrez-Menoyo, Emilio Ichikawa, Larry LaFountain-Stokes, Yolanda Martínez SanMiguel, Eyda Merediz, Sylvia Molloy, Francisco Morán, Juan Carlos Quintero-Herencia, Ivette Rodríguez, Ana Serra—many of the insights in this book could not have been made without them. In Cuba, the extended family includes but is not limited to Carlos Aguilera, Norge Espinosa, Víctor Fowler, Pedro Marqués de Armas, Antonio José Ponte, Reina María Rodríguez, and Roberto Zurbano.

My gratitude to Galerie Lelong in New York for the very efficient and generous permission to use the Ana Mendieta prints, as well as to Leandro Katz for his speedy work in procuring materials from his exhibition. María de los Ángeles Torres read an initial version of this manuscript and pointed out errors of fact and omission, though none of the errors in the final version are hers, of course. Isabel Barbuzza introduced me to Hans Breder, with whom I spent a wonderful afternoon in Iowa. Antonio Benítez Rojo also backed this project at the beginning, when it was a proposal with a different focus. His death in 2005 is an immense loss to Cuban culture.

Editor extraordinaire Richard Morrison was patient beyond the call of duty and has had a keen eye to rescue me from my ramblings. I concur with Jane Blocker: he is a prince. The staff at the University of Minnesota Press was also stellar, in particular Heather Burns and David Thorstad, who did an impeccable job editing the manuscript.

Lourdes Martínez Echazabal gave me a chance to try out my essays with students at the University of California, Santa Cruz, and has been a fellow *cubana* in body and spirit. José Muñoz is not only the best *cubano* in Miami and New York, but he is the best *cubano* in Hialeah—and that's no small accomplishment. Félix Jiménez read most of the manuscript and I could have never hoped for a sharper eye from a friend who should know that my writing is just a pale reflection of his.

María Mercedes Carrión is one of a stellar group of colleagues at Emory University who have made many positive changes in my life. María pushed me, brought me to Cuba, believed in this work, and spent many afternoons talking about all these things in a house in Havana that will always hold a special place in my heart. Sarah Shortt helped with my computer clumsiness, and Zinnia Johnston has been invaluable in making so many aspects of my life easier at Emory and also in being her usual extraordinary self.

Gerardo Calderón-Juliá turned my life into an origami when I needed it most.

José Castelló took pictures on short notice; Tom Graham sent them fast on the computer. Hilario Martínez provided a lot of love, and also coffee and fresh-squeezed orange juice and mango shakes. Lourdes Quiroga kept me sane, as always, and José Quiroga, my father, has always turned our attachment to Cuba into the stuff of everyday bantering on Cubans and their quirks.

My first trip to Cuba after many years I made with my mother, Rita Molinero. Not merely this book, but all books to come, are dedicated to her, even if I don't say it out loud.

Notes

PREFACE

1. Reinaldo Arenas, *Before Night Falls,* trans. Dolores M. Koch (New York: Penguin Books, 1993), 165.

2. "Las maderas cubanas, que cerca de Madrid, en el Escorial, tenían su templo y cerraban en la propia ciudad la basílica de San Francisco el Grande, penetraban por la boca a llenar el apetito" (Antonio José Ponte, *Las comidas profundas* [Angers: Éditions Deleatur, 1997], 24; unless otherwise indicated, translations from Spanish are my own).

3. For the best analysis of Operation Pedro Pan, see María de los Ángeles Torres, *The Lost Apple: Operation Pedro Pan, Cuban Children in the U.S., and the Promise of a Better Future* (Boston: Beacon Press, 2003).

4. Román de la Campa, *Cuba on My Mind: Journeys to a Severed Nation* (New York: Verso, 2000), 22.

INTRODUCTION

1. "The flight of a tyrant, the defeat of his minions, the capture of power by young men, the miraculous culmination of a brave gesture, the attention of the world; an honest army guarding public buildings; great projects for reform ahead; young men ready for any job, any undertaking, whatever their experience or lack of it: these things gave Cuba in early 1959 an extraordinary mood of hope, confidence, enthusiasm, comradeship. Certain companies such as José Bosch's Bacardí Rum Company and the Hatuey Beer Company offered to pay their annual taxes in advance" (Hugh Thomas, *Cuba: The Pursuit of Freedom* [New York: Harper & Row, 1971], 1065.)

2. See Michael Burawoy and Katherine Verdery, *Uncertain Transition: Ethnographies of Change in the Postsocialist World* (Lanham, MD: Rowman and Littlefield, 1999), 14–15. Transition, they argue, cannot be conceived as either "rooted in the past or tied to an imagined future." They define it as a process suspended between those

two possibilities, in which policy and reaction interact according to the levels of resistance each of them finds. For them, it is not the kind of "unilinear" process conceived in neoliberal plans, but rather "a combined and uneven one having multiple trajectories." This is why they prefer the term "transformation" instead of "transition," whereby "policies combine with preexisting circumstances in different ways to produce different outcomes and reactions. This combination means the process is also uneven, affecting different regions and, within regions, different sectors at different rates." I think this is an adequate way of understanding the present Cuban moment, and it has the added benefit of disrupting a facile temporal narrative that has been constructed both by the state and by its opposition in the United States.

3. Andreas Huyssen, *Present Pasts: Urban Palimpsests and the Politics of Memory* (Stanford, CA: Stanford University Press, 2003), 96–97.

4. Hugh Thomas already noted it in 1971: "Castro frequently described the Revolution as a 'process', beginning with the first Cuban war of independence, and the propaganda of the regime always so depicts it. Thus 1968 was celebrated as the culmination of a 'hundred years of struggle' . . . Though history has been distorted since 1959, Castro's Revolution was the culmination of three generations of 'revolutionary activity', verbal violence, extravagant hopes of redemption and further embroidery on the idea of freedom" (Thomas, *Cuba,* 1491–92). Thomas also notes that this is true of exiles, and he quotes Castro's estranged sister Juanita, interviewed in 1969 in Miami, commenting on the need to create a "new Cuba . . . a Cuba which has nothing to do with the past or the present" (1491).

5. Cuban slogans have always underscored the open-ended nature of that struggle, generally by pointing out that it was, indeed, never-ending. Thus, the repeated appeals to an "eternal Baragua" (the site of the Cuban cry for independence in the nineteenth century) or the insistence that "every day" is the 26th of July (a reference to the July 26 attacks on the Moncada barracks). This idea of the eternal struggle is also underscored by the fact that young schoolchildren are *pioneros* (pioneers) and are constantly urged to emulate Che Guevara.

6. Eliseo Alberto, *Informe contra mí mismo* (Mexico City: Alfaguara, 1997), 172. Eliseo Alberto left the island during the 1990s and is the son of the prominent Cuban poet Eliseo Diego (1920–94).

7. See Julie M. Bunck, "Market Oriented Marxism: Post-Cold War Transition in Cuba and Vietnam" in *Cuban Communism,* ed. Irving Louis Horowitz and Jaime Suchliki, 10th ed. (New Brunswick, NJ: Transaction Publishers, 2003), 186.

8. Carmelo Mesa-Lago, "Assessing Economic and Social Performance in the Cuban Transition of the 1990s," in Horowitz and Suchliki, *Cuban Comunism,* 119.

9. Juan M. del Águila, "The Cuban Armed Forces: Changing Roles, Continuing Loyalties," in Horowitz and Suchliki, *Cuban Communism,* 513.

10. The best account of these changes can be found in Max Azicri, *Cuba Today and Tomorrow: Reinventing Socialism* (Gainesville: University Press of Florida, 2000), 138–39.

11. An account of Ochoa's trial and execution is given in Norberto Fuentes, *Dulces guerrilleros cubanos* (Barcelona: Seix Barral, 1999). It is a memoir written by an important Cuban novelist who was implicated in the tale because of his friendship with Ochoa and the de la Guardia twins. Fuentes was captured in 1993 while trying

to escape from Cuba, and he went on a hunger strike in 1994. He finally left Cuba on September 2, 1994, on a private plane, property of the Mexican president Carlos Salinas de Gortari, after Gabriel García Márquez intervened on his behalf. Fuentes later published an exposé that linked Cuban armed forces to the drug trade in the Caribbean, in a complicated narrative involving not only Arnaldo Ochoa, but also Robert Vesco, Manuel Noriega, and the Colombian drug kingpin Pablo Escobar. Although I cannot verify all this information independently, it does reveal how delicate the armed forces' loyalty was for the government throughout the late 1980s—hence, their being retrained in order to manage many sectors of the tourism industry was not uncalled for. See Norberto Fuentes, *Narcotráfico y tareas revolucionarias: el concepto cubano* (Miami: Ediciones Universal, 2002).

12. In 2003, Eloy Gutiérrez Menoyo, former combatant in Castro's army and then political prisoner, surprised his critics by using one of the yearly visits to Havana to which he is allowed as a member of the Cuban community living abroad as the platform from which to launch his most ambitious project yet: opening an office in Havana for his political organization. At the last minute, Gutiérrez Menoyo bid farewell to his wife and his children, and decided to stay in Havana, reclaiming his right as a Cuban citizen to live in his own country. It was clear from the outset that it presented the Cuban state with a problem in a context of growing internal unrest resulting from the 2003 prison sentences handed out to writers, independent journalists, members of human rights groups, and other segments of the internal opposition.

13. Ann Louise Bardach, *Cuba Confidential: Love and Vengeance in Miami and Havana* (New York: Random House, 2002), xviii–xx.

14. Some economic changes were advocated within the Centro de Estudios de América (CEA), an economic think tank closely associated with the government that was nevertheless closed down because its analyses were increasingly incisive and disturbing. This is impressively reconstructed in Maurizio Giuliano, *El caso CEA. Intelectuales e inquisidores en Cuba ¿Perestroika en la isla?* (Miami: Ediciones Universal, 1998).

15. Although for some time Cuba has had a market for foreign goods bartered for sexual favors—as happened in most socialist countries, at least since the 1970s—it became a problem in the 1990s and was evident on the streets of Havana in a way unseen for the previous decades.

16. See Homero Campa and Orlando Pérez, *Cuba: los años duros* (Barcelona: Plaza y Janés, 1997), 157–218, for a fuller account of the economic situation in the early 1990s.

17. See the film *Balseros* directed by Carlos Bosch and Josep Ma Domenech (Bausan Films, 2002) for a good account of this situation. It focuses on the lives of a number of Cubans who left during the *balsero* crisis of 1994 and follows them to the United States. The film avoids taking a critical stance toward the Cuban government and sees the refugee crisis as part of a worldwide migration from poor to rich countries. The first part of the film, which takes place in Havana, underscores the degree to which the *balsero* crisis was a media event, as the government gave free and unimpeded access to journalists the world over to photograph events as they were unfolding. The film was shown in Cuba once during the Havana Film Festival, but other

shows had to be added by popular demand. Within the Cuban context, the film gave further argument to the government's warnings against leaving the island, and generally portrayed life outside of Cuba as difficult and bleak.

18. Eliseo Alberto is particularly embittered by this, and part of his memoir is also an account of what the city meant to his circle of friends, most of whom were artists or writers: "The Havana that is now photographed by visitors is a broken city, attacked by lack of efficiency, mistreated by administrative incapacities, abandoned, besieged from the inside and the outside, bitten by the vermin of despondency; an old, naked city . . . a pure fossil . . ." (Alberto, *Informe contra mí mismo*, 130–31).

19. Books that have been useful in general terms include Bardach, *Cuba Confidential*, Campa and Pérez, *Cuba*, and Manuel Vázquez Montalbán, *Y Dios entró en La Habana* (Madrid: Grupo Santillana de Ediciones, 1998).

20. Pedro Juan Gutiérrez, *El Rey de La Habana* (Barcelona: Anagrama, 1999), 148–50.

21. Arturo Arango, "To Write in Cuba, Today," *South Atlantic Quarterly* 96:1 (winter 1997): 118.

22. See Roberto Fernández Retamar, *Calibán: Apuntes sobre la cultura en nuestra América* (Mexico City: Editorial Diógenes, 1971).

23. "The devaluation of our own culture has its roots in the frustration of individual expectations during the second stage of the revolutionary process, from 1970 to 1980" (Fernando Martínez Heredia, "In the Furnace of the Nineties: Identity and Society in Cuba Today," *boundary 2* 29:3 [2002]: 144).

24. For Padilla's own account of these times, readers should consult his memoir *La mala memoria* (Barcelona: Plaza y Janés, 1989). For a complete dossier of all the documentation on the case, see Lourdes Casal, ed., *El Caso Padilla: literatura y revolución en Cuba* (Miami: Ediciones Universal, n.d.).

25. The exhibition Volumen 1 in 1981 represents, according to many critics, the founding moment of the New Cuban Art. The first Havana Bienal took place in 1984, with prizes for painting, engraving, dancing, and photography. However, in October 1988, the last Arte Calle show was shut down; exhibitions at the Proyecto Castillo de la Real Fuerza in 1989 were closed down and the vice minister of culture was removed from office. In spite of these initial conflicts, the government has considerably opened the space for visual arts as a source of cultural revenue and prestige abroad. As Coco Fusco has remarked, by 1995 the government was very interested in "launching work by Cuban nationals into the mainstream world of the United States" (Coco Fusco, *English Is Broken Here: Notes on Cultural Fusion in the Americas* [New York: New Press, 1995], 125).

26. See, for example, *La Gaceta de Cuba*, no. 5 (September–October 1996), with a sample of writings by Louis A. Pérez Jr., Ruth Behar, María de los Ángeles Torres, Cristina García, and Gustavo Pérez Firmat.

27. In the September–October 1996 issue of *La Gaceta de Cuba*, Ambrosio Fornet attacks Antonio Vera-León's questioning of the writer's cultural autonomy vis-à-vis governmental cultural projects. The question of cultural autonomy was a particularly contentious point, and Vera-León argues—correctly, in my mind—that subjects do not necessarily think of culture from monolithic referents to a presumed "Cuban" way

of thinking. Vera-León also critiques Fornet's insistence on separating culture and language versus Rine Leal's more open gesture of trying to understand Cuban theater regardless of the language in which it is written.

28. *Encuentro de la cultura cubana* has been a controversial journal. Joining in the dispute, John Beverley stated in his preface to a special issue of *boundary 2* (2002) that "*Encuentro* has become in effect an exile publication, which rarely has anything good to say about Cuba and which publishes primarily those intellectuals in Cuba who are explicitly identified with a dissident or 'liberal' position, like its own"(8). This statement underscores his decision to publish the special issue without including Cuban authors who do not live in Cuba—although by the time the issue went to press, some of the authors he included had left the island. See also, from Cuba, Pedro de la Hoz's very negative reading of *Encuentro,* in which he accuses it of being a right-wing journal ("Desencuentros y lejanías," *La Gaceta de Cuba,* no. 5 [September–October 1996]: 56–58). His polemics against *Encuentro* need to be underscored by the displeasure of Cuban authorities at the addition of Antonio José Ponte to the journal's editorial board. The National Union of Cuban Writers and Artists considered expelling Ponte from its ranks because of this. That it did not was certainly because of gestures of solidarity by his colleagues in the face of yet another instance of governmental intransigence.

29. Fidel Díaz, "Pero los dientes no hincan en la luz," attacks Ponte for "minimizing" Martí and turning him into an object of ridicule, undermining "the thoughts, heroes, and symbols of the nation" (*Temas: Cultura-Ideología-Sociedad,* no. 29, [April–June 2002]: 112). Ponte's piece is a stunningly sensitive meditation on Martí. The article "introduces" Ponte's "El abrigo de aire," which is reproduced immediately afterwards. See 111–23 for the whole polemic, including Ponte's essay.

30. Debates about the "diaspora" have become more numerous over the course of the past decade. See also Ernesto Rodríguez Chávez, "Notas sobre la identidad cubana en su relación con la diáspora, *Temas: Cultura-Ideología-Sociedad,* no. 28 [January–March 2002], 44–55). Cuban identity, he explains, at this point is found not only within the island, but also in its diaspora.

31. The question of nomenclature in itself is a political minefield, as is discussed at other points in this book. For example, in "The Cuban Literary Diaspora and Its Contexts: A Glossary," Ambrosio Fornet argues against using the term "exile," which in Cuba carries a long history of radical and revolutionary connotations, for the "semantic neutrality" of "diaspora," though he also has reservations in this regard (*boundary 2* 29:3 [2002]: 92). For Fornet, literary nationality is also a question of language and context. He reads Cuban "diaspora" literature as part of a migratory, rootless mode of writing within the context of the First World, and not within the Cuban context: "If we are going to talk seriously about the literary discourse of the diaspora, if we want to know in what way it resembles and differs from the literature that is produced here, we must begin by trying to understand what is most specific to it, including its own historical and cultural contexts, *which are not our own*" (103; emphasis added). All these polemics show to what extent it is important to recognize the growing body of work produced by Cubans outside the island, while at the same time they show to what extent Cuban intellectuals try to discipline—in a Foucauldian sense— what is considered properly "Cuban."

32. *Areíto* was published in the United States. Its first issue appeared in 1974, and it openly supported the egalitarian policies of the Cuban Revolution. Its editors accused the exile community and its media of racial intolerance, sexism, and political conservatism. The editors considered themselves above all Cuban, and insisted that *cubanía* was found in the island itself. They did not consider themselves Cuban-Americans, nor exiles, but rather Cubans who lived in the United States. This position produced enormous hostility in Miami especially, and their ethnic and political identification would change over time. They were an alienated group of young people, and they encountered enormous hostility within the Cuban exile community. See María Cristina García, *Havana, USA: Cuban Exiles and Cuban Americans in South Florida, 1959–1994* (Berkeley: University of California Press, 1996), 201–2. *Areíto* went so far as to criticize those who left Cuba via Mariel in the 1980s, which in turn prompted Reinaldo Arenas to call them "the official organ of the Cuban state police in New York" (ibid., 203).

33. The Stockholm Encounter brought together members of the generation divided by the 1970s, and their two collective statements were that (1) Cuban culture was a unified whole, regardless of where it was produced, and (2) the U.S. embargo had to be lifted. The Olof Palme center also published two volumes, dividing Cubans living on the island from those who lived abroad, edited by René Vázquez Díaz and titled *Cuba: voces para cerrar un siglo* (Stockholm: Centro Internacional Olof Palme, 1999). Volume 1, which contains writers living on the island, includes essays by Abilio Estévez, Ena Lucía Portela, Francisco López Sacha, and Leonardo Padura Fuentes, among others. Volume 2, dedicated to those who live abroad, features Mayra Montero, José Kozer, Pío Serrano, Rafael Rojas, and Daína Chaviano, among others.

34. The fact that there are few women essayists in Cuba these days points to how gendered the Cuban cultural space is after more than four decades of social experimentation. Two notable exceptions are Margarita Mateo Palmer, *Ella escribía poscrítica* (Havana: Casa Editora Abril, 1995), and, outside of Cuba, Madeline Camara, *La letra rebelde: estudios de escritoras cubanas* (Miami: Editorial Universal, 2002). Although magazines such as *Encuentro* in Madrid have devoted essays to the questions of feminism in Cuba, most attention is centered on questions of nationality, politics, and the public sphere defined principally in male-centered terms. See the insightful article on women by Madeline Cámara, "Una promesa incumplida: la emancipación de la mujer cubana," *Encuentro*, no. 6/7 (fall/winter 1997): 212–16. In the most recent index published by the journal from the summer of 1996 to the spring of 2002, there are only two articles on Cuban women, one under the entry "Women in Literature—Latin America," and no entries on "Feminism."

35. For an assessment of this situation see, among others, Holly Block, ed., *Art Cuba: The New Generation* (New York: Harry N. Abrams, 2001).

36. The best recent analyses of this tradition can be found in Rafael Rojas, *Isla sin fin: Contribución a la crítica del nacionalismo cubano* (Miami: Ediciones Universal, 1998).

37. Judith Butler, *The Psychic Life of Power: Theories in Subjection* (Stanford, CA: Stanford University Press, 1997). For Butler, power is not necessarily external to the subject but, rather, is what makes the subject *possible* in the first place. Internalized

power is what gives the subject a sense of agency. Although the subject may fight power in order to achieve liberation, it also *uses* power in order to become a subject in the first place. The subject, as Butler defines it, is an entity that incorporates things— not merely a being that rejects and delimits all that does not conform to its vision of self. Subjection, usually defined as "a power exerted on the subject," is also a power "assumed by" the subject in order to *become.*

38. Gustavo Pérez Firmat, *Next Year in Cuba: A Cubano's Coming of Age in America* (New York: Doubleday, 1995), 20.

39. Ibid., 37.

40. A narrative about this film can be found in Jean-François Fogel and Bertrand Rosenthal, *Fin de siglo en La Habana: los secretos del derrumbe de Fidel,* trans. Helena Uribe de Lemoine (Bogotá: Tercer Mundo Editores, 1994), 468.

41. Antonio José Ponte, "A Throw of the Book of Changes," in *In the Cold of the Malecón,* trans. Cola Franzen and Dick Cluster (San Francisco: City Lights Books, 2000), 40.

42. All quotes are from Reina María Rodríguez, "—Al menos, así lo veía a contraluz—," in *La isla en su tinta: Antología de la poesía cubana,* ed. Francisco Morán (Madrid: Ediciones Verbum, 2000), 252–56.

43. "la foto también morirá / por la humedad del mar, la duración; / el contacto, la devoción, la obsesión / fatal de repetir tantas veces que seríamos como él."

44. I am here echoing Román de la Campa's excellent book *Cuba on My Mind: Journeys to a Severed Nation* (New York: Verso, 2000), from which I have learned a lot.

HISTORY ON THE ROCKS

1. As just one example, Fernando Ortiz's *Contrapunteo cubano del tabaco y el azúcar* uses the musical term "counterpoint" to great effect, by engaging the contrapuntal dynamic as one of "transculturation"—in broad terms, the way in which vernacular culture emerges, as a recasting of foreign elements. In Ortiz's text, the counterpoint at its most fundamental level deals with tobacco and sugar as contrasting products that, over the course of Cuban history, have defined as well as determined Cuban character, an allegorical counterpoint in which history and chance pair off. Ortiz had in mind not only how Cuban history and culture could be represented for Cubans, but also how they had inscribed themselves within broader international representation. Other critical and literary works that deal with history and representation include Nicolás Guillén's *Motivos de son* (1930), one of the most important Afro-Caribbean texts of all time; Jorge Mañach's *Indagación del choteo* (1928), which examines how Cubans deflate the worthy sentiment of national uplift; and Antonio Benítez Rojo's *The Repeating Island* (1992). For an excellent account of Cuban critical discourse during the republic, see Gustavo Pérez Firmat, *The Cuban Condition: Translation and Identity in Modern Cuban Literature* (Cambridge: Cambridge University Press, 1989).

2. I am quoting from Virgilio Piñera, *La isla en peso,* ed. Antón Arrufat (Havana: Ediciones Unión, 1998), 33.

3. Actually, Piñera was first republished in the 1980s in Spain by Editorial Alfaguara, which brought out his *Cuentos* (1983), *La carne de René* (1985), and *Pequeñas*

maniobras, along with *Presiones y diamantes* (1986). The contentious nature of these new editions was evident when an English translation by Mark Schafer for Eridanos Press (1988) was removed from circulation because it contained a prologue by Guillermo Cabrera Infante, titled "The Death of Virgilio," in which the Cuban novelist presented Piñera as a writer pursued by the state in the 1970s. In 1989, Eridanos Press reprinted the translation, at this point with a prologue by Antón Arrufat, who since then has been the person most responsible for the reprints of Piñera's work in Cuba as well as abroad. That this was a particularly contentious process, involving copyright restrictions, intellectual memory, and cultural capital, can be seen in my essay "Piñera inconcluso" in *Virgilio Piñera: la memoria del cuerpo,* ed. Rita Molinero (San Juan: Editorial Plaza Mayor, 2002), 163–80.

4. Toward the end of the 1990s, and once Piñera had been firmly entrenched within the Cuban canon, a magazine such as *La isla en peso,* taking its title from his poem, was launched as part of a growing list of literary magazines and cultural sites that can be accessed via the Web. Its editor is Roberto Zurbano.

5. Rafael Rojas, "Alegorías de la revolución," in *Isla sin fin: Contribución a la crítica del nacionalismo cubano* (Miami: Ediciones Universal, 1998), 188–215, particularly 209. Rojas also mentions Castro's speech of October 10, 1968, in which Castro pushes back the revolutionary struggle by stating that there had been only one revolution in Cuba, and this had originated in 1868 against slavery and for independence from Spain, and that this was continued in 1959, against North American imperialism and for socialism.

6. Ibid., 191.

7. Fidel Castro, *History Will Absolve Me* (Havana: Editorial de Ciencias Sociales, 1975), 5.

8. Eduardo Cadava, *Words of Light: Theses on the Photography of History* (Princeton, NJ: Princeton University Press, 1997), 72, 73.

9. Castro, *History Will Absolve Me,* 195.

10. Slavoj Žižek, *The Sublime Object of Ideology* (London: Verso, 1989), 142.

11. Friedrich Nietzsche, *On the Genealogy of Morals,* trans. Walter Kaufmann and R. J. Hollingdale, ed. Walter Kaufmann (New York: Vintage Books, 1969), second essay, sec. 19, 89.

12. Rafael Rojas, "El peso del olvido," in *El arte de la espera: notas al margen de la política cubana* (Barcelona: Editorial Colibrí, 1998), 29–32.

13. Louis Pérez Jr., "Toward a New Future, from a New Past: The Enterprise of History in Socialist Cuba," *Cuban Studies/Estudios Cubanos,* 15:1 (winter, 1985): 1–13.

14. For a very moving account of what this period meant, see Antón Arrufat's *Virgilio Piñera entre el y yo,* published in 1994, in the midst of the Special Period. The fact that already by that time this period was openly talked about gives a good idea of the extent to which past repressions could be talked about in Cuba in the 1990s. See especially: "We were not only dead in life, we seemed never to have been born, nor written. New generations were educated to despise all that we had done, or to ignore it. We were taken out of our jobs and sent to work where no one would know us" ([Havana: Ediciones Unión, 1994], 42). For nine years, between 1971 and 1979, Arrufat was ordered to work at the Marianao Public Library, and he was not allowed to write nor read the materials he archived. This was punishment for his having

written *Los siete contra Tebas,* which won the prestigious UNEAC theater prize in 1968. Arrufat did not publish again in Cuba until 1984, when his novel *La caja está cerrada* appeared. For useful information, including Arrufat's statements, see the special issue of *Encuentro de la cultura cubana* dedicated to Antón Arrufat (no. 20 [Spring 2001]).

15. Abel Prieto's comments on resistance as state policy are from a speech titled "Cultura, cubanidad, cubanía" and given at a conference titled "La nación y la emigración" that took place April 22–24, 1994, in Havana.

16. This site appears not only in Hitchcock's *Topaz,* but also in a different, more farcical register, in Woody Allen's *Bananas.*

17. Contrary to the protocolar structure of Cuban-U.S. relations, the United States had not been Fidel's first visit abroad. He went first to Venezuela, a country that had also recently thrown out the dictator Marcos Pérez Jiménez. This has been important lately, given the close relations that have developed between Fidel and Venezuela's Hugo Chávez.

18. The account of this visit appears in Hugh Thomas, *Cuba: The Pursuit of Freedom* (New York: Harper & Row, 1971), 1208–13. The public relations part was organized by Bernard Reilling of New York, and, apart from a lunch with the acting secretary of state, the only official meeting was with Nixon, because President Eisenhower was playing golf in Carolina. After the meeting with Nixon, the latter concluded that a force of Cuban exiles should be armed immediately to overthrow Castro, although at this point, according to Thomas, "Castro's heart was with the West in the cold war" (1211). Castro was irritated with the constant U.S. concern about communism: "it was as if the U.S. did not care what Cuba was, provided it was not Communist" (ibid.).

19. Van Gosse, *Where the Boys Are: Cuba, Cold War America, and the Making of a New Left* (London: Verso, 1993), 112. Van Gosse adds that the first visit "reinforced the subversive appeal of *fidelismo*" to youth, and, curiously, that *Life* reported, on April 13, "a toy manufacturer had 100,000 Fidel cap-and-beard sets ready to hit the market." Van Gosse adds that the "accompanying photos of a gang of little boys running around the New Jersey woods pretending to ambush each other seem familiar to any North American of a certain age, except that instead of Davy Crockett coonskin caps or plastic GI Joe helmets, their khaki fatigue caps sport a 26th of July movement logo and the legend 'El Libertador'. Even odder, though, is that the caps' chin-straps are covered in thick black hair, for a moment creating the illusion that a host of tiny, grinning barbudos has sprouted from North American soil" (113).

20. Louis Pérez Jr., *On Becoming Cuban: Identity, Nationality, and Culture* (Chapel Hill: University of North Carolina Press, 1999), 490. The irony of the situation was further compounded by the fact that most of the liberals in the first revolutionary administration had been educated in North American schools. As Pérez puts it, "the U.S. dispute with Cuba in 1959 was, ironically, largely with the policies and programs enacted by men and women most closely identified with North American practices" (488). This U.S. opposition, in fact, was one of the decisive contributing factors in undermining the internal position of the liberals. If, in the nineteenth century, to be a patriot was to be anti-Spanish, after 1960, as Pérez remarks, "to be Cuban implied increasingly to be anti-American" (490).

21. According to Thomas, Castro's own plane "was impounded under writs of attachment obtained in Miami against Cuban debts" (*Cuba*, 1295). Castro left behind more than half of his delegation, and the visit, Thomas concludes, "had served little purpose" (ibid.).

22. Van Gosse, *Where the Boys Are*, 150.

23. Carlos Franqui, *Retrato de familia con Fidel* (Barcelona: Seix Barral, 1981).

24. Ralph Crowder also mentions the fact that Malcolm helped in bringing the delegation to Harlem, and that an anonymous Harlem gangster gave the Fair Play for Cuba Committee one thousand dollars for the room deposit. See Ralph Crowder, "Fidel Castro and Harlem: Political, Diplomatic, and Social Influences of the 1960 Visit to the Hotel Theresa," *Afro-Americans in New York Life and History* 24:1 (2000): 79.

25. According to Van Gosse, Gibson "deserves the credit for making African-Americans some of the most prominent spokespersons in defense of the Cuban revolution and for FPCC [Fair Play for Cuba Committee]" (*Where the Boys Are*, 147).

26. The issue included original contributions by LeRoi Jones, Langston Hughes, James Baldwin, Harold Cruse, John Hendrik Clarve, and Alice Childress. Van Gosse adds that "the magazine's visuals made the clearest possible analogy between reaction at home and abroad" (ibid., 147–48).

27. Van Gosse just recounts the situation: "C. Wright Mills, Allen Ginsberg, I. F. Stone and Henri Cartier-Bresson joined 250 other luminati of the left and the arts in the Theresa ballroom, where Richard Gibson handed Fidel a small bust of Lincoln, ad-libbing 'from one Liberator to another' and Ginsberg asked security chief Major Ramiro Valdés, 'What does the Cuban Revolution think about marijuana?'" (ibid., 151). There is also an account of the question in Franqui, *Retrato de familia con Fidel*, (172). There is no record of what Valdés replied. Ginsberg was notoriously upset at the Cubans' antimarijuana policy, as befit his antigovernment stance. In his "Prose Contribution to the Cuban Revolution," written in Athens in October 1961, Ginsberg explained: "I'm NOT down on the Cubans or anti their revolution, it's just that it's important to make clear *in advance, in front,* what I feel about life. Big statements saying Viva Fidel are/would be/meaningless and just 2-dimensional politics" (quoted in Van Gosse, *Where the Boys Are*, 191). In his 1965 visit when he was deported from Cuba, Ginsberg explained to Allen Young: "I took one stick of grass one day, walking along a shady street with a bearded fellow who said he's been up in the mountains with Castro and that they had smoked up there" (Allen Young, *Gays under the Cuban Revolution* [San Francisco: Grey Fox Press, 1981], 21). In general, the alliance between the Beats and the revolutionaries did not bear fruits in the case of Ginsberg, who accused the revolutionaries of being "Self-seeking squares, not at all spiritually communist . . . setting themselves at odds against the people who screw with their eyes open, listen to the Beatles and read interesting books like Genet, and *fought* at the Bay of Pigs against the Americans" (20). More recently, Huber Matos, one of Fidel's most important collaborators in the revolutionary war, and later condemned to twenty years in prison, mentioned in his memoir that Fidel entered into pacts with marijuana growers in the Sierra who were also collaborating with the rebel army. See Huber Matos, *Cómo llegó la noche* (Barcelona: Tusquets Editores, 2002), 123–24.

28. Allen Young quotes a big part of Allen Ginsberg's interview with Gay Sunshine Press in 1974 in which he explained what got him deported: "Well, the worst thing I said was that I'd heard by rumor that Raúl Castro was gay. And the second worst thing I said was that Che Guevara was cute . . ." (Young, *Gays under the Cuban Revolution*, 20).

29. Franqui recounts the street scenes in front of the Hotel Theresa, as he does his story throughout the book, in short paragraphs, sometimes composed of just one sentence. But there is no doubt that only after Harlem was completely sold on the idea of the young *barbudos* did Fidel bring out Juan Almeida and Celia Sanchez: "And a thankful Fidel sent out for Juan Almeida, the *comandante* from the sierra, a hero who was the Virgin of Charity's little black boy. // The rest of the delegation was all white and masculine. // Almeida and Celia were the symbols" (*Retrato de familia con Fidel*, 163).

30. Guevara's words are from a talk to *Nuestro Tiempo* association and they are quoted by Thomas, *Cuba*, 1038–39. Subsequent references are given in the text.

31. Louis Perez Jr. makes the further point that most of the reforms initiated by the new administration at that time were put in place by liberals who had been educated at American schools. "Almost all of them would resign by the end of the first eighteen months, as radicals took over the government" (*On Becoming Cuban*, 488). For Pérez, the historical irony of the situation is that the United States isolated "policies and programs enacted by men and women most closely identified with North American practices" and thus undermined their positions (ibid.).

32. Van Gosse, *Where the Boys Are*, 165.

33. Louis Pérez Jr., *Cuba and the United States: Ties of Singular Intimacy* (Athens: University of Georgia Press, 1990).

34. Pérez, *On Becoming Cuban*, 492.

35. Michel Foucault, "Of Other Spaces," *Diacritics* (spring 1986): 22–27.

36. Katherine Verdery, *The Political Lives of Dead Bodies: Reburial and Postsocialist Change* (New York: Columbia University Press, 1999).

37. Foucault, "Of Other Spaces." At the same time, it is important to warn against understanding the notion of "site" in a very literal manner. They are not sites with "no real place" like utopias, while at the same time it is clear that they include sites, such as cemeteries, churches, brothels, and others, yet are not limited to these.

38. Thomas was one of the first serious historians to be fascinated with the social changes brought about since 1959, and with the fact that a strategically located island had managed to affect world events to an extent previously unseen. In many ways, his book is a fascinating object in and of itself. It is partly the result of Europe's romance with the revolution during its first decade, but it is also a case study in how colonialism affected one particular place that had managed to insert itself in the midst of a broad net of issues, culminating with the showdown produced during the missile crisis.

ESPIONAGE AND IDENTITY

1. As Persephone Braham has perceptively noted in *Crimes against the State, Crimes against Persons* (Minneapolis: University of Minnesota Press, 2004), in 1972 the

Cuban ministry of the interior instigated the creation of a new genre, the socialist detective novel. It was a "medium for advancing government ideology, promoting conformity with revolutionary norms, and reinforcing the unmasking and suppression of antisocial tendencies" (29), but it was also a way of shifting literary discourse away from what Cuban Marxist critics called "formalist," which in this context was understood as avant-garde experimentalism and portrayed in gendered terms as "not virile" (associated with homosexuality), and thus bourgeois and decadent.

2. All references to *Spy vs. Spy* and to Prohías's work in Cuba originate from *Spy vs. Spy: The Complete Casebook* (New York: Watson-Hill Publications, 2001). These include interviews with Prohías's editors as well as family members and are given in the text.

3. These dailies were in turn compromised to varying degrees with the government—Batista himself was the owner of the newspaper *Pueblo* and the weekly *Gente*—so this is not to argue that "freedom of the press" prevailed, although Cubans did possess a lot of information in terms of events in other parts of the world.

4. He added: "I think words are superfluous. In fact, even in Cuba I used Spanish as little as possible. All the power was in the drawings" (*Spy vs. Spy*, 8).

5. All information about this game comes from Ilana Rudnik's unofficial *Spy vs. Spy* home page. See www.itsgames.com/usr/ilana/mad/svsgame.htm.

6. The number of 612 attempts comes from an interview with Division General Fabián Escalante, former head of Cuban State Security, in *CIA Targets Fidel: Secret 1967 CIA Inspector General's Report on Plots to Assassinate Fidel Castro* (Melbourne, Australia: Ocean Press, 1996), 8. María Cristina García, in *Havana, USA: Cuban Exiles and Cuban Americans in South Florida, 1959–1994* (Berkeley: University of California Press, 1996), says that there were "eight different CIA plots to assassinate Fidel Castro from 1960 to 1965" (241 n. 16).

7. García, *Havana, USA*, 130–31.

8. Ibid., 131.

9. Ernest Volkman, *Espionage: The Greatest Spy Operations of the Twentieth Century* (New York: John Wiley and Sons, 1995), 16–17.

10. In Miami, during the contentious end of the 1970s and the beginning of the 1980s, the Reverend Manuel Espinosa delivered a broadside, carried live by many Miami radio stations, "exposing" a number of members of the Cuban-American community as having been, or being, Cuban spies and agents. This information, as well as that up to the end of this section, comes from Rafael de la Cova's very thorough Web site. See www.rose-hulman.edu/~delacova/cuba.htm.

11. Cuba's espionage apparatus figures come from a report written by the Endowment for Cuban American Studies of the Jorge Mas Canosa Freedom Foundation, which is, admittedly, a very partisan attempt to convince U.S. lawmakers that Cuba still represents a threat to U.S. and hemispheric security. See *Cuba: Assessing the Threat to U.S. Security*, ed. Adolfo Leyva de Varona (Miami: Endowment for Cuban American Studies, 2001), 13. The movement of the attachés and the USIA can be found in Garcia, *Havana, USA*, 216–17.

12. García, *Havana, USA*, 241 n. 16.

13. In 1982, the Miami City Commission "unanimously approved a resolution calling upon the U.S. Attorney General to require that the Maceo brigade—composed of

Cubans more sympathetic to the Revolution—register as a 'foreign agent of the government of Cuba'" (ibid., 204).

14. Ibid., 141.

15. Ibid., 141–43. Cuban exiles' relationship with the CIA came to light once again when Luis Posada Carriles, accused of planting the bomb that killed seventy-three Cubana Airlines passengers in Barbados, surfaced in the United States in May 2005. As a known terrorist suspect who had been on the CIA payroll in Central America, his case has proven embarrassing to U.S. authorities, especially as it concerns the U.S. "war on terror."

16. Their identities were divulged by the defense attorneys on December 6, 2000; they had refused to identify themselves and the FBI had been unable to determine their real names. In turn, the Cuban state published a more complete report on them on June 20, 2001, three years after they were charged. It alleged that, given the heroic character of their mission, it had felt the need to wait that long so as to unmask and denounce the blatant acts of the Miami police and judicial authorities ("era necesario esperar el desarollo del largo y tenebroso período que duró el proceso desde el arresto hasta la injusta decisión del jurado, para desenmascarar y denunciar la impúdica actuación de las autoridades policiales y judiciales de Miami"). See *Cinco patriotas cubanos rehenes del imperio* (Buenos Aires: Ediciones Colihue, 2002), 137.

17. They were the first secretary, Eduardo Martínez Borbonet; counselor Gonzalo Fernández Garay; and the third secretary, Roberto Azanza Paez.

18. There are two versions of this tale. One claims that the officer who was going to defect was José Imperatori, whom Faget had met with at a bar at the Miami airport. The other version names Luis Molina as the agent whom Pesquera said was about to defect.

19. See "USA INS Spy Working for Castro's Government" at http://home.swipnet. se/~w-93068.htm.

20. It was not clear what Imperatori's connection was to the case. Imperatori knew Font, and it was through Font that he met Antonio Faget. In the drama that ensued, it is not clear who at this point was going to defect. Initial reports said it was Luis Molina, but other reports said it was José Imperatori. Molina had held Imperatori's position previously.

21. Although Cuban officials at the UN mission in New York have been accused of espionage, Imperatori said that the Cuban government had expressly forbidden spying by diplomats at the Cuban Interests Section in Washington.

22. *Washington Post*, February 27, 2000, 1, 24.

23. The immediate background to the Web of the Wasp was the shooting down by Cuban MiGs of two civilian aircraft belonging to the group Brothers to the Rescue in international waters. Cuba alleged continuous violations of its airspace by the group, which had been founded in 1991 by exile José Basulto in order to rescue the growing numbers of *balseros* (rafters) fleeing Cuba's desperate economic and political conditions for Florida. The flights were clearly a provocation to the Cuban government, with Basulto and his group going so far as to drop leaflets over Havana. On February 24, 1996, Castro directly ordered that the planes be shot down, and in the ensuing confrontation four Cuban-Americans, including three U.S. citizens, were killed. According to Ann Louise Bardach, Castro at this point disregarded the pleas

of Ricardo Alarcón and other moderates of the regime (*Cuba Confidential: Love and Vengeance in Miami and Havana* [New York: Random House, 2002], 133). The event prompted President Clinton to brand the Cuban government as "repressive" and it produced the famous press conference were Madeline Albright attacked the Cubans as having no *cojones*. The fracas also had an espionage component to it, as Cuban agent Juan Pablo Roque, who had come to Miami to infiltrate the organization, fled to Cuba hours before the shoot-down, leaving a jilted wife, Ana Margarita Martínez, who would in turn sue the Cuban government for "rape." In Cuba, Roque denounced the exile organization and accused it of planning terrorist attacks against the island.

24. González Sehwerert's wife, Olga Salanueva Arango, was deported at the end of 2000 back to Cuba. Cuban official accounts state that she managed to join her two daughters in Cuba after she was taken prisoner and blackmailed in order to force her to testify against her husband ("despues de estar prisionera y ser chantajeada para que declarase") (*Cinco patriotas cubanos rehenes del imperio*, 130).

25. Although it was founded in 1991 to rescue *balseros*, over the years Brothers to the Rescue has played a more proactive political role.

26. The infiltration at the more modest levels of the Cuban-American community led some to believe the implausible, in the ever more implausible world of Cuban paranoia: first, that the spies were set up in order to be discovered, and then that the spies themselves were part of an elaborate joke played at the expense of the Cuban exile community.

27. The reason Gerardo received such a tough sentence was that he collaborated in another part of the running narrative of this spy case, another tangled web in the network: he was involved in the shooting down of the Brothers to the Rescue plane in 1996, in which Carlos Costa, Armando Alejandre, Mario de la Peña, and Pablo Morales died. Within the narrative of exile, these four are heroes—just as the five condemned spies are heroes in Cuba.

28. One such case was that of Orlando Bosch, who was accused of a bombing in 1976, and served eleven years in prison in Venezuela before being acquitted in 1988. Bosch traveled to Miami; the associate attorney general ordered him deported but was overruled by federal authorities, who ordered him to stay. Bosch was pardoned on July 18, 1990, after Rep. Ileana Ros-Lehtinen intervened on his behalf by meeting with then-President George Bush to negotiate his release. The meeting was arranged by Jeb Bush, the president's son and now Florida governor.

29. See Bardach, *Cuba Confidential*, 207–14.

A CUBAN LOVE AFFAIR WITH THE IMAGE

1. Although she focuses on the allure of nightlife, and the touristy packaged return of Havana as a city of fashionable sin, Rosalie Schwartz's *Pleasure Island: Tourism and Temptation in Cuba* (Lincoln and London: University of Nebraska Press, 1999) establishes the disconnected experience of tourists in Havana, who are taken around in air-conditioned buses and housed in luxurious hotels, actors in a drama that "plays to a worldwide audience eager to know the fate of Cuba's socialist and tourist experiments" (xv).

2. Susan Sontag, *Regarding the Pain of Others* (New York: Farrar, Straus and Giroux, 2003), 8.

3. *Our Islands and Their People as Seen with Camera and Pencil,* ed. William S. Bryan, introduction by Major General Joseph Wheeler, with special descriptive matter and narratives by José de Olivares (New York: N. D. Thomson Publishing Company, 1899).

4. See James R. Mellow, *Walker Evans* (New York: Basic Books, 1999), 202–4, 223–25.

5. Ibid., 176. In an undated diary entry, Evans wrote that "The political situation was critical at the moment" but then he crossed it out. His biographer adduces ambivalence on Evans's part as to whether the assignment was a political or a professional mission.

6. Ibid.

7. See Gilles Mora, "Havana 1933: A Seminal Work," trans. Christie McDonald, in *Walker Evans: Havana 1933* (New York: Pantheon, 1989), 9.

8. According to his biographer, this gave him "some measure of flexibility with the quicker hand-held shots and the inevitably more static shots necessitated by the setting-up of the tripod exposures" (Mellow, *Walker Evans,* 176).

9. "In later years, Evans would claim that he had not read the Beals book before his trip to Cuba. That was essentially true—Beals had not completed the manuscript by the time Evans left for Cuba in the middle of May" (ibid., 175).

10. In the end, as his biographer states, "[t]he photographs are not, in the most emphatic sense, indictments, statements of innocence or guilt, but images of the observant eye. The sequence ends with a picture of words, political slogans scrawled on a wall: 'We support the strike of the cigar workers,' probably from some labor party, and 'Down with the Imperialist War,' signed P.C. for the Communist Party" (ibid., 192). The photographs received a minor commendation in the *New York Times Book Review,* though it did reproduce "a full-width horizontal of his photograph 'Villa of Havana Poor'" (ibid.).

11. Antonio José Ponte, *In The Cold of the Malecón,* trans. Cola Franzen and Dick Cluster (San Francisco: City Lights Books, 2000).

12. Juan Antonio Molina, researcher and curator at the Centro Wifredo Lam in Havana, quoted in "Cuba: Image and Imagination," special issue of *Aperture* 141 (fall 1995): 18.

13. "Foreword," in Osvaldo Salas, *Fidel's Cuba: A Revolution in Pictures* (New York: Thunder's Mouth Press, 1998), 6.

14. Ibid.

15. Ibid.

16. According to Tim B. Wride, who wrote the notes to *Shifting Tides: Cuban Photography after the Revolution* (Los Angeles: Los Angeles County Museum of Art, 2001), the first generation created the indelible image of the heroic, whereas the second generation was most concerned, from the mid-1960s to the mid-1970s (also called the "golden age" of Cuban photojournalism), with the heroism of its almost anonymous citizens. The same narrative may also be found in Gareth Jenkins, ed., *Havana in My Heart: 75 Years of Cuban Photography* (Chicago: Chicago Review Press, 2002).

17. Alberto "Korda" Díaz Gutiérrez died in May 2001, and five days later his elder daughter, Diana Díaz López, claimed inheritance rights to his work. This claim was contested by some of Korda's other children, including Dante Díaz, who fled with his family in 2002 and asked for political asylum in Miami after he was threatened with eviction from his house for supposedly contesting the will. In July 2003, French courts prohibited the French organization Reporters sans Frontières from distributing copies of Che's image to tourists embarking on Cuba flights, as a result of the organization's position opposing the incarceration of journalists in Cuba. Diane Díaz had sued the organization for about $1.4 million, but French courts forced Reporters sans Frontières to pay $7,344.

18. Paradoxically, the most innovative recent artistic works in Cuba do not involve photography, but rather installation art. Because photography became so linked to the representation of the social process, it has been particularly difficult for photographers to disengage from this link. Because the canvas was always somehow "insufficient," Cuban artists have more recently turned to a hybrid mixture of sculpture, photography, and installation in order to represent projects that critically engage the dictates of the state.

19. Miguel Castro Muñiz, "Micronotas fotográficas," in *Cuba: 100 años de la fotografía cubana, 1898–1998* (Madrid: Mestizo, 1998).

20. Ibid., 21.

21. Ibid.

22. Emma Álvarez-Tabío Albo, *Invención de La Habana* (Barcelona: Editorial Casiopea, 2000), 18.

23. Nancy Stout and Jorge Rigau, eds., *Havana* (New York: Rizzoli International Publications, 1994); "Cuba Theme Issue," *Journal of Decorative and Propaganda Arts* (Miami: Wolfson Foundation of Decorative and Propaganda Arts, 1996).

24. *Cuba*, ed. Rachel Carley, with photographs by Andrea Brizzi (New York: Whitney Library of Design, 1997) (published in Spanish, English, and other languages; I am using the Spanish translation, by Caroline Phillips); Juliet Barclay, with photographs by Martin Charles Barclay, *Havana: Portrait of a City* (London: Cassell, 1993).

25. Barclay, *Havana*, 76.

26. George Yúdice has studied how culture—particularly the new definitions it has and the claims fostered on its behalf—interacts with new configurations of global capital in his indispensable *The Expediency of Culture: Uses of Culture in the Global Era* (Durham, NC: Duke University Press, 2003). The mode in which these pacts were implemented in Cuba and how they were pursued with transnational actors is beyond the scope of this study, and awaits a comprehensive treatment. But it is important at this point to make the link between images and tourism, as well as to insist on the role that images have played in assuaging the political frictions the island still provokes. The notion of culture that I am arguing the Cuban state has followed falls into line with other claims for culture as an "engine of capital development" (the term is Yúdice's [17]) and as being capable of producing some measure of social peace.

27. See http://paradiso.soycubano.com/ofertas.asp. At one point, according to sources in Cuba, the government considered setting up theme restaurants using the work of some of the island's most famous painters. Thus, Amelia Pelaez was to have a

restaurant named after her, as was Wifredo Lam. Some of these projects were later dropped because of their limited appeal, though artists working in advertising went so far as to design color-coordinated menus and interior decorations.

28. One can see these images foreshadowed in the streets empty of pedestrians and people in Paolo Gasparini's photographs for Alejo Carpentier's *La ciudad de las columnas*. Although Carpentier talks about streets full of people and houses built to provide solace from the street, the pictures focus on architecture, on empty spaces, peopled by only one or two pedestrians (Alejo Carpentier and Paolo Gasparini, *La ciudad de las columnas* [Barcelona: Editorial Lumen, 1970], n.p.).

29. Eduardo Luis Rodríguez, *The Havana Guide: Modern Architecture, 1925–1965,* trans. Lorn Scott Fox (New York: Princeton Architectural Press, 2000), v.

30. Ibid., 1.

31. Ibid., iv

32. *Shifting Tides: Cuban Photography after the Revolution,* with essays by Tim B. Wride and Cristina Vives, foreword by Wim Wenders (Los Angeles: Los Angeles County Museum of Art, 2001).

33. Gareth Jenkins, ed., *Havana in My Heart: 75 Years of Cuban Photography* (Chicago: Chicago Review Press, 2002); subsequent references are given in the text. James Michener and John Kings, *Six Days in Havana* (Austin: University of Texas Press, 1989).

34. *Cuban Photography after the Revolution,* 20. Subsequent references are given in the text.

35. María Luisa Lobo Montalvo, *Havana: History and Architecture of a Romantic City,* prologue by Hugh Thomas (New York: Monacelli Press, 2000), 16. Subsequent references are given in the text.

36. The Julio Lobo collection is now housed in "La Dolce Dimora," Orestes Ferrara's Florentine villa built in 1927 by one of the best Cuban architectural firms of the time, Govantes & Cobarrocas. As Lobo Montalvo explains, "The property was taken over in 1961, destined to house the Julio Lobo Napoleonic Collection, as the museum it is today—which entailed removing almost the entire contents of my father's house to that address. While he and Ferrara lived in Cuba, they were on indifferent terms; but once in exile [Ferrara died in 1971], the matter of the house brought them together to ignite a genuine friendship. In old age—Ferrara in Rome, my father in Madrid— they exchanged a copious correspondence on the subject of Cuba's future" (Ibid., 210).

MIGRATIONS OF THE BOOK

1. Ángel Rama, *The Lettered City,* trans. and ed. John Charles Chasteen (Durham, NC: Duke University Press, 1996), 104–5.

2. Ana Serra has carefully examined Daura Olema's novel in the context of the state's creation of a revolutionary identity in her dissertation titled "Ideology and the Novel in the Cuban Revolution: The Making of a Revolutionary Identity in the First Decade," George Washington University, 1999.

3. "la Revolución, porque la libertad de un pueblo va en relación directa con su cultura" (Daura Olema, *Maestra voluntaria* ([Havana: Casa de las Américas, 1962], 141).

4. Interviewed by Néstor Rodríguez, Antonio José Ponte sums up this situation precisely: "Think about the differences in the Cuban literary world in relation to any other country, as to what a book within Cuba means. That is less noticeable at this point, though a number of years ago, when none of us traveled or we traveled very little and we had no contacts with foreign visitors, having a book by a writer we liked was like having an amulet. To share that amulet has turned us into brothers. A chain of conspirators gets established. The book becomes a conspiratorial object in a context in which it is censored, prohibited, or simply one does not talk about it" ("Un arte de hacer ruinas: Entrevista con el autor cubano Antonio José Ponte," *Revista Iberoamericana* [January–March 2002]: 179).

5. Technically, the booksellers in the Plaza de Armas cannot sell any book that has been published within the past few years. But sellers constantly circumvent this law, and are able to produce copies of books that they buy in pesos and sell at a price considerably lower than the official price in the dollar bookstore.

6. See, for example, Waldo Pérez Cino commenting on Antonio José Ponte's *Las comidas profundas,* or Antonio Benítez Rojo's *Mujer en traje de batalla,* and even Eliseo Alberto's *Informe contra mi mismo,* in a friendly polemic against Ambrosio Fornet on the "dual" nature of Cuban culture—meaning what is produced inside or outside Cuba. Pérez Cino agrees that classifying authors according to their place of residence is useful, though he would rather examine texts themselves, without privileging external referents such as where the author lives or publishes. See Waldo Pérez Cino, "Sentido y paráfrasis," *La Gaceta de Cuba,* no. 6 (November–December 2002): 22–28.

7. Juan Valdés Paz, "Todo es según el color del cristal con que se mira," *Temas: Cultura-Ideología-Sociedad,* special issue, no. 18–19 (July–December 1999): 150–53.

8. Jorge Castañeda, *Compañero: The Life and Death of Che Guevara* (New York: Vintage, 1998).

9. In 2002, when Castro was furious over the fact that Mexico was voting to condemn Cuba at the UN Human Rights Commission meeting in Geneva in April, he insulted Fox (who had cast a tie-breaking vote), as well as Castañeda, and allowed media access to a private conversation with Fox in which the Mexican president advised Castro to speed up his visit to a world poverty conference in Monterrey. The fact that Castro had recorded Fox and that he played it to the media was an obvious breach of etiquette, which Castro defended by insisting that "A conversation between two heads of state is not a love letter. It is a political exchange. It is not a secret of the confessional" (Ann Louise Bardach, *Cuba Confidential: Love and Vengeance in Miami and Havana* [New York: Random House, 2002], 255). He aimed to embarrass Fox, on the one hand, and, on the other, to manifest his displeasure with Castañeda, who had met with Cuban exiles in Miami. The latter's visit provoked yet another diplomatic contretemps.

10. "un acto de difamación política con ropaje académico" (Valdés Paz, "Todo es según el color del cristal con que se mira," 152).

11. In Zoé Valdés's *La nada cotidiana,* the Cuban intelligentsia behaves like a literate high class, one that lives off the international prestige possessed by the revolution. Her satire takes place in the 1970s, but it is clear that it also applies to the present.

12. Gutiérrez has since published *Animal tropical* (Barcelona: Anagrama, 2000), which won the Alfonso García-Ramos Prize in 2000, conferred by the Tenerife Cabildo and Editorial Anagrama.

13. See Rama, *The Lettered City,* particularly his last chapter, "The City Revolutionized," in which he explains how, in the mid-twentieth century, and without depending on the state, the city of letters was transformed in three important ways: "the incorporation of social doctrine, the rise of the self-educated, and professionalism" (117). Rama's example concerns Mexico, but he also comments on the Cuban situation in the early 1960s throughout the book.

14. Esther Katheryn Whitfield, "Fiction(s) of Cuba in Literary Economies of the 1990s: Buying in or Selling Out?" Dissertation, Harvard University, May 2001.

15. Ibid., 7. Whitfield's project is concerned, among other things, with the relationship between the novels and the writers' place of residence. In this section, I am more interested in the relationship between the novel as object and its Cuban readers, but it is appropriate to quote part of her comments: "The genre's almost inherent displacement calls into question the location of Cuban literature, for the distinction between exiled writers versus those 'at home' gives way to a more continuous panorama when commercially-resonant patterns and practices reproduce themselves in different sites, and when a Cuban author living in Paris, another in Miami and another in Havana manipulate the same set of 'special period' images. In this newly fluid space the writer cedes to the novel; or, rather, the former's place of residence becomes less important than the latter's setting and place of publication and, if we are to be especially cynical, than the currency in which it is sold" (9–10).

16. See Katherine Verdery's insightful work on Romanian politics: "National Ideology under Socialism: Identity and Cultural Politics in Ceausescu's Romania," in Michael Burawoy and Katherine Verdery, *Uncertain Transition: Ethnographies of Change in the Postsocialist World* (Lanham, MD: Rowman & Littlefield, 1999 [online publication]), 22.

17. Magaly Muguercia, "The Body and Its Politics in Cuba of the Nineties," *boundary 2* 29:3 (2002): 176.

18. In Jorge Castañeda's *Utopia Unarmed: The Latin American Left after the Cold War* (New York: Alfred A. Knopf, 1993), there is an unsurpassed account of the culture that the revolution exported to Latin America. Castañeda explains that Latin American students found answers to questions their parents would not dare ask "in the teachings, writings and preaching of the social scientists, in the novels and poems of the writers of the 'literary boom,' in the lyrics of Violeta Parra and Victor Jara and the rhythms of Caetano Veloso and the Nueva Trova Cubana" (192). He also observes that "Every left-wing intellectual in Latin America had his or her own private Cuba, which fitted his or her own preferences and priorities" (ibid.). See also his account of Arnaldo Orfila, who founded the publishing concern *Siglo XXI* (175–77).

19. The cultural effervescence in Cuba during the first decade of the revolution, and particularly during the first five years, still needs a fuller treatment. Havana was one of the Latin American cities most thoroughly saturated by media. The sheer amount of newspapers, radio stations, magazines, television programs, and film presented the scene of a thoroughly modernized society by Latin American standards.

20. According to Hugh Thomas, *Revolución* was started by Franqui in 1955, and it appeared publicly on January 2, 1959. On January 4, it carried a photograph of Castro with the caption: "The Hero-Guide of Cuban Reform. May God continue to illuminate him." Surveying the first issues of the paper, Thomas adds, "Here was a nation which hungered at least for heroism" (Hugh Thomas, *Cuba: The Pursuit of Freedom* [New York: Harper & Row, 1971], 868, 1032). See also Franqui's account of his problems with the bureaucracy and *Revolución* in his *Retrato de familia con Fidel* (Barcelona: Seix Barral, 1981), especially 267–73 and 450–73.

21. See Thomas, *Cuba*, 1076.

22. In a more recent update of his famous *Historia personal del "Boom"* (1972), José Donoso ponders the relationship between Cuba and the Boom—whether writers used the Cuban Revolution as a launching pad for their work, or whether it was the revolution that used writers to gain worldwide publicity. Donoso leans toward the latter option, though he does not fully discount the first. See his appendix to *Historia personal del "Boom"* (Barcelona: Seix Barral, 1983),146–47.

23. Idelber Avelar, in *The Untimely Present: Latin American Fiction and the Task of Mourning* (Durham, NC, and London: Duke University Press, 1999), explains that some of the elements that created a continental canon at this time were "a systematic intercommunication in a common Latin American field, the unifying presence of Cuba, and the belief in a common Latin American cause" (36). In literature, Randolph Pope explains that "The triumph of the Cuban guerrillas in January of 1959 over Batista's dictatorship was seen as an affirmation of Spanish American independence. The participation of the Argentinean Ernesto Che Guevara in the insurrectionary movements in Cuba and Bolivia became a symbol of internationalism, while the example of a cultural center in 1960s, the Casa de las Américas, with its yearly awards and aggressive marketing of the Revolution among Spanish American intellectuals, created a shared sense of purpose" ("The Spanish American Novel, 1950–1975," in *The Cambridge History of Latin American Literature*, ed. Roberto González Echevarría and Enrique Pupo-Walker [Cambridge: Cambridge University Press, 1996], 230).

24. An interesting account of these intellectual disputes during the 1970s can be found in Angel Rama, *Diario 1974–1983*, ed. Rosario Peyrou (Montevideo: Ediciones Trilce, 2001). See especially his comments on Cortázar ("I am aware of his lack of political, not to say economic and social, information, as well as his lack of understanding of international problematics" [153]) and on García Márquez, whose views of the Cuban situation are guided more by affection than analysis ("a relationship that seems to me more affective than analytic, which is my own" [158]). I thank Juan Carlos Quintero-Herencia for calling my attention to this book.

25. See Juan Carlos Quintero-Herencia, "Una parada: *Casa de las Américas* y *Mundo Nuevo*," in *Fulguración del espacio: Letras e imaginario institucional de la Revolución cubana (1960–1971)* (Buenos Aires: Beatriz Viterbo, 2002), 512–20. Quintero-Herencia understands that the polemic was part of a debate about who had the editorial legitimacy to offer a unified vision of Latin American reality. The opening salvo seems to have been a series of articles appearing in the *New York Times* between April 25 and 29, 1966, that detailed how the CIA financed Latin American foundations and intellectual centers by circuitous means. One of its indirect beneficiaries was

the Instituto Latinoamericano de Relaciones Internacionales (ILARI), which partially financed *Mundo Nuevo*. Although Rodríguez Monegal explained in 1967 that, to his knowledge, the journal was financed by private donations and foundations, still he resigned from it and the journal then moved to Buenos Aires (513–14). In his *Historia personal del "Boom,"* Donoso underscores that *Mundo Nuevo* was the most exciting journal of the "Boom" while Rodríguez Monegal ran it (85–86). More recently, Cuban authorities launched a campaign against the journal *Encuentro de la cultura cubana,* directed until 2002 by Jesús Díaz, accusing it of being like *Mundo Nuevo,* a review financed by U.S. imperial capital. See Pedro de la Hoz's comments against *Encuentro* in "Desencuentros y lejanías," *La Gaceta de Cuba,* no. 5 (September–October 1996): 56–58. The full response from the journal's editors can be found in the Web page version of the magazine, at www.cubaencuentro.com.

26. See Avelar, *The Untimely Present,* 30.

27. Roberto González Echevarría has explained this in *Alejo Carpentier: The Pilgrim at Home* (Ithaca, NY: Cornell University Press, 1977): Carpentier's "entire literary enterprise issues from the desire to seize upon that moment of origination from which history and the history of the self begin simultaneously—a moment from which both language and history will start" (32).

28. As mentioned earlier, this architectural fixation can be seen in the picture book by Alejo Carpentier and Paolo Gasparini, *La ciudad de las columnas* (Barcelona: Editorial Lumen, 1970, n.p.).

29. Lezama's work was memorialized in the 1990s in a way that Carpentier's was not, and thus it acquired a value of political resistance to the errors of the revolution that was important for most contemporary writers. Within the dense fabric of memorialization, one of the issues debated was how the state absorbed the baroque project as a fundamental element for its notions of aesthetics. Lezama's project could only be digested by reading its more profound notions of *cubanía* within a deeply nationalistic vein, and embalming it within the arrested temporality of a city that was preserved as a monument against time. Severo Sarduy's more radical readings of Lezama would only be given an official presence much later, but by that time, in the 1990s, new readings of Lezama separated the writer from his work's inherent institutionality. This can be seen more recently in Antonio José Ponte, *El libro perdido de los origenistas* (Mexico City: Editorial Aldus, 2002).

30. See Avelar, *The Untimely Present,* 50, and Quintero-Herencia, *Fulguración del espacio,* who provides a fuller account of the editorial work of the revolution and how it differed from the prerevolutionary era (153–58 and 177–82). The number of editions, new publications, and even cultural centers reveals the dimensions of this change (179).

31. It is important to state that fragmentation was also a hallmark of the modern project of the revolution, and that disparate works such as Guillermo Cabrera Infante's *Tres Tristes Tigres,* Norberto Fuentes's *Los condenados de Condado,* and Reinaldo Arenas's *Celestino antes del Alba,* as works that reflected the revolution in some way, also used the poetics of the fragment in a very different time period and context.

32. Prieto's remarks were distributed as "Cultura, cubanidad, cubanía," part of a conference titled "La nación y la emigración" that took place April 22–24, 1994, in

Havana and during which cultural policy with Cubans abroad was codified to a certain extent. This was the first of two conferences on this topic. The second was held in 1995, and there was even a third meeting, in 1997, to denounce the Helms-Burton act. See also Max Azicri, *Cuba Today and Tomorrow: Reinventing Socialism* (Gainesville: University Press of Florida, 2000), 247.

33. "Carta de los Diez," in Manuel Vázquez Montalbán, *Y Dios entró en La Habana* (Madrid: Grupo Santillana de Ediciones, 1998), 464.

34. Cruz Varela's was one of the most notorious cases of governmental persecution in the early 1990s. A prize-winning poet, she helped found a human rights organization called Criterio Alternativo (Alternative Criterion) in 1991. She was assaulted in her Havana apartment by a mob, obviously orchestrated by government thugs. She was dragged out of the apartment, beaten on the street, and forced to eat papers of her writings before she was arrested. She was named a "prisoner of conscience" by Amnesty International and was finally granted a visa to leave Cuba. She lives in Madrid.

35. "Se apaga un municipio para que exista otro. / Ya mi vida está hecha de materia prestada. / Cumplo con luz la vida de algún desconocido. / Digo a oscuras: otro vive la que me falta" (Antonio José Ponte, *Asiento en las ruinas* [Havana: Editorial Letras Cubanas, 1997], 45). This mood was captured by Francisco Moran in his "La generación cubana de los 89: un destino entre las ruinas," *Cuadernos hispanoamericanos,* no. 588 (June 1999): 15–29.

36. Included in Pedro Marqués de Armas, *Los altos manicomios (1987–1989)* (Havana: Casa Editora Abril, 1993).

37. *Retrato de Grupo,* ed. Carlos Augusto Alfonso Barroso, Víctor Fowler Calzada, Emilio García Montiel and Antonio José Ponte; preface by Víctor Fowler Calzada and Antonio José Ponte (Havana: Editorial Letras Cubanas, 1989).

38. "Ésta será la única mentira en la que siempre creeremos" (ibid., 165).

39. "Es una historia triste / jugar a ser perfectos" (ibid.). Calderón's text also appears in *Poesía cubana: la isla entera,* ed. Felipe Lázaro and Bladimir Zamora [Madrid: Editorial Betania, 1995], 362–63).

40. "Estos son los plátanos que ha mandado / mi hermana desde Oriente, y un poco de café / porque imagina / que a la hora de comer cae la penuria / como un relámpago" ("La hora de comer," *Retrato de Grupo,* 66).

41. "yo deseaba un viaje, un largo y limpio viaje para no pudrirme" (*Retrato de Grupo,* 53).

42. "Seguramente pensados para el vuelo / ya éramos pájaros de cansadas formas" (Alessandra Molina, *Anfiteatro entre los pinos* [Havana: Ediciones Extramuros, 1998], 8).

43. "Todo el que parte, regresa . . . Todo el que regresa: arde" (Norge Espinosa, "Dejar la isla" in Rolando Sánchez Mejías, *Mapa Imaginario* [Havana: Embassy of France in Cuba and the Instituto Cubano del Libro, 1995], 25–27).

44. See, for example, Lázaro and Zamora, *Poesía cubana,* and *La poesía de las dos orillas,* ed. León de la Hoz (Madrid: Libertarias, 1994). The way in which many poetry anthologies originated can be seen in the introduction to Lázaro and Zamora's *Poesía cubana,* which reproduces an exchange of letters: first Lázaro wrote to Zamora on February 18 1994, and then Zamora replied from Havana on March 21. The

letters themselves create the illusion of a flow, between Cuba and Spain, and aim to give a sense of immediacy, transparency, and fairness, as each writer insists that Cuban poetry should not be separated by political circumstance; at the same time, they aim to achieve a totalizing effect while viewing national tradition from multiple vantage points.

45. "Casal es todavía un misterio" (Víctor Fowler Calzada, *Rupturas y homenajes* [Havana: Unión, 1998], 89). The best account of the critical dialectics between Martí and Casal is found in Francisco Morán, *Casal a rebours* (Havana: Casa Editora Abril, 1996).

46. In this sense, the title of the last section of Francisco Morán's anthology *La isla en su tinta* is an adequate one, "Palma negra," for there was an open bitterness directed at what was happening.

47. See, for example, "Vigía: The Endless Publications of Matanzas," a conversation between Rolando Estévez, María Eugenia Alegría, and Alfredo Zaldívar that appeared in *Bridges to Cuba,* ed. Ruth Behar (Ann Arbor: University of Michigan Press, 1995), 316–22. *Vigía* was started in 1985 by the director of La Casa del Escritor in Matanzas, Alfredo Zaldívar, with the cooperation of Rolando Estévez, who was the designer. Its creators assert that *Vigía* was not really born out of material need, but out of aesthetic choices, because Cuban publishing houses were not publishing the work they liked. Because the print runs were small, and the aesthetic materials simple, they were able to survive during the Special Period in a way that other editorial concerns could not. Zaldívar explains: "Our resources were scarce: a mimeograph machine that someone from a press was able to lend us, and a typewriter—also borrowed—because we owned neither. These are the only two machines we have used in the history of *Vigía*" (317).

48. The Stockholm Encounter was a meeting of the generation divided by the 1970s—the most contentious period in Cuban arts and letters—and it issued two collective statements: first, Cuban culture is a totality, a unified whole, and it extends beyond the territorial borders of the island; second, that the embargo be lifted. During the 1990s, there were also two conferences on the topic "La nación y la emigración" in 1994 and 1995, and a third meeting in 1997 that denounced the Helms-Burton act. These encounters signaled the Cuban government's desire to talk to selected members of its external opposition. The 2003 meeting was canceled after the government arrested the leaders and participants of small dissident organizations. The background to all these meetings was the 1977–78 dialogue, in Spanish referred to as the "Diálogo," with members of the Cuban community abroad. Many observers have questioned why it took so long (seventeen years) to produce a rapprochement between the government and the exile population.

49. Fowler Calzada has published more poetry—*Visitas* (Havana: Ediciones Extramuros, 1996), *Malecón Tao* (2001), but also has produced impressive work in literary criticism and as an essayist. He wrote the first comprehensive account of homosexuality in Cuban literature in *La maldición: una historia del placer como conquista* (Havana: Editorial Letras Cubanas, 1998), and *Rupturas y homenajes* (Havana: Ediciones Unión, 1998). In the first book, he notes in his nine essays the way homosexuality is embedded in the Cuban nation as an "other"; the second consists of essays

on various topics of Cuban literature. Fowler emerged as an acute observer of Cuban literary trends, and he has kept himself well-informed about the major trends happening in the outside world. He has explicated questions of postmodernism, cultural studies, and performance studies to a Cuban audience, and has served as an interlocutor between the world "outside" and the Cuban literary community.

50. This story was published as part of a broader collection: *In the Cold of the Malecon*, trans. Cola Franzen and Dick Cluster (San Francisco: City Lights Books, 2000). The collection includes other stories that portray life during the Special Period, without lapsing into the sort of folkloric account of exotic hardship that one finds in Pedro Juan Gutiérrez.

51. The essay has been reprinted most recently in Rita Molinero, *Virgilio Piñera: la memoria del cuerpo* (San Juan: Editorial Plaza Mayor, 2002), 103–8.

52. In the short story, the groundbreaking collection was published by the late Salvador Redonet and titled *Los últimos serán los primeros* (Havana: Editorial Letras Cubanas, 1993).

53. Esther Katheryn Whitfield, "Fiction(s) of Cuba in Literary Economies of the 1990s: Buying in or Selling Out?" Dissertation, Harvard University, May 2001, 3.

54. It is important to contrast the treatment of homosexuality in these works with others in Cuba, such as Norge Espinosa's in his poetry book *Las estrategias del páramo* (Havana: Ediciones Unión, 2000), which won an important prize from the magazine *El Caimán Barbudo*. In his poem "Vestido de novia," which is a classic of contemporary Cuban literature, Espinosa portrays the sad yet defiant subjectivity of contemporary Cuban male homosexuals.

55. Esther Katheryn Whitfield, "Cuba through the Narrative Looking Glass," 2 (conference paper read in Iowa). Víctor Fowler Calzada devoted a book to the issue, and this was followed, from the diaspora, by Emilio Bejel, whose *Gay Cuban Nation* (Chicago: University of Chicago Press, 2001) is the first comprehensive account of this subject in Cuban letters in English.

56. See Whitfield, "Fiction(s) of Cuba," 10.

57. Ena Lucía Portela, "Literatura versus lechugitas, breve esbozo de una tendencia," in *Cuba: voces para cerrar un siglo,* ed René Vázquez Díaz [Stockholm: Centro Internacional Olof Palme, 1999), 1: 78–79.

58. Although I have not discussed theater, it is important to note that in the 1990s theater openly addressed the destruction of family structures in Cuba, by rescuing a number of plays that were important during the early years of the revolution and then banned, such as Piñera's *Electra Garrigó* and José Triana's *La noche de los asesinos.* In 1989, playwright Raúl Alfonzo openly presented a play that dealt with the Mariel exodus.

59. "Rodríguez states frankly that the greatest challenge to any poet writing on the island today is the absence of the others who have left. Readers can sense this concern in her writing; common themes include spatiality, motion and stasis, interpersonal relationships, and loss. If the island *chisme,* or gossip, says any number of things behind closed doors in a way that's both powerful and indirect, then it might be said that Rodríguez's poetry adopts a similar manner of speaking about issues affecting both her daily life and her understanding of aesthetics." (Reina María

Rodríguez, *La detención del tiempo*, trans. Kristen Dykstra [San Diego: Factory School, 2001], 38–39.

60. See his interview with Arturo Arango, "No hay modo de ignorar la vida," *La Gaceta de Cuba*, no. 6 (November–December 2002): 29–33.

THE BEAT OF THE STATE

1. See George Yúdice's important chapter "The Globalization of Latin America: Miami" in his *The Expediency of Culture: Uses of Culture in the Global Era* (Durham, NC, and London: Duke University Press, 2003), 192–93. Yúdice remarks that the Cuban presence in Miami is not as overwhelming as it once was, and he explores the effects that Latin American capital has had in the city: "By the early 1990s the major music multinational corporations like Sony and Warner reestablished offices there, and throughout the 1990s all the majors had their regional headquarters (i.e., headquarters for Latin America) in Miami, specifically in South Miami Beach" (199). He also provides figures showing that, "For the past five or six years, Latin music has enjoyed robust growth unseen in any other segment of the music business, with a 12 percent jump from 1998 to 1999" (200).

2. Eugene Robinson, *Last Dance in Havana: The Final Days of Fidel and the Start of the New Cuban Revolution* (New York: Free Press, 2004), 31.

3. Ibid,. 7.

4. The extent to which popular music and globalization have affected state policies can be ascertained by the debates around *Buena Vista Social Club* (the movie and the compact disc) that took place in Cuba in the late 1990s and early 2000s. Two debates appeared in the journal *Temas*. The first, commented on in more detail later, "Buena Vista Social Club y la cultura musical cubana," was reproduced in *Temas*, no. 22–23 (July–December 2000); the second, "La música popular como espejo social," a broader conversation on trends in Cuban popular music and their relationship to recent historical and economic processes, appeared in *Temas*, no. 29 (April–June 2002). Between the first and the second, two more essays appeared on the Buena Vista phenomenon that also involved representation and state policies: Román de la Campa, "El sublime encanto de la nostalgia cultural," *Temas*, no. 27 (October–December 2001): 126–32; and Rufo Caballero, "La excusa: Semiosis, ideología y montaje en Buena Vista Social Club," *Temas*, no. 27 (October–December 2001): 133–50.

5. Antonio Benítez Rojo, *La isla que se repite: El Caribe y la perspectiva posmoderna* (Hanover, NH: Ediciones del Norte, 1989), xiii–xiv. The English translation is *The Repeating Island: The Caribbean and the Postmodern Perspective*, 2d ed., trans. James Maraniss (Durham, NC: Duke University Press, 1996).

6. These are the observations of Roberto Zurbano in the *Temas* debate "La música popular como espejo social," 66.

7. See Natalio Galán, *Cuba y sus sones* (Valencia: Pre-Textos, 1997); Alejo Carpentier, *La música en Cuba* (Mexico City: Fondo de Cultura Económica, 1972 [1946]); in English, *Music in Cuba*. trans. Alan West-Durán, ed. and intro. Timothy Brennan (Minneapolis: University of Minnesota Press, 2001).

8. Fidel Castro, "Palabras a los intelectuales," in *Política cultural de la revolución cubana* (Havana: Editorial de Ciencias Sociales, 1977), 41–42.

9. As Yúdice has remarked in *The Expediency of Culture*, the relationship between "cultural and political spheres or cultural and economic spheres is not new" (10). Culture, as he has defined it, is "expedient" and there is no point in dismissing this expediency for a "nostalgic or reactionary desire for the restoration of the high place of culture" (25)—and, it is important to add, of entertainment as a nonpolitical category.

10. An observer hostile to the Cuban revolution such as Natalio Galán put it best: "The revolution came and morality started castrating popular music . . . Havana was then not a city of bongo players . . . but rather a military center that could export its soldiers to Africa, but not one mulatto rhythm to New York" (Galán, *Cuba y sus sones,* 350).

11. See David García's *"From son montuno to Salsa: Arsenio Rodríguez, Race, and Latin Popular Music in Havana and New York City* (forthcoming) for an excellent discussion of the networks of social and communal life—and the difficulties produced by new economic and social realities—that Cuban musicians and artists encountered in New York after the revolution.

12. Since 2002, EGREM has a Web site (www.egrem.com.cu) and a commercial director as well as a public relations department. It has various commercial divisions, including international ones, including one called Agencia Musicuba that represents Cuban artists who want to tour abroad. It also rents out its studios to musicians who want to record in the island. I have profited immensely for this chapter from the work of Ariana Hernández-Reguant, which I have consulted in manuscript form ("Radio Taíno and the Globalization of the Cuban Culture Industries," dissertation, Department of Anthropology, University of Chicago, March 2002, 94). The book is forthcoming from Duke University Press.

13. Sylvio Rodríguez has described in an interview the kinds of difficulties he encountered during the revolution. He was told at one point not to sing his song "Rifle against Rifle" because it did not pass muster with a commission of the Central Committee of the Party that was in charge of approving "songs, poems and anything that had to do with Che Guevara," and he was suspended from the ICR (Cuban Radio Institute) because of positive opinions he had expressed about the Beatles. He states, however, that reports of his early problems with the state have been generally exaggerated. See "Silvio Rodríguez: Folk Music, Revolutionary Style," in *Culture and the Cuban Revolution: Conversations in Havana,* ed. John M. Kirk and Leonardo Padura Fuentes (Gainesville: University Press of Florida, 2001), 9, 10. Allen Ginsberg offered the following account: "I suggested to Haydee Santamaria that they invite the Beatles and got the answer: 'They have no ideology; we are trying to build a revolution with an ideology.' Well, that's true, but what was the ideology they were proposing?" (Allen Young, *Gays under the Cuban Revolution* [San Francisco: Grey Fox Press, 1981], 21).

14. See Hernández-Reguant, "Radio Taíno and the Globalization of the Cuban Culture Industries," 94, for a fascinating account of the accounting practices of EGREM and independent corporations such as Artex and BIS set up by the Ministry of Culture in the 1990s.

15. *P.M.* was shot in 1961, though Cabrera Infante places it toward the end of 1960. See Guillermo Cabrera Infante, "*P.M.* Means Post Mortem," in *Mea Cuba,* trans. Kenneth Hall and Guillermo Cabrera Infante (New York: Farrar, Straus and Giroux, 1994), 52–54. Hugh Thomas establishes that the film was the background for the debate on commitment in the arts that took place in July 1961. He also states that the film was not publicly shown: "one reason was that it gave a free and easy impression of life in Havana at a time when the whole city was supposed to be alert and expecting an invasion. The only reviewer to praise it, Néstor Almendros, was sacked from his job at *Bohemia*"(Hugh Thomas, *The Cuban Revolution* [New York: Harper & Row, 1977], 564 n. 9; this is a shortened version of Thomas's *Cuba: The Pursuit of Freedom* [1971]). However, Pablo Armando Fernández claims that he showed the film on television: "Sabá Cabrera and Orlandito Jiménes [*sic*] made a film called *P.M.,* which was about night life in Havana. I had a television program at that time, *Lunes en la Televisión,* and I showed the film on it. There was no problem when I showed it" (Kirk and Padura Fuentes, *Culture and the Cuban Revolution,* 83). Another account can be found in a series of memoirs commemorating the forty years that had passed since Fidel Castro's 1961 "Palabras a los intelectuales." Roberto Fernández Retamar revisited the polemics around *P.M.* and recalled statements by Arturo Guevara in 1992 that are less condemnatory of the film, but that also tend to minimize its importance. Forty years later, and undoubtedly because of the fracas created around Fidel's speech and Cabrera Infante's tireless campaigns, the film and the controversy were still very much on people's minds. See Roberto Fernández Retamar, "Cuarenta años después," *La Gaceta de Cuba,* ño. 4 (July–August 2001): 47–53.

16. See Sigfredo Ariel's liner notes to the CD compilation *A Riot of Women* (Cuba XXI Music, S.L., 2000). It is important to mention those who disappeared, for they are not known outside Cuba, if only to highlight the difference between the music that is heard in Cuba and music that is marketed as Cuban music abroad: Los Meme (a Cuban blend of the Four Tops, one might say), or Martha Strada (a chanteuse not unlike the French Barbara or Mireille Mathieu), or Luisa María Guell (who left Cuba in the 1960s), and others such as Farah María. They supplemented the absence of other, more popular stars (Benny More died early in the revolution, and Celeste Mendoza, Omara Portuondo, and others were not necessarily popular during the pre-revolutionary period, but later).

17. Germán Piniella: "That is why I don't like the image Omara Portuondo gives in that documentary, singing a repertoire that she always rejected" ("De Buena Vista al Mundo," *Temas* [July–December 2000]: 178).

18. See Silvio Rodríguez's statements in Kirk and Padura Fuentes, *Culture and the Cuban Revolution,* 1–16. Things have changed, of course. Between October 1996 and November 1997, Cuba hosted two conferences on the Beatles legacy. In 2000, a John Lennon statue was unveiled in Havana, in a ceremony attended by Fidel Castro himself. Lennon is now seen as an artist who suffered because of his relentless campaign against the Vietnam War, and because he was aggressively pursued by the U.S. government. There are two books on the Beatles in Cuba: Ernesto Juan Castellanos, *El Sargento Pimienta vino a Cuba en un submarillo amarillo* (Havana: Letras Cubanas, 2000), and his *Los Beatles en Cuba* (Havana: Ediciones Unión, 1998).

19. Margarita Mateo Palmer alludes to the fact that the *trova* was in fact a movement created by the youth mass organization UJC (Unión de Juventudes Cubanas) in the 1970s, and points to the fact that the spaces where it could be heard in 2002 were few. See "La música popular como espejo social," 77.

20. Grupo Moncada, *Credenciales,* Discos Pueblo DP 1041. There is no year, but it is from the late 1970s.

21. "las mujeres perfectas y las mujeres 'traicioneras', los amores imposibles, los paisajes bucólicos de etiquetas, el tropicalismo turístico y otros engendros similares."

22. "su música fácil, sus temas banales, sus textos repletos de cursilerías, sus ídolos fabricados por los monopolios disqueros." For a different kind of reading of bolero, as fostering new forms of sociability, see the excellent study by Rafael Castillo Zapata, *Fenomenología del bolero* (Caracas: Monte Avila, 1990), and José Quiroga, "Tears at the Nightclub," in *Tropics of Desire: Interventions from Queer Latino America* (New York: New York University Press, 2000), 145–68. This essay focuses on the 1990s and new readings of the bolero made possible by different inflections of gender and sexuality. It also includes a section on the Cuban singer La Lupe, who left Cuba at the beginning of the revolution.

23. "de la historia y la guerra, de la Patria y los héroes, de la lucha cotidiana contra los enemigos del pueblo, del trabajo anónimo de cualquier obrero."

24. In the discussion sponsored by the journal *Temas* on the topic "La música popular como espejo social," Danilo Orozco points out that the Nueva Trova was not a simple genre, but rather a kind of "creative attitude," and that it used different genres and styles. He points out, for example, Pablo Milanés's way of putting together genres ranging from the late 1950s *filin* to folk rock or jazz (64).

25. "en escuelas universitarias, fábricas, secundarias en el campo, preuniversitarios, talleres, comunidades campesinas, festivales estudiantiles y obreros."

26. "Perdonen los que se sitúan fuera del juego / ahora que jugamos a la muerte con la vida."

27. There is, in general terms, less an emphasis on the leader of the group, or on individual personalities, and the Grupo Moncada also de-emphasizes the kind of showmanship that was present, in the 1990s, in the new orchestras that played the fast-paced Cuban beat known as *timba.*

28. See, for example, Natalio Galán in *Cuba y sus sones:* "Salsa is a music of the past . . . a very curious regressive phenomenon that announces a pact with rock and roll" (352–53). Also see Guillermo Cabrera Infante: "In the worst of cases, salsa is a copy of old Cuban *sones,* and even its name comes from a son . . . by Ignacio Piñero of the 1920s that was titled precisely 'Échale salsita.' In the best of cases, it is a retro copy" ("Bienvenida, Lady Salsa," in *Mi música extremada,* ed. Rosa M. Pereda [Madrid: Espasa Calpe, 1996], 182).

29. Helio Orovio in "Buena Vista Social Club y la cultura musical cubana," 175.

30. One of the important strains in urban popular music of the Caribbean that Cubans "missed" was the cross-fertilization that would ultimately produce the hip-hop zone in the 1970s and 1980s in the United States, including the collaboration between Puerto Ricans and African Americans that can be heard in the Latin *bugalú* of the 1960s (a mix of mambo with African American rock and roll), as well as Latin

Soul and funk. See Raquel Rivera, *New York Ricans from the Hip-Hop Zone* (New York: Palgrave Macmillan, 2003), 32. This cross-fertilization may be happening at present, but mostly between the Cuban scene and the Afro pop directly related to the African continent and to Africans' migration to European capitals such as Paris. A recording such as *A lo cubano* by Orishas owes a lot to the French African Parisian nightclub scene.

31. Hernández-Reguant, "Radio Taíno and the Globalization of the Cuban Culture Industries," 78.

32. See Paquito D'Rivera, *Mi Vida Saxual* (San Juan: Plaza Mayor, 2001).

33. *Diablo al Infierno,* Luaka Bop, WEA 9–45107–2.

34. *Cuban Counterpoint: History of the Son Montuno,* Rounder CD 1078, 1992.

35. In the *Cuban Counterpoint* liner notes, for example, Morton Marks remarks: "While the son montuno is usually thought of as Afro-Cuban in origin, it may come as a surprise that Cuban musicologists group the son, at least in its 'folk' origins, not with their African-based musical heritage, but with the Iberian side of musical culture." But he also adds: "Besides its predominantly white guajiros, Oriente also had a large black population, descendants of freemen and slaves" and explains how the *changüí,* the Afro-Cuban variant of the *son,* was born around Guantánamo and Santiago. This shows the compiler taking issue with the way the music is classified in Cuba. The direct allusion to Fernando Ortiz's *Cuban Counterpoint* in the title of the CD underscores the academic and cultural direction of the CD as a whole.

36. Hernández-Reguant, "Radio Taíno and the Globalization of the Cuban Culture Industries," 77–78.

37. Hernández-Reguant points out how this transnational capitalism appeared in Cuba as "a varied array of entrepreneurs, media-workers, bureaucracy's employees, artists, cultural workers, mid-level managers, free-lance producers, and others who mediated among the interests of transnational capital, the Cuban state bureaucracy, and their own goals and ideals. They were agents within chains of institutions constituting a global economy of unprecedented flexibility, affecting the pattern of development of the Cuban music industry, the use of certain marketing strategies, and the forms of audience segmentation. These individuals decided in many cases the pool of cultural products made available to the public" (ibid., 77).

38. Ibid., 82.

39. This was, in many ways, cultural capitalism. At the same time, as yet another intellectual remarked in the forum on *Buena Vista Social Club,* Cuba had no control over the kinds of materials disseminated by virtue of the commercial transactions involved. In this way, and in order to market a product, foreign impresarios started using the name Cuba as a hook, proposing all kinds of combinations and producing all kinds of visions that did not always reflect the reality that some intellectuals wanted to project, since these gazes were too foreign.

40. Deborah Pacini Hernández, 111–12.

41. Pacini's comments that the rest of the Caribbean de-emphasizes its African roots must be nuanced a bit. There has also been a process of trans-Caribbean migration that simply did not happen during the preceding decades in Cuba. At the same time, the long-standing Cuban bias against salsa, seen by many as a pallid imitation

of traditional Cuban music, separated the Cuban musical circuit from the major currents in Caribbean music. Pacini does not take into account the Cuban government's dismantling of its musicians, the state rationalization, especially during the 1970s, though she does make this point in her later discussion of the Buena Vista Social Club. In addition, one cannot separate musicianship (and the Cubans, as is well known, invested heavily in music schools) from the fact that many of the tunes popular in the Caribbean area carried a level of sexual innuendo that was absent from the more innocuous Cuban songs recorded at the time.

42. In the United States, this presented particular problems, because Cuban musicians are (or were) barred from performing in dance halls, and so they could never develop contact with other communities. The Smithsonian, for example, brought Cuban bands and groups to the United States—Company Segundo, of *Buena Vista Social Club* fame, gave a concert at the Smithsonian because for a long time these artists could only perform in cultural venues as opposed to commercial ones. The musical relationship was at all times a government-to-government affair, as musical appearances were mediated by all sorts of governmental restrictions, including whether the musicians were employed by the state—which technically they were—or were members of the Communist Party. These restrictions were slowly lifted, as Pacini mentions.

43. Valera's beginnings as a somewhat oppositional figure belie his later transformation into an ubiquitous figure within the context of the Nueva Trova during the 1990s. In December 2003, he sang in Venezuela with Silvio Rodríguez in support of Hugo Chávez. He has asserted, though, that he is not "an instrument of anyone or any project." He belongs to a second generation of Nueva Trova singers who began writing at the end of the 1970s. Margarita Mateo, in "La música popular como espejo social," mentions the way in which the Trova could engage difficult issues such as economic collapse, migration, and the prostitution that accompanied the beginnings of the tourist economy. She mentions Varela's "Robinson" (which was collected in his *Monedas al Aire*, Cubadisc, 1993) as a particularly important piece (66). She is also clearly thinking of Pedro Luis Ferrer, who penned important songs that circulated more or less underground at the beginning of the decade. Varela recorded "Guillermo Tell" in his *Jalisco Park* (1989) and also in *Varela en vivo* (1991), which is the recording made at the Karl Marx Theater in Havana. An interesting discussion of Varela in the context of Cubans' representation of migration and other difficult issues at the beginning of the decade can be found in Yolanda Martínez San Miguel, *Caribe Two Ways* (San Juan: Editorial Callejón, 2003), 215–17.

44. De la Campa, "El sublime encanto de la nostalgia cultural," 126–32. It is the spectral combination of images (in the film) and music that prompts de la Campa to observe how the event places itself between memory and desire, while also noting its immense international appeal at that juncture.

45. See Robinson, *Last Dance in Havana*, 27–29. Robinson points out that Cooder received the credit, though at no point is Juan de Marcos González resentful of this. It was simply a good business decision that paid off, including the myth of Cooder's discovering these musicians in Havana when in fact they had already been contacted by de Marcos.

46. "su vulgaridad, su superficialidad, su incapacidad para explicarse un olvido presentado como total" (its vulgarity, its superficiality, its inability to explain for itself an amnesia presented as absolute) (136).

47. Caballero's tirade against history in Wenders's film, and his historical revision of Omara Portuondo—whom he insists he admires—are on pages 136, 139–40.

48. Hernández-Reguant, "Radio Taíno and the Globalization of the Cuban Culture Industries," 87.

49. Chanan is one of the foremost historians of Cuban cinema and his book *The Cuban Image,* published in 1985 by the British Film Institute, has appeared in a new edition, *Cuban Cinema* (Minneapolis: University of Minnesota Press, 2004). That the essay was published simultaneously in two places demonstrates how different the Cuban literary circuit has become.

50. *Temas* has been published since January 1995. Its stated mandate is to be a space where intellectuals can reflect critically on Cuban issues. It aims to include arts and letters, social science, political theory, and ideology. It states that it is not the official publication of any institution, and it expressly underscores the fact that the editorial board alone is responsible for its editorial line. Published four times a year, it is financed by the Fondo para el Desarrollo de la Cultura y la Educación, an agency of the Ministry of Culture. Its Web page (which began in September 2002) states that it has received contributions from OXFAM, UNESCO, the John D. and Catherine T. MacArthur Foundation, and other institutions. Its director is Rafael Hernández, who works at the Centro de Investigación y Desarrollo de la Cultura Cubana "Juan Marinello."

51. "el contraste de La Habana con esa Nueva York—que no es la Nueva York correspondiente a esa Habana, porque, efectivamente, hay otra Nueva York—también me parece una agresión" (165). A more just representation, some of these academics argue, would have placed on the same level Fifth Avenue and reconstructed spaces in Old Havana.

52. Piniella argues that a shot in the film juxtaposing the revolutionary slogan "La revolución es eterna" to shots of dilapidated cars pulled by donkeys, or to the Karl Marx Theater with a broken letter, is not merely an artistic fact but a thesis that says something negative about the context: as an image that communicates, and in spite of the fact that it could be analyzed in terms of artistic statement by specialists, he considers it "badly intentioned" ("yo, como comunicador, tengo que analizarlo como un hecho de comunicación y lo considero mal intencionado" [171]). This is first mentioned by Julio García Espinosa with regard to all the efforts Wenders made to create the illusion of objectivity: "He tries, in all kinds of ways, to make sure that people don't think he is in favor of this system, of this country, of politics, and he makes a rather big effort to demonstrate some kind of balance from this point of view" ("Él trata, de todas maneras, que no vayan a pensar que está a favor de este sistema, de este país, de la política, y hace un esfuerzo bastante grande por mostrar un equilibrio desde ese punto de vista" [164]).

53. Ibid., 175.

54. The same internal problem applies to the relationship between the music and the dancers for whom the music is presumably done. García Espinosa laments the

absence of dancers in this documentary (the only dancers who do appear are little girls and boys learning ballet). But he also talks about the absence of dance halls and spaces in Cuba in general: "the dancers were part of the evolution of popular music. That was finished later on and it's been a big deficit—that would also be a good topic for discussion, because we have practically finished with all of this country's dance halls" (166). There are other, more striking comments, always made indirectly, in this debate. For example, Germán Piniella discusses the fact that Omara Portuondo presents an image of herself doing a repertoire that she always rejected ("Por eso no me gusta la imagen que da Omara Portuondo, en ese documental, haciendo un repertorio que siempre rechazó" [178]). But above and beyond such issues, what is most striking about this roundtable debate is the undercurrent of resentment that runs throughout it.

55. Ibid., 173. González Castro implicitly equates Cuba with the state, and wants it to design the image of its musicians. In his view, the state is an intermediary between the musician and the commercial enterprise, implying that the impresario should not be the one who pays the musicians, but that all transactions should be done through the intermediary of the state ("Mientras Cuba no diseñe la imagen de todos sus músicos, de su obra, y dependa de que los empresarios comercializadores de los músicos sean quienes paguen, tendremos esto [commercialization]).

56. Roberto Zurbano's comments are paraphrased from pages 75–76.

57. Rufo Caballero quotes approvingly Alan West's statement that the Buena Vista phenomenon is part of a merchandising of nostalgia for a prerevolutionary Cuba, as well as his negative comments on Gloria Estefan and the Miami sound (though he chides West about West's irreverence). By contrast, Zurbano does not comment negatively on the music, as Caballero does. See Caballero, "La excusa," 140.

58. P18's name refers to the Parisian arrondissement in which keyboardist and graphic designer Tom Darnal (formerly part of Mano Negra) is located. In 1996 he traveled to Havana and came into contact with the music scene there. He specifically did not want to create a "Latin house" type of fusion and wanted to ground it specifically in Cuba.

59. P18's first concert took place in France on December 4, 1998, on a day sacred to the Afro-Cuban deity Chango, at the Transmusicales de Rennes.

60. According to Juan Formell, leader of the group Los Van Van (one of the most important in Cuba during the past four decades), *timba* is a cross between the Cuban *son* and salsa, though salsa as a term has always been frowned upon by Cubans, who prefer the term "Cuban" music and regard salsa as a New York creation. The *son* was originally a beat from the eastern part of Cuba that migrated west, to Havana, in the early twentieth century, where, after initial rejection, the music was quickly adopted.

61. Robinson focuses on the failed efforts of an all-female *timba* band called Ebano. They had to refashion themselves a number of times and incorporate men into the group. Robinson narrates poignantly the scene of its final disintegration (*Last Dance in Havana*, 87, 91, 94, 181, and 253).

62. Apparently, the *tembleque* dance style has now been validated by the National Folkloric Ballet, which has included it in its repertoire.

63. García Espinosa, "La música popular como espejo social," 167.

64. Robinson, *Last Dance in Havana,* 69.

65. Zurbano, "La música popular como espejo social," 70. I saw the old Charanga in Madrid in 1998, and the new Charanga at S.O.B. in New York in 1999. Gone were the furious pelvic thrusts that drove the audience in Madrid crazy, as well as the flashy presentation. I asked one of the Cuban managers whether it was the same band, and he responded that it was, but the musicians were not, and he left it at that.

66. See "La música popular como espejo social," 77–78.

67. The revolution had always steered away from creating separate mass organizations based on race. Revolutionary discourse always took note of racism but interpellated both whites and blacks as part of the same Cuban nation, whose cultural boundaries were synonymous with the territorial boundaries of the island. The transatlantic African American diasporic cultural milieu was not anathema to the revolution per se (the African wars that Cuba fought in the 1970s and 1980s had underscored these transatlantic links), but it was a point of contention with regard to the United States and its popular or mass culture.

68. See Rivera, *New York Ricans from the Hip-Hop Zone,* 15, 17.

69. Ibid., 3.

70. Ibid., 14.

71. See Robinson, *Last Dance in Havana,* 118–19. Robinson speculates about the reasons for the change, though he cannot come up with a definite answer. What is clear, he states, is that "no reversal of this magnitude could ever happen without Fidel's personal approval" (119).

72. Ibid., 120.

73. Ibid., 121. In an interview with Herrera posted on AfroCuba Web, he explains that he does not want Cuban hip-hop to go "down the drain with consumerism," but rather would like the hip-hop voice to be important for the world community, in the same way that Cuba represents hope for leftists the world over.

74. Eugene Robinson, "The Rap Revolución," *Washington Post,* April 14, 2002, G1.

75. Annelise Wunderlich, "Cuban Hip-Hop, Underground Revolution" http://journalism.berkeley.edu/projects/cubans2001.

76. The scene is recounted in Robinson, *Last Dance in Havana,* 209–10.

77. Ibid., 212–13. The denouement is sadly described by Robinson: "Aside from Café Cantante on Saturdays and one recreation center every other weekend, all the hip-hop venues had been closed. Maybe once a month there would be a special event at one of the big halls, but there was no regular schedule and no publicity . . . Of the roughly two hundred hip-hop groups in metropolitan Havana, only three had been taken under the wing of the new state-run hip-hop enterprise. For the moment, only those three were receiving state support" (214).

78. Wunderlich, "Cuban Hip-Hop, Underground Revolution."

STILL SEARCHING FOR ANA MENDIETA

1. The best account of this operation is María de los Ángeles Torres, *The Lost Apple: Operation Pedro Pan, Cuban Children in the U.S., and the Promise of a Better Future* (Boston: Beacon Press, 2003).

2. Olga Viso, in *Ana Mendieta: Earth Body (Sculpture and Performance 1972–1985)* (Washington, DC: Hirschhorn Museum, 2000), 78.

3. Quoted in Charles Merewether, "From Inscription to Dissolution: An Essay on Consumption in the Work of Ana Mendieta," in *Ana Mendieta*, ed. Gloria Moure (Barcelona: Ediciones Polígrafa, 1996), 98.

4. Mendieta enrolled in the artists' program at the University of Iowa. She received a BA in art in 1969 and an MA in painting in 1972. She also received a Master of Fine Arts in multimedia and video in 1977. In the Iowa program she was exposed to visiting artists such as Robert Wilson, Vito Acconci, and Nam June Paik, and it was there she met the artist Hans Breder, with whom she lived and traveled a number of times to Mexico and who was an early collaborator in her work, taking many of the uncredited photographs of Mendieta's performances. The program was very receptive to opening up the boundaries between art and museums, by questioning art's commodity status.

5. Ana Mendieta, "The Struggle for Culture Today Is the Struggle for Life," in Moure, *Ana Mendieta*, 175.

6. In her comprehensive account of Mendieta's art, titled *Where Is Ana Mendieta? Identity, Performativity, Exile* (Durham, NC: Duke University Press, 1999), Jane Blocker compares this piece, correctly, in my view, to Bruce Nauman's 1969 *Pulling Mouth*. Both pieces show the influence of what Blocker calls "conceptualism," though Nauman sees the body as a closed system, whereas Mendieta engages and interrogates gender and the female body. Nauman documented his contorted face-making by using a slow-motion film (11).

7. Quoted in Mary Sabbatino, "Ana Mendieta: Identity and the Silueta Series," in Moure, *Ana Mendieta*, 150. The volume reproduces a piece called *Self-Portraits* with the same quote.

8. Ana Mendieta, "Self-Portrait," in Moure, *Ana Mendieta*, 179.

9. For these and other details on Mendieta in Cuba I am extremely grateful to Olga Viso, curator at the Hirschhorn Museum in Washington, DC, who allowed me to read the chapter titled "Engagement with Cuba" of the major Mendieta retrospective that traveled around the United States in 2004–5.

10. Part of this context can be seen in the documentary *55 hermanos,* by the late Cuban intellectual Jesús Díaz, who left Cuba in the 1990s. Díaz filmed the return of those members of the Cuban group Areíto who were allowed a three-week tour of the island. See María de los Ángeles Torres, *In the Land of Mirrors: Cuban Exile Politics in the United States* (Ann Arbor: University of Michigan Press, 1999), 92, 178.

11. Miami Cubans coined the term *dialoguero* to refer to these people, who in fact held quite divergent views among themselves.

12. Much of this information, unavailable up till now, comes from Olga Viso's research in *Ana Mendieta: Earth Body,* 77–99.

13. Ibid., 79.

14. Mendieta recorded her *Rupestrian Sculptures* in a number of formats: slides, Super-8 film, and black-and-white photographs. The photographic record of her work in Jaruco was exhibited at the A.I.R. gallery in November 1981.

15. In "Traces of Ana Mendieta, 1988–1993," Coco Fusco remarks that "Ana's understanding of Afro-Cuban ritual and music and of Latin American history was the

result of self-conscious research more than osmosis" (in *English Is Broken Here: Notes on Cultural Fusion in the Americas* [New York: New Press, 1995], 122).

16. Viso confirms that Mendieta talked to Arrom, who was at that point involved with the Círculo de Cultura Cubana in New York.

17. Moure, *Ana Mendieta*, 186.

18. Ana Mendieta plunged (she fell or was pushed) twenty-seven floors to her death in Lower Manhattan in 1985. Her husband, Carl André, was aquitted of the crime after two trials.

19. See the account in Coco Fusco, ed., *Corpus Delicti: Performance Art of the Americas* (New York: Routledge, 2000). In *English Is Broken Here*, Fusco remarked in 1995 that the art world in Cuba had moved away from the kind of dialogue that Mendieta was interested in, away from a Cuban-to-Cuban dialogue "that does not disrupt age-old schisms." She pointedly observed that "the flow of cultural exchange has been directed largely at launching work by Cuban nationals into the mainstream world of the United States" (125).

20. See Viso, *Ana Mendieta: Earth Body,* 98–99].

THE CUBAN BOOK OF THE DEAD

1. "For many exiles, the real Cuba had died with the revolution, and could only live on in their minds" (Coco Fusco, in *Bridges to Cuba,* ed. Ruth Behar [Ann Arbor: University of Michigan Press, 1995], 199).

2. Eduardo Aparicio, "Fragments from Cuban Narratives," in Behar, *Bridges to Cuba.*

3. Gustavo Pérez Firmat, *Next Year in Cuba: A Cubano's Coming of Age in America* (New York: Doubleday, 1995), 152.

4. Antón Arrufat, *Virgilio Piñera entre él y yo* (Havana: Ediciones Unión, 1994), 57.

5. See John Lee Anderson, *Che Guevara: A Revolutionary Life* (New York: Grove Press 1997), 744–45.

6. "A mi pueblo cubano caminante por el exilio del mundo, los Cubanos dentro de la isla que se imponen contra viento y marea y hacen que mi voz pasee por toda Cuba." She added a message of hope and strength: "y Dios permita que nos volvamos a encontrar" (and may God will that we all find each other again) (*Regalo del alma,* Sony Entertainment, 2003 TRK 70620).

7. Joan Didion, *Miami* (New York: Simon and Schuster, 1987), 1.

Index

José Quiroga, born in Havana and raised in San Juan, Puerto Rico, is professor and chair of Spanish and Portuguese at Emory University. He is author of *Understanding Octavio Paz* and *Tropics of Desire: Interventions from Queer Latino America,* as well as coeditor of the series New Directions in Latino American Cultures. He has traveled often to Cuba since 1980.